QUALITY OF SERVICE IN IP NETWORKS:

Foundations for a Multi-Service Internet

Grenville Armitage

MACMILLAN
TECHNICAL
PUBLISHING
U·S·A

Quality of Service in IP Networks:
Foundations for a Multi-Service Internet

by Grenville Armitage

Published by:
MTP
201 West 103rd Street
Indianapolis, IN USA

FIRST EDITION: April 2000

International Standard Book Number: 1-57870-189-9

Library of Congress Catalog Card Number: 99-63275

03 02 01 00   7 6 5 4 3 2 1

Interpretation of the printing code: The rightmost double-digit number is the year of the book's printing; the rightmost single-digit number is the number of the book's printing. For example, the printing code 00-1 shows that the first printing of the book occurred in 2000.

Printed in the United States of America

Trademark Acknowledgments

All terms mentioned in this book that are known to be trademarks or service marks have been appropriately capitalized. MTP cannot attest to the accuracy of this information. Use of a term in this book should not be regarded as affecting the validity of any trademark or service mark.

Warning and Disclaimer

This book is designed to provide information about Quality of Service. Every effort has been made to make this book as complete and as accurate as possible, but no warranty or fitness is implied.

The information is provided on an as-is basis. The authors and MTP shall have neither liability nor responsibility to any person or entity with respect to any loss or damages arising from the information contained in this book or from the use of the discs or programs that may accompany it.

PUBLISHER
David Dwyer

ASSOCIATE PUBLISHER
Brad Koch

EXECUTIVE EDITORS
Linda Ratts Engelman
Al Valvano

MANAGING EDITOR
Gina Brown

PRODUCT MARKETING MANAGER
Stephanie Layton

ACQUISITIONS EDITORS
Karen Wachs
Leah Williams

DEVELOPMENT EDITORS
Ami Frank Sullivan
Lisa M. Thibault

PROJECT EDITOR
Laura Loveall

COPY EDITOR
June Waldman

INDEXER
Tim Wright

TEAM COORDINATOR
Jennifer Garrett

MANUFACTURING COORDINATOR
Jim Conway
Chris Moos

BOOK DESIGNER
Louisa Klucznik

COVER DESIGNER
Aren Howell

PROOFREADER
Debbie Williams

COMPOSITION
Amy Parker

OVERVIEW

CONTENTS

About the Author

Grenville Armitage has been involved in IP- and ATM-related research for the past nine years. Grenville is an active member of the Internet Engineering Task Force (IETF) and has co-authored several protocols and standards documents in the area. For the past few years, he has been focusing on IP over ATM, IP multicast, IPv6, Integrated Services, Differentiated Services, and Multiprotocol Label Switching (MPLS) issues and protocol development. He was a senior scientist in the Internetworking Research Group at Bellcore before moving to the High Speed Networks Research department at Bell Labs Research (Lucent Technologies) in 1997. In the past two years, he has also traveled internationally, giving talks to customers and general audiences on the latest QoS and MPLS solutions. Grenville received his bachelor and Ph.D. degrees in electronic engineering from the University of Melbourne, Australia. He now lives in the San Francisco Bay Area and has a weakness for social activities involving beer and/or pool. He has been known to hit tennis balls (poorly), roller-blade (once breaking his arm), and play volleyball (before having a beer). The guitars in his closet haven't been used in years.

About the Technical Reviewers

These reviewers contributed their considerable practical, hands-on expertise to the entire development process for *Quality of Service in IP Networks*. As the book was being written, these dedicated professionals reviewed all the material for technical content, organization, and flow. Their feedback was critical to ensuring that *Quality of Service in IP Networks* fits our reader's need for the highest quality technical information.

Ken Carlberg has been involved in the design and development of computer networks for the past 15 years. The first five years involved developing embedded software for U.S. Department of Defense networks. For the last 10 years, he has led research efforts and developed designs and prototypes for networks and protocols involving routing, multicast, mobility, and QoS. Most of this work was done as a principal investigator for U.S. agencies such as the Naval Research Laboratory (NRL), the National Science Foundation (NSF), and the Defense Advanced Research Projects Agency (DARPA). In addition, he has conducted internal research for Science Applications International Corporation (SAIC), of which he is an employee. Ken has also been involved with various working groups of the IETF since 1990.

Ken received his Ph.D. in computer science, focusing on QoS Multicast, from University College London and received earlier degrees of BSc and MSc from Loyola College in Baltimore, Maryland. He currently lives in northern Virginia and always looks forward to being with his family in Baltimore and Chile.

Bryan Gleeson has 16 years of experience as a software engineer in the computer networking industry. He received a BAI degree in computer engineering and a BA degree in mathematics from Trinity College Dublin in Ireland. He started his career by developing a file transfer protocol for the National Research Network, and later projects included the development of a number of X.25, X.400, email, and satellite communication products. After four years, Bryan moved to Silicon Valley where he continued to work on the implementation of ISO protocols and the design of specialized transport protocols. Later he led the design and implementation of products for wide-area wireless mobile computing and for enterprise ATM networks. After joining Cisco Systems, he worked on the design and development of next-generation enterprise routers and ATM products. He was a frequent contributor to the ATM Forum, where he helped develop the LANE and MPOA protocol specifications. Bryan was one of the early engineers at Shasta Networks, a startup developer of a new type of carrier-class Internet product that enables the large-scale deployment of networking services for broadband subscribers.

He currently works for Nortel Networks on the design and implementation of new types of VPNs on the Shasta platform. Bryan holds a number of patents in the networking software area and is also active in the IETF, where he developed a general framework and architecture for VPNs. He lives in Cupertino, California, and enjoys music, travel, motor racing, and playing at being a sound-recording engineer.

Dedication

This book is dedicated to my parents—God blessed me with great ones. Their early investment in my hobbies and interests allowed me to create my career of being paid to do cool stuff.

Acknowledgments

I am no longer certain of my own sanity. Writing this book turned out to be far harder than I envisaged and would have been impossible if not for the support of the MTP team and my employer (Lucent Technologies). I also owe thanks to my two technical reviewers —Ken Carlberg and Bryan Gleeson—who frequently disregard their own personal safety by daring to point out my goofs. I also thank my many friends who no doubt became tired of hearing that I was "still working on my book" throughout the past year. Ann Roberts in particular kept reminding me that there's more to life than writing. Linda Engelman deserves thanks for persisting with me during the early days of defining the book and launching the project—without her, this book would never have been.

In a much broader sense, I must thank the IETF's IntServ, DiffServ, MPLS, IPng, ION, ISSLL, and PILC working groups, and the IRTF's End2End working group. They have provided us all with many of the tools and developments that will bring IP QoS to the Internet. They have also taught me much and provided me many opportunities for debates—some futile, some furious, and many educational. Although much of this book is based on the work of others, the errors and misconceptions are all mine. Finally, Bell Labs Research has proven that it is a great place to work, having supported my goal to write this book and allowed me to pursue my interests in QoS-related research.

Feedback Information

At MTP, our goal is to create in-depth technical books of the highest quality and value. Each book is crafted with care and precision, undergoing rigorous development that involves the unique expertise of members from the professional technical community.

Readers' feedback is a natural continuation of this process. If you have any comments regarding how we could improve the quality of this book, or otherwise alter it to better suit your needs, you can contact us at www.newriders.com/contact. Please make sure to include the book title and ISBN in your message.

We greatly appreciate your assistance.

INTRODUCTION

The Internet has been given many labels—ranging from the enthusiastic "information superhighway" to the pessimistic "World Wide Wait." As an impressive interconnected collection of networks around the world that ships vast quantities of information to varied locations and at all sorts of speeds, perhaps the Internet deserves the highway analogy. Yet most of us have suffered through the unpredictability of service offered by this so-called highway and can hardly deny that the second label is also well deserved. The information superhighway at times appears more like a water-logged, unpaved back street—dragging down traffic with scant regard for the importance of the packets it chooses to delay or lose entirely. Quality of service (QoS) is an effort to minimize those types of problems.

Why Do We Want Quality of Service?

When playing a word association game, most of us would probably respond with "Internet!" when faced with the phrase *Best Effort*. The history of the Internet Protocol (IP) suite shows a clear focus on developing a network technology that seeks out and establishes connectivity through rain, hail, and shine. Given knowledge of a packet's ultimate destination, the network will (if at all possible) find a path through any available internal links that enables the packet's ultimate delivery. The actual time it takes to achieve delivery (the transmission delay) is at best a secondary consideration. If no path is available, because of either long-term or short-term problems within the network, a packet might be discarded (a fairly extreme form of delay). In either case, nothing is passed from the network back to the packet's source indicating success or failure. Not unlike posting a regular letter, the service says "leave it to me" and simply tries to do its best. If guaranteed delivery is required, the source and destination must utilize additional end-to-end mechanisms (for example, the Transmission Control Protocol, or TCP) to determine whether their packets are being delivered successfully and, retransmit lost packets if they are not.

Of course, in the real world importance is attached to the timeliness of events. The applications generating packet traffic across an IP network have their own requirements to meet, and it is rarely sufficient for a packet to merely be delivered sometime. An automated, once-a-day file backup application, which has minutes or even hours to complete its task, might not be overly concerned about packets taking a long circuitous path. If you are surfing the Web or querying a remote database, you might tolerate delays measured in seconds, but the service is totally unacceptable if packets are taking minutes. The most demanding applications, such as chat sessions or real-time voice and video, must satisfy human requirements for interactivity—where tolerable delays are measured in the fractions of a second. The delay imposed by a network is often referred to as end-to-end *latency*.

Another common real-world requirement is to preserve the temporal ordering of packets (the time between arrivals of packets from the same source). If an application sends a stream of regularly spaced packets and they arrive at the far end as bursts of packets clumped together in time, the network has disrupted the source's temporal ordering—a phenomenon often referred to as *jitter*. This can impose troublesome requirements on applications involving real-time video and audio delivery (although it is typically of little concern to non-real-time applications such as file transfers and email transport). We humans generally like our video and audio transmissions to exhibit smooth and regular rendering of media content at the receiving end.

To combat jitter, many existing network video and audio applications include play-out buffers to reinstate the original temporal ordering before decoding the video or audio content. However, a play-out buffer increases the average time for a packet to be sent from source to receiver. Interactive applications (such as Internet Telephony) involve a careful balancing act between large buffer sizes to cope with network vagaries and small buffer sizes to ensure an acceptable sense of interactivity. It may even be valuable to discard packets that have been delayed too long within the network. For noninteractive applications (such as Internet television broadcasts), the play-out buffers may be relatively large without affecting the end user's experience.

Today's Internet guarantees neither transmission timeliness nor preservation of temporal ordering—the Internet focuses more on *where* to send packets and little on the *when*. During the early days, this practice was acceptable—applications usually were not done in real time, or the network was designed to "usually be good enough" for simple interactive services such as remote login. Network provisioning was driven by the simple adage "add more bandwidth when things get congested," and sharing the available bandwidth was left to the random laws of statistical multiplexing. As long as the available bandwidth along any one link was significantly larger than the average traffic load, everyone was generally happy.

However, times have changed. Corporate IP intranets and commercial IP backbones alike are facing demands for more predictability in their network's end-to-end behavior. These demands are driven by a range of factors from the explosive growth of PCs running network-based multimedia applications to corporations attempting the migration of their mission-critical applications from proprietary to IP-based networks. Mid- and top-level IP backbone providers are feeling pressure to provide predictable and guaranteed service levels on their wide area IP networks. As long as customers can shop around for IP connectivity, service providers are under significant pressure to continuously improve their own network's service quality—both to take customers from others and to retain the ones they already have.

The Basic Problem with IP

As with most things in life, there are different perspectives on QoS. For people with a traditional network operations background, QoS is a question of long-term network reliability and availability. (Is my connectivity present more than a few hours a day, a few days a week, or a few months a year?) The alternative is the consumer's view of the network behavior over much shorter time spans, during the periods when connectivity exists and applications are transmitting packets. QoS then becomes a question of transmission speed, timeliness of packet delivery, amount of jitter the network introduces into packet streams, and the probability of outright packet loss.

Between these two extremes are engineering questions about how gracefully a network degrades in the face of internal component failures. How reliable are the individual components (routers, switches, or links) within the network? Are critical components replicated in a redundant fashion so that connectivity is maintained? What happens to the quality of the connectivity (available bandwidth, delay, burstiness, or probability of packet loss) as redundant components are brought into use? How much degradation can be tolerated before a short-term problem with the quality of connectivity becomes a long-term loss of connectivity?

The average user ignores the internals of an IP network when sending his or her packets. However, you need to understand the weaknesses of existing IP networks before you can competently decide which additional techniques are suitable for enhancing a network's QoS. These weaknesses can be summarized as

- Routers provide unpredictable temporal response to transient congestion

- Inability to provide priority service to different classes of traffic

- Inability to dynamically request (or modify) end-to-end service quality

- Limited mechanisms for auditing usage of network resources

Packets follow paths made from sequences of *links* and *routers*. Routers and links may be connected to form any arbitrary topology, requiring the use of routing protocols to discover appropriate paths toward every packet's desired destination. Routers may find themselves acting as the convergence and divergence points for tens, hundreds, and thousands of unrelated flows of packets. Data applications may generate streams of packets clumped into bursts (with periods of silence in between) or spaced out evenly. When the simultaneous arrival of packet bursts leave a router with more packets than it can immediately deliver, all the packets attempting to pass through it experience additional delays. (This is not unlike checking in at the airport close to flight departure time or attempting to drive through a congested intersection, toll-road, or tunnel during peak periods.) Such a router or switch suffers from *transient congestion* and buffers excess packets internally until they can be sent onward. (When the transient congestion becomes too severe, buffers may even overflow resulting in packets being completely discarded.) Two critical factors in the provision of QoS are:

- How routers treat different types of packets during periods of transient congestion

- How routers utilize the QoS characteristics of underlying links

The latency any given packet experiences is a combination of the transmission delays across each link and the processing delays (which includes buffering or queuing) experienced within each router.

Jitter is introduced by the unpredictability of a router's congestion-induced buffering delays—varying from one moment to the next even for packets heading to the same destination. Routers built for the Best Effort Internet provide no means to differentiate between packets belonging to different applications or customers. Yet what we need are routers that can provide different latency and jitter characteristics to different classes or types of packets.

Airline check-in procedures are a useful analogy. Several agents process passengers as quickly as possible, yet the airline has a number of classes of passengers for whom it would like to provide expedited check-in service. To achieve this goal, the airline may establish multiple queues, or lines, in front of the check-in counters—one for each class of service on the plane (and often for the airline's frequent fliers). The segregation of passengers into distinct lines (queues) allows the agents to expedite the check-in of the airline's premium customers. The net effect is that premium-class customers experience faster (shorter lines and, thus, lower latency) and more predictable (lower jitter) check-in service than economy-class customers. To create a QoS-capable Internet, network designers need to develop and deploy routers capable of classifying packets into different classes, queuing each class separately during periods of congestion, and assigning unique levels of processing priority to each class. With these tools at hand, network designers can begin to control the end-to-end latency and jitter experienced by premium-class customers.

However, merely providing differentiated packet-handling capabilities within individual routers is not sufficient. Two more developments are required before a QoS-enabled Internet becomes a reality: signaling and accounting. In the broadest sense, *signaling* refers to the establishment of packet-classification and servicing rules across an end-to-end path. (In practice a number of mechanisms exist, varying in the time spans over which they operate.) In addition, there must be an accounting for everyone's use of resources. Router capacity and link bandwidths are neither free nor limitless. Any provision of priority service to some traffic classes implies that other traffic classes are commensurately penalized. Without mechanisms to account for (and control) a customer's usage of different traffic classes, everyone would ask for the premium service, putting us right back where we started.

Accounting for resources has two components. First, requests for specific resources must be authenticated (to accurately record legitimate requests and to protect against malicious attempts to subvert the resource allocation process by those without the appropriate entitlements). Second, a user's actual resource utilization should be monitored and tracked (to enable profiling of a user's actual network demands), and possibly authenticated (to ensure that the packet is using resources requested by a specific user are in fact coming from the user). Service providers ultimately utilize accounting information to bill their customers in accordance with their marketing and sales "plan du jour." However, the topic of pricing models for different levels of QoS is an area unto itself and outside the scope of this book.

Who This Book Is For

This book is for anyone who has spent time puzzling over the technological constraints and considerations that conspired to bring us today's Internet and for anyone who has wondered what we must add to improve things. Are you

- Trying to understand the delivery of video and audio services over a corporate or enterprise LAN?

- Looking to generate more revenue by providing guaranteed service levels to customers of your IP service?

- Just hoping to stay abreast of the claims and counterclaims being made by vendors?

By the end of this book, you will have a clear understanding of Internet technology's state of the art, and you will have developed a framework for evaluating each new QoS technology that promises to create a better Internet.

How This Book Is Organized

By starting with a basic refresher on IP networking (addressing, network hierarchy, and Best Effort routing), this book explains the technological issues that have led to the limitations of today's IP networks. These limitations include unpredictable and variable transmission delays (known as latency and jitter), unpredictable packet loss, network failures, and an inability to guarantee bandwidth to individual services sharing parts of a network. Together these represent the poor QoS exhibited by today's IP networks.

Motivated by the service requirements of emerging video, voice, and mission-critical applications, this book explores the various evolution paths open to IP routers and packet-switching devices and their relative trade-offs. You will become empowered to evaluate and understand existing and future QoS schemes within a framework of traffic classification, scheduling algorithms, link technologies, routing protocols, signaling methods, approaches to accounting and authentication, and robustness against network component failures.

Focus is brought to bear on the roles of emerging technologies such as IP routing switches, Multiprotocol Label Switching (MPLS), Resource Reservation Protocol (RSVP), Dense Wave Division Multiplexing (DWDM), Gigabit Ethernet, Asynchronous Transfer Mode (ATM), and Packet over SONET/SDH (POS).

In addition to the discussion of specific technologies, two network-level architectures developed for IP QoS by the Internet Engineering Task Force (IETF) will be evaluated.

The IETF began work on a relatively complex Integrated Services (IntServ) end-to-end model and then embarked on the much simpler edge-to-edge Differentiated Services (DiffServ) model. The differences and similarities between both schemes are explained and shown to be specific examples of general design principles that lie behind any scheme that aims to deliver predictable service quality.

This book provides a clear description of the engineering issues associated with specifying, providing, and managing service quality within the context of today's IP architecture. Following is a chapter breakdown of what you can expect to learn from each chapter:

- Chapter 1, "The Internet Today," begins with a basic introduction to the Internet's current Best Effort architecture, its use of shortest-path routing, and the end-to-end principle of flow control and reliable transport. We then look at how this existing architecture is failing to meet the demands of real-time multimedia applications and of service providers aiming to efficiently support paying customers who desire premium service.

- Chapter 2, "The Components of Network QoS," explains the broad developments that must occur before any IP-based network can meaningfully begin to support different levels of QoS to users. This chapter analyzes the hierarchical nature of IP networking and breaks the requirement for end-to-end QoS into a more manageable sequence of edge-to-edge QoS requirements. Chapter 2 also explains the need for routers to Classify, Queue, and Schedule (CQS) packets in accordance to their class, examines the limitations of existing shortest-path IP routing protocols, and outlines the value of traffic engineering non-shortest-path routes. A description of the key role played by signaling and accounting mechanisms wraps up the chapter.

- Chapter 3, "Per-hop Packet Processing," provides a detailed description of how per-router and per-switch QoS behavior can be controlled. Specific information is provided on the pros and cons of different classification schemes, queue management schemes (such as random early detection, or RED), and scheduling schemes (such as Weighted Fair Queuing, or WFQ). This topic leads to Chapter 4, " Edge-to-Edge Network Models," and a discussion of end-to-end network models based on a variety of per-router and per-switch solutions. The IETF's IntServ, DiffServ, and MPLS models are used as examples.

- Chapter 5, "Establishing Edge-to-Edge IP QoS," reviews the current state of the art with respect to signaling—especially the use of RSVP in enterprise networks.

- Chapter 6, " Link Layers Beneath IP," describes the issues associated with scheduling on low speed links, provides an overview of PPP and ATM link technologies, and high-lights the use of tunneling to provide virtual links.

- Chapters 7 and 8 provide insights into the architectures and QoS characteristics of a number of link technologies upon which end-to-end QoS solutions will depend. Chapter 7, "Low-Speed Link Technologies," looks specifically at dial-up, ISDN, ADSL, and CableModem link technologies. Chapter 8, "High-Speed Link Technologies," looks specifically at ATM over SONET/SDH, IP over ATM, Packet over SONET/SDH, and the fiber multiplication role of Wave Division Multiplexing (WDM).

- Chapter 9, "Dynamic Efficiency and Robustness," evaluates the robustness of edge-to-edge QoS schemes in the face of network component failures, and describes how TCP's own end-to-end behaviors interact with a network's internal QoS mechanisms.

- The book concludes with Chapter 10, "Reflections on the Future."

The Internet Today

Before embarking on an investigation of Internet quality of service (QoS), a review of the state of Internet Protocol (IP) networking today and the applications driving its evolution is in order. This chapter covers the basics of Best Effort IP technology, looks at how its roots influence its evolutionary path, and outlines its present limitations when faced with next-generation applications such as Internet Telephony, IP virtual private networks (VPNs), and multimedia Webcasting.

> **Note**
>
> You might want to skip this chapter if you already understand IP networking basics such as IP addressing, subnets, prefixes, shortest-path routing, the role of routers and routing protocols, and the reasons that the Internet currently provides only Best Effort service. My primary goal in this chapter is to refresh your memory and provide a backdrop for discussing the next generation of technologies required to add QoS to the Internet. Because the current Internet is based on IP version 4 (IPv4), that version is the focus of this review.

One of the fundamental philosophies underlying IP networking is that the network ought to be as "simple" as possible—providing the minimal set of functions required to enable relatively "smart" edge devices to communicate. This philosophy stands in stark contrast to the philosophy of the traditional telecommunications providers, whose networks are smart in order to accommodate extremely simple end-user devices (such as consumer telephones).

The Internet has benefited from the stunningly rapid evolution in processing power and sophistication of miniature electronic systems, especially embedded computers and the ubiquitous Personal Computer (PC). Such devices have made the simple network/smart edge model viable and, indeed, put the tools for developing the Internet's applications (intelligent services) into the hands of thousands of engineers and enthusiasts since the 1980s. By contrast, the telephony industry's intelligent network services could progress only as fast as developments were rolled out of professional, closely controlled engineering labs in the private and government sectors. The proliferation of PC platforms for smart end devices is arguably one of the reasons for the success of the Internet in the 1990s (despite all the efforts of traditional telecommunications bodies to develop and introduce their own digital networking services).

The minimal function required from the simple IP network was connectivity—that is, delivery of data packets from a source to a destination in some reasonable period of time if any possible path existed. The definition of *reasonable* could range from milliseconds to seconds, and ultimately there was no guarantee that any given packet would arrive at all. Nevertheless, everyone assumed that smart-edge devices, and the applications they supported, would somehow cope. This principle was, and is, the definition of the *Best Effort* network.

Even a simple network requires some degree of internal intelligence to find the appropriate paths between a source and any desired destination—in this case IP routing protocols. Although it is exciting to think of IP routing dynamically adapting to network failures induced by war or natural calamity, today's IP routing protocols are usually coping with the predictable changes (caused by reconfigurations) and unpredictable failures that bedevil any large-scale system.

However, a strong demand exists for IP networks to expand their range of minimal functions to include more than simple connectivity. End-user applications that involve real-time information flow or interactivity are placing demands on the network for fast and predictable response times. Customers of commercial IP networks are demanding reliable bandwidth guarantees. Such new applications need a network that includes timeliness and predictability as its primary characteristics.

1.1 Simple Network, Smart Edges

The traditional postal service might be considered an example of a simple network. The act of placing letters into envelopes, addressing them to the final destination, and placing them into a local post box is a familiar process. After that we, the end users, simply trust "the postal network" to transport the envelope to its destination in some reasonable time. We neither know nor care how the envelope gets to the destination, the delivery time is usually days, and we acknowledge that every so often envelopes are lost. Being aware of the service's limitations, we implement our own end-to-end strategies to confirm delivery (such as a phone call to the recipient some days later, or re-posting a copy of the original letter every few days until the recipient responds). The network itself neither looks inside the envelope to decide what to do nor performs any modification of the envelope's contents. All additional services (for example, content translation if the letter is going to a foreign country, filing the letter away for safekeeping, or making copies to be forwarded) are performed by humans at each end—the "smart edge."

From the perspective of end users, a Best Effort IP network is a similarly simple, self-contained entity whose primary role is to transport packets of data from one point to another. The end user is often an application running on an endpoint attached to the IP network, and these endpoints are identified by numerical *IP addresses.* The current Internet is based on IPv4; and in this protocol, 32-bit (4 byte) values represent endpoint IP addresses. By convention we write these addresses in dotted-quad form—four decimal numbers representing each of the four bytes making up the IP address, separated by periods. For example, the 32-bit binary address 1000 0000 0101 0000 1100 0101 0000 0011 is written as 128.80.197.3 in *dotted-quad* form. In theory, up to 2^{32} unique IPv4 addresses exist, but as you'll see later in this section significantly fewer are actually available for use.

Endpoints are sometimes colloquially referred to as *hosts,* although this is not entirely precise because it is possible for a host (a PC, workstation, or any physical entity capable of attaching to an IP network) to actually support multiple IP endpoints (a *multi-homed host,* where each endpoint is represented by a unique network interface attached to the host). The IPv4 address assigned to a particular endpoint depends on where it attaches to the IP network. IPv4 addresses, therefore, denote both location and identity. If an application moves from one host to another, or the host changes its attachment point to the IP network, the IP address used to identify the application must also change.

The average application neither knows nor cares about the internals of an IP network—all the application needs is the IP address(es) of the other endpoint(s) with which it plans to exchange packets. (Figure 1.1 shows one endpoint sending packets to another endpoint, and the only information the sender needs is the target's address—w.x.y.z.) The contents of a packet can represent anything expressible in digital form—pictures, text, sounds, movies—the list is limited only by the sophistication of the applications. The IP network itself is not concerned with the meaning of whatever each endpoint's application is sending. With the simple network/smart edge approach, anything important happens at the ends of the network, not in the middle—this approach is also known as the *end-to-end* model.

Note

IP addresses are closely related to fully qualified domain names (FQDNs)—human readable addresses of the form www.lucent.com or whitehouse.gov. Although these textual addresses are sometimes referred to as IP addresses, they are not. If a user supplies an application with an FQDN, the address is resolved into an IP address using a system known as the domain name system (DNS), operating transparently to the application's user. The application uses the resulting numeric IP address to establish packet communication with other hosts.

Figure 1.1   An IP cloud—the simple network.

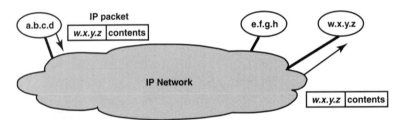

1.1.1   Transport Services

In general, every application has the potential to implement its own protocols for adapting to, and recovering from, an IP network's vagaries in packet delivery. However, early in the development of the Internet, people recognized that this practice would lead to a lot of redundant design and implementation effort. Many of the early applications were things like email, File Transfer Protocol (FTP), and Telnet (a remote login service)—sensitive to packet loss (everything sent had to be received), but not overly sensitive to timeliness (tolerating delays from tens of milliseconds to a few seconds). The applications shared a common end-to-end *transport* requirement for reliable ordered transfer of bytes from one endpoint to another. A sensible approach, therefore, was for these applications to share a common protocol that would emulate a reliable transport service on top of the unreliable IP network service. Ultimately this technology led to the development of what is known today as the Transmission Control Protocol (TCP).

Sitting between an application and the IP network (see Figure 1.2), TCP breaks an application's data into packet-sized units, uses acknowledged IP packet transmissions to detect losses, and retransmits IP packets to recover from losses. TCP uses windowed flow control mechanisms to adapt in a network-friendly manner to possible congestion within the IP network. A multiplexing method based on *port numbers* allows thousands of independent application flows to be supported between any two endpoints. By hiding the unreliability of the IP network from applications, TCP allows developers to focus on the actual goals of their applications—be they database updates, email exchanges, file transfer services, remote login services, Web page downloads, and so on. Most important, the IP network is generally unaware that a TCP entity is generating and exchanging IP packets on behalf of other applications. An analogy is a group of managers sharing an administrative assistant. The managers care only about communicating with their peers, which leaves the assistant to battle the vagaries of phones, voice mails, and postal services to transport the actual messages.

Figure 1.2   Transmission Control Protocol runs transparently across the IP network.

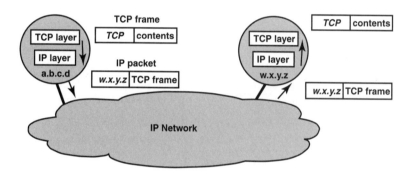

Not all applications required the reliable service or flow control that TCP offered or could tolerate its initial start-up delays. For such applications, the User Datagram Protocol (UDP) was developed to provide a connectionless, datagram-oriented transport service. Although in principle raw IP access may have sufficed, UDP was created to provide a common application-level interface to the IP layer within each endpoint's operating systems. Like TCP, UDP includes multiplexing based on port numbers, allowing thousands of unique, unreliable application-to-application datagram flows to be established between any two IP endpoints. Unlike TCP, in UDP no windowing flow control affects transmission speeds, and no synchronized acknowledgment scheme detects or recovers from lost packets. If required, the applications look after such matters on their own.

The term *application flow* (or just *flow*) is frequently used to mean a sequence of packets being exchanged between the same TCP or UDP ports on the same two endpoints. Various proposals for network QoS involve the network looking inside the IP packets and differentiating flows based on the source/destination IP addresses and the source/destination TCP or UDP port numbers. (Many applications use "well-known" port numbers, and so it is sometimes possible to infer the identity of the application from the port numbers used by a flow.)

1.1.2 Simplicity of State

Because its service definition is so simple, the IP network avoids much of the internal complexity associated with traditional telecommunications. In traditional networks, signaling establishes "state" information along the end-to-end path to ensure that the network's internal components could recognize and appropriately handle the subsequent data traffic. With a Best Effort IP network, no end-to-end signaling is required—endpoints simply attach and start sending packets.

The IP philosophy is to decouple the smart edge from the simple network. This practice means minimizing the interactions between the existence of any single endpoint and the network's internal state. End-user signaling and the attendant fluctuations in network "state" have traditionally been considered *bad things* in the IP world. On a philosophical level, such behavior weakens the edge/network decoupling. On a practical level, maintaining state information consumes memory in every router (almost always a scarce resource), and changing state information regularly on every router soaks up CPU capacity that, in many routers, would otherwise be available for forwarding packets. (Regular changes in state information are also usually associated with extra signaling communication between routers, consuming bandwidth otherwise available for user packets.)

1.1.3 Unicast and Multicast

The discussion so far has assumed the transmission of IP packets from one source to one destination—a *unicast* service. In the late 1980s, the IP service model was expanded to include a new service—*multicast*. With IP multicast, a source sends one packet into the network, and identical copies of that packet are delivered to multiple destinations (each destination receiving only one copy). The destinations that receive copies are considered to be members of a *multicast group*. In keeping with the general notion of decoupling edge and core behaviors, a source neither knows nor specifies the actual endpoints of a multicast group. The group's members are identified indirectly through a special IP multicast group address. The source simply places an IP multicast address (representing the desired target group) into a packet's destination field, and the network is expected to perform the appropriate replication and delivery. A source may or may not be a group member itself.

Figure 1.3 shows a packet being sent to a group identified only by the destination address g.g.g.g. The group's members include endpoints e.f.g.h and w.x.y.z, but only the network (not the packet's sender) knows this information.

Figure 1.3   Multicasting replicates a single packet to group members.

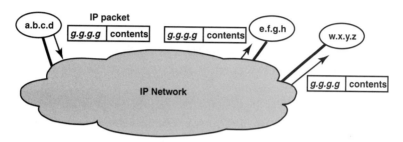

The IP multicast service is essentially an "any to many" service. Anyone is supposed to be able to transmit to a multicast group from anywhere on the network, and the multicast group can consist of many members. Because it imposes quite complex requirements on the network's internal operation, IP multicasting has taken a long time to become understood. Yet, it promises to be an extremely important service for efficiently delivering content that is intended for multiple simultaneous recipients (for example, stock exchange ticker information, streaming video and audio for real-time news reports, music clips, and so on), or for discovering services whose IP addresses are often not known a priori. If only unicast service is available, a source would have to transmit packets multiple times (once for each recipient), consuming additional bandwidth by filling the source's link into the network with redundant traffic. Although multicasting is valuable for real-time distributed multimedia, it does not inherently address the QoS requirements for these applications. QoS techniques are largely orthogonal to multicasting techniques.

1.1.4 Fairness

The "simple network" has traditionally not included many mechanisms to ensure that its resources are shared equitably between endpoints. Indeed, strict application of the end-to-end principle has meant that TCP is the main source of "fairness" within today's Internet. TCP's windowed flow control algorithm dynamically adjusts itself to ensure that it is using as much bandwidth as possible before the onset of packet loss. Every TCP connection interprets packet loss to mean there is congestion somewhere within the network, and in response it throttles back the rate at which it is transmitting a particular application's data. Even though endpoints are all independent, there is an expectation that if all TCPs run similar flow control algorithms, everyone will get along just fine and share the network's capacity fairly.

However, this approach has an important Achilles' heel—it leaves network "fairness" in the hands of the endpoints. It may be acceptable when a single administrative entity controls both the network and the software running at each endpoint. But in the real world, anyone can modify their endpoint's software to create a more aggressive TCP, or turn off its flow control entirely. The Internet has already seen examples of popular PC operating systems patched to do just that. The net effect is that one person starts seeing wonderfully good performance at the expense of others whose TCPs *are* backing off. Quickly, more people deploy the aggressive TCPs, or write their applications to use UDP in the first place (which has no inherent flow control). From a good business perspective, you cannot allow a network's resource utilization to be controlled by the unconstrained whim of the endpoints. This is one of the key reasons service providers are looking for network-based mechanisms for controlling endpoint-to-endpoint traffic flows, independently of what the endpoints may attempt to use.

1.2 Network Connectivity and Routing

Of course, even a "simple" IP network may contain a large degree of intelligence. The requirement that a packet be delivered over any available path, if at all possible, suggests some mechanism for discovering these paths in the first place. Because the network is expected to be ready for packet transport at any time without a priori warning from the end-to-end applications (no end-user signaling), the path discovery mechanism must operate continuously behind the scenes. Pick your favorite postal service, and behind the scenes you'll find someone (or a committee) deciding how to route letters and bundles of letters from town to town and city to city via train, plane, and bicycle. Within any IP network, you'll find the Internet's equivalent—IP *routing protocols*.

Any IP network is basically an arbitrary interconnection (topology) of links and routers. Links provide packet transport between routers, and routers act as nodes in the topology where packets may be forwarded (or routed) from one link to another.

When a router receives an IP packet, the router's primary job is to pick another link (the *next-hop* link) on which to forward (transmit) the packet and then to do so as quickly as possible. Depending on the nature of the network's topology, multiple possible next-hop links may be available. IP routing protocols ensure every router has enough local information to make the correct choice of next hop based solely on the IP destination address carried in each packet. This approach is known as *hop-by-hop forwarding*, where each hop makes an independent next-hop choice based solely on the globally significant destination address. In general, each hop's forwarding decision is not dependent on where the packet came from.

Figure 1.4 shows a simple network where multiple paths exist to take a packet from a.b.c.d to w.x.y.z. Router R1 could send the packet to R2 or R3, both of which have the capability to forward the packet even closer to w.x.y.z. However, in this case the routing protocol has informed R1 to use R2 as the next hop toward w.x.y.z and has informed R2 to use R5 as its next hop toward w.x.y.z.

Figure 1.4   An arbitrary topology may have multiple next hops.

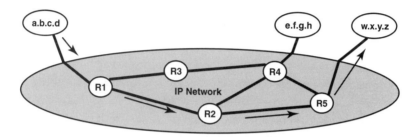

An IP network is not stateless, even though it is inherently connectionless, and no end-to-end-user signaling is involved. Each router's set of next-hop information represents part of an IP network's state at any given time. Taken together, this state information represents the set of all source-to-destination paths currently considered optimal by the routing protocols. Given that the network is required to provide "any to any" connectivity, the amount of information might be quite large. Because the network's basic topology can change dynamically (either through component failures or reconfiguration), the routing protocols must also operate dynamically. The following section briefly describes a number of specific routing mechanisms that have been developed over the years.

1.2.1 Aggregation and Hierarchy

A close interaction exists between the format of IP addresses, the allocation of addresses to specific endpoints, the way that IP routing protocols establish appropriate paths, and the way each router performs its per-packet forwarding decisions. The goal of an IP network is expressed in terms of its ability to deliver an IP packet from anywhere to anywhere based on a globally meaningful IP destination address. For a network containing only a handful of possible endpoints, allowing every router to simply know the identity and location of every endpoint might seem reasonable. However, this approach becomes untenable for large networks in which the number of endpoints begins to reach thousands or tens of thousands. This practice is virtually impossible (given reasonable assumptions about the memory space in IP routers) in the context of a network connected to the wider Internet, which has millions of potential endpoints.

Clearly it is necessary for routers to carry a much smaller amount of information and, yet, still be able to accurately forward a packet towards any specified destination. The solution is to introduce a hierarchy into the IP address space—one that maps closely related IP addresses onto topologically localized sets of actual IP endpoints. Doing this allows routers to carry summarized information for different regions of the network with the level of summarization increasing the further away from the actual endpoints you get. (This hierarchy is orthogonal to the classic network "layering" hierarchy—the two should not be confused. Address hierarchy is for efficient packet routing *within* a layer.) A traditional postal address contains a similar hierarchy: country (localization to a large section of the planet), state (localization within the country), town (within the state), street (within the town), and street number (within the street). Your local post office usually does not know specific forwarding information for letters outside the local town, it merely recognizes that out of town mail goes to a more central post office in a nearby city. As your letter is forwarded across the postal network, it eventually reaches postal centers with more specific knowledge of the intended final destination. In a similar way, IP routers can forward packets without really knowing complete information about destinations not local to themselves.

Class-Based Hierarchy

In the early days of IPv4, the unicast address space was blocked into three classes—A, B, and C (see Table 1.1). Specific combinations of an address's most significant 3 bits explicitly identified the class to which the address belonged. The next most significant 7, 14, or 21 bits of the IP address represented a network number or identifier. The Internet itself at the time (known as ARPAnet) was modeled as a backbone (a network of routers) with multiple independent networks attached. Each attached network was assigned a specific class A, B, or C network number. The actual IP address for any given IP endpoint within a network was the combination of class bit(s), network number bits, and a locally significant choice of value for the remaining 24, 16, or 8 host bits.

Table 1.1 Early IPv4 Space Divided into Fixed-Size Classes

Class	Address Format in Binary (Endpoints)	Networks and Hosts
A	0nnnnnnn.hhhhhhhh.hhhhhhhh.hhhhhhhh	2^7 nets, 2^{24} hosts
B	10nnnnnn.nnnnnnnn.hhhhhhhh.hhhhhhhh	2^{14} nets, 2^{16} hosts
C	110nnnnn.nnnnnnnn.nnnnnnnn.hhhhhhhh	2^{21} nets, 2^8 hosts

This convention provided a simple method to establish hierarchy in the address space. All endpoint addresses belonging to a specific network would have the same network number. Because the class of an IP address could be determined simply by looking at the top 3 bits, a router could easily determine which part of a packet's destination address represented the destination network. An IP address such as 128.80.197.3 clearly belongs to a class B network whose network number is 128.80, whereas an IP address such as 192.80.197.3 belongs to a class C network whose network number is 192.80.197. As a consequence, the backbone routers only needed to know the network numbers of each attached network.

In Figure 1.5 the sample backbone has three networks attached—Network 1 is a class B net with network number 128.80, Network 2 is a class A net with network number 64, and Network 3 is a class C net with network number 192.24.80. The backbone routers can assume that the IP packets it sees will contain destination address fields with network numbers 192.24.80, 128.80, or 64. Routing within the backbone is limited to getting the packets from one network's attachment point to another.

Figure 1.5   Early Internet considered a backbone with attached networks.

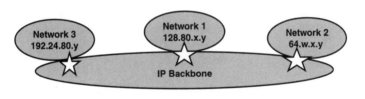

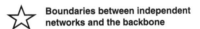

Of course, everything in life is a trade-off. As the Internet started to grow, concerns were raised about the rate at which the 32-bit address space was being exhausted. If the address space had been unstructured, 2^{32} addresses would have been available for unique endpoints—an extremely large number. Sparse utilization of the 32-number space was the price that was paid for introducing hierarchy and thereby making the routing tractable. However, the existing class structure was not necessarily the most efficient way to assign top-level networks. Many companies were building networks that either started out larger than a single class C address space or would very quickly do so. Yet few companies or institutions would fill the class B address space, let alone fill a class A address space. However, any institution planning a network slightly larger than a class C space faced two options— request and consume an entire class B network or request multiple class C networks. The former choice was wasteful of addressing space, whereas the latter choice added multiple entries into the backbone routing tables where only one would have been preferable.

Classless Inter-Domain Routing

Classless Inter-Domain Routing (CIDR) was introduced to improve the Internet's utilization of top-level prefixes. Primarily focused on the backbone routing between major networks (domains), CIDR threw out the previous A, B, and C class rules (hence, *classless*). Instead of the original three fixed-prefix sizes, the number of bits representing the network number could be anything. Networks would be specified by a 32-bit value containing their network number in the top bits and a prefix-size value indicating how many of the top bits was valid (counting down from the most significant bit). A network's CIDR prefix specifies how many of the most significant bits in an IP address are unique to that network. For example, using the new CIDR notation of network number/prefix size, the old class B network 128.80 is now expressed as 128.80/16. The class C network 192.80.197 would be written as 192.80.197/24. Table 1.2 shows that in general, a prefix size of X results in a network that can theoretically contain up to $2^{(32-X)}$ endpoints.

Table 1.2   CIDR Relaxes the Network Prefix Lengths

Address Format in Binary	Networks and Hosts (Endpoints)
nnnnnnnn.nnnnnnnn.nnnhhhhh.hhhhhhhh	
|< - - - - X - - - - - >|	2^X nets, $2^{(32-X)}$ hosts

Most important, variably sized networks could now be built from the old class C space. For example, 192.80.192/22 represents a single network with a 22-bit prefix and a network number of 192.80.192. Given the 22-bit prefix, it is equivalent to four contiguous class C networks (192.80.192.*, 192.80.193.*, 192.80.194.*, 192.80.195.*).

This process of creating a single network from multiple old class C networks is also known as *supernetting*. By assigning prefixes to more accurately reflect the needs of new companies and institutions, CIDR significantly slowed the consumption rate of the IPv4 address space and the growth rate of the backbone routing tables. (Indeed, it was calculated that had CIDR not been introduced, the last class B address would have been assigned in early 1994!)

Although CIDR might seem obvious in retrospect, the original network class system existed because of the evolutionary way the Internet was created. Engineers built routers and routing software to meet the demands they saw at each point in the Internet's history and modified them as the scope of their creation grew. (Arguably this approach is what enabled the Internet to become a functional proof of concept while the traditional international standards bodies where still designing their own data networking solutions in committee rooms.)

Subnetting

Hierarchy also exists inside each backbone-attached network, dividing each one into subnetworks. The endpoint addresses within a network are assigned according to internal locality, and localized groups of endpoints are said to exist on a subnetwork (commonly referred to as *subnets*). Individual subnets contain endpoints whose addresses all fall under a common prefix (or *subnet mask*), a prefix that is itself a subset of the class or CIDR prefix assigned to the network of which they are a part. The process of creating subnets is referred to as *subnetting*. In a classless world, a subnet is nothing more than a local section of the network that can be described by a longer (that is, more precise) prefix or mask than the one that describes the network itself.

Note

The term *subnet* is often colloquially applied to Layer 2 networks used as links between routers—particularly for Ethernet or similar local area networks (LANs). A single Layer 2 subnet (link) may support multiple IP subnets. However, an IP subnet cannot span more than one inter-router link (by its very definition).

Figure 1.6 shows a simple example where the network 128.80.0.0/16 (as known to the IP backbone) is internally broken into two subnets—each with a 24-bit prefix (in other words a subnet mask of 255.255.255.0). Subnet 1 covers all endpoints with addresses in the range 128.80.1.0 to 128.80.1.255, whereas subnet 2 covers endpoints in the range 128.80.9.0 to 128.80.9.255.

Figure 1.6   Subnetting allows aggregation within a network.

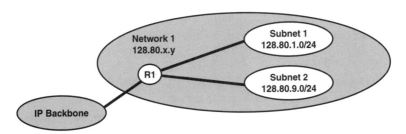

1.2.2 Shortest-Path Routing

IP networks use *shortest-path routing*. Each hop within the network, from one router to the next, is assigned a relative weighting (called a *metric*). Having discovered the network's topology and every hop's associated metric, each router in the network calculates the possible paths from itself to all known networks, subnets, or destinations. If multiple possible paths exist, the routing protocol calculates the sum of the metrics of the hops in each possible path and picks the path for which this sum is lowest—the shortest path.

Each router summarizes the results of these calculations in a set of forwarding rules. For each known network/prefix pair X/Y, a forwarding rule states, "For packets destined to endpoints covered by X/Y, use link Z as the next hop." When a packet arrives, the router executes the following process:

- For each X/Y pair:

    1. Create a 32-bit value (a *bitmask*) containing ones in the top (most significant) Y positions and zeros in the rest.

    2. Apply this bitmask to the destination IP address.

    3. Compare the result to X.

    4. If a match exists, the packet is forwarded out on link Z, and the process is complete.

    5. Otherwise, repeat this entire process.

- Discard the packet if it never matches any entry.

The table of X/Y/next-hop information is typically referred to as a *forwarding table*, or a *forwarding information base* (*FIB*).

The simplest network topology would be a tree—a hierarchy of subnetworks with each subnetwork hanging off a larger subnetwork with a shorter prefix. However, a network's real topology may contain links that cut across the tree implied by the prefix hierarchy. The shortest path chosen by the routing protocol might even use these links for certain network/prefix pairs. To ensure that routers always utilize the most precisely specified path, they are required to implement a *longest prefix match* when forwarding packets. This rule basically states that the forwarding table's X/Y pairs be searched in descending order of Y, ensuring that the most precise match is always found if it exists.

When building a shortest-path tree, the routing protocol may also choose to use (or be required to account for) two extreme network/prefix pairs—*default routes* and *host routes*. Default routes are represented by the network/prefix 0.0.0.0/0—a guaranteed match to any IP address. Because the prefix length is zero, this route is the last entry in a router's forwarding table. It represents the ultimate in aggregation—if only one link provides the path out of the local network, a default route entry can point to that link (instead of having explicit forwarding rules for all the network/prefix pairs that can be reached in the world outside the local network). For example, in Figure 1.6 router R1 would have specific routes pointing into Network 1 for destinations under 128.80/16, and a default route entry point out towards the IP backbone. Host routes are represented by the network/prefix w.x.y.z/32—a rule that matches only packets actually destined for endpoint w.x.y.z. Host routes are highly discouraged because they are the ultimate in nonaggregated routing information.

Each destination prefix known to the local network's routing protocol is said to be the root of its own particular *shortest-path tree*. The tree has branches passing through every router in the network, although not all links in the network are branches on every shortest-path tree. No matter where a packet appears within the network, the packet will find itself on a branch of a shortest-path tree leading toward its desired destination. The challenge for a dynamic IP routing protocol is to keep these shortest-path trees current in the presence of router failures, link failures, or deliberate modifications to the network's topology. Any link failure usually requires the recalculation of trees for many destination prefixes.

Most IP routing protocols use only a single metric in their calculations, and the same metric must be used across the entire topology of a self-contained network. Metrics may reflect physical characteristics such as available bandwidth, link delays, and link costs or simply represent the administrator's relative preference for traffic to be on a particular link. Assigning metrics is a nontrivial task for network operators because the result can have a profound affect on a network's behavior.

1.2.3 Routing Protocols

Because it is not the goal of this book to detail the history and operation of IP routing protocols, this section provides only a brief overview of how existing solutions meet the preceding requirements. Doing justice to the art of IP routing requires a book of its own—a number of suggestions are listed in the "Further Reading" section of Chapter 10, "Reflections on the Future."

Although network failures could be induced by war or natural calamity, most network changes occur due to the random human interventions and unpredictable failures that bedevil any large-scale system. Routing protocols must meet a number of simultaneous requirements:

- Dynamically discover a network's topology

- Build shortest-path trees forwarding trees

- Handle summarized information about external networks, possibly using different metrics to those used in the local network

- React to changes in the network's topology and update the shortest-path trees

- Do it all in a timely manner

The two main approaches to controlling networks are centralized and distributed. The centralized approach is common in "intelligent networks" where even the network nodes themselves (for example, routers) are kept relatively simple. Routes are calculated centrally at a route processor and then distributed out to the network's routers whenever updates are required. However, two problems exist with the centralized approach:

- It presumes the a priori establishment of communication paths between the centralized route processor and the network's routers. If a section of the network is cut off from the centralized route processor, it stops functioning reliably.

- The processing load of recalculating routes for the entire network is focused on a single machine, which reduces the timeliness with which routes can adapt to changing network conditions. On the contrary, distributed approaches assume that each router participates in the topology discovery and route calculation process. The processing load is shared across all the routers, and if sections of the network become isolated, they adapt locally to their new conditions but still keep functioning. The Internet uses distributed routing protocols.

An additional form of distributed processing exists due to the delineation of the Internet into regions known as autonomous systems. An *autonomous system* is defined loosely as a self-contained, independently administered network or internally connected set of networks. Within an autonomous system the routing is managed by an Interior Gateway Protocol (IGP) (because a gateway is an old name for what are now called *routers*). The arbitrary interconnection of autonomous systems makes up the Internet itself. Routing of traffic between autonomous systems is managed by an Exterior Gateway Protocol (EGP). Interior and exterior protocols have quite different goals and requirements.

Interior Gateway Protocols

Two distinct classes of distributed routing algorithms have been used as the basis of IGPs. They are known as *distance vector (DV)* and *link state (LS)* algorithms. Each approach has its benefits and limitations—DV algorithms tend to be simpler to implement than LS algorithms, but conversely are also less robust in the face of regular topology changes within a network.

DV algorithms operate by having each router advertise information to its neighbors about the relative distance to each network the router knows about (a vector of distances). The advertisement basically tells the neighbor: You can reach network X through me with distance Y. To learn about distant networks, all routers listen to these same advertisements from their neighbors. A router may receive multiple advertisements for the same network

X, each from a different neighbor, in which case the router remembers the advertisement with the lowest distance. The neighbor advertising the lowest distance toward X becomes the chosen next hop for packets heading to X. The effective distance from the local router toward X is the lowest advertised distance received from a neighbor plus the additional distance (metric) of the link to that neighbor. The local router then regularly re-advertises (to its neighbors) its own distance to all the networks it has previously learned about (typically with intervals in the tens to hundreds of seconds). The re-advertising process ensures that information about new networks, or new distances to existing networks, ripples out across the local network whenever changes occur. Because each router creates forwarding rules from the shortest distances it receives, a shortest-path tree is created toward every known network.

LS algorithms do not distribute relative distances to all known locations. Rather, the algorithms distribute maps of the local network's entire topology (along with the state and metrics of all the links in the topology)—that is, its neighbors. The maps are distributed by flooding link state advertisements, whereby each router informs its neighbors about sections of the network topology that the local router knows about. When a state change occurs (for example, a link goes up or down, or a new route is associated with an existing link), the new link state information is flooded across the local network to ensure all router's have up-to-date link state maps. Each router then uses these maps to locally calculate the shortest-path trees to all listed destination networks and, hence, to determine the appropriate next hops out of the router itself. Because the next-hop calculations are based on complete knowledge of the network's state, every router can be expected to agree on the shortest-path trees.

Although the most basic DV protocols are simple to describe and implement, they result in a network whose shortest-path trees can get tangled up in transient loops. It can take tens of seconds to minutes for a DV-based network's routes to converge on a loop-free topology. Slow convergence is a fundamental limitation of any scheme in which the local router has only secondhand, interpreted information about the nature of the network beyond the router's local interfaces. Relative, rather than absolute, information is derived from neighbor advertisements because the advertisement process is designed to directly create shortest-path trees. In contrast to DV protocols, LS protocols are more complex to describe and implement even in their most basic form. They contain two separate functions—maintenance of a distributed link state database and standalone shortest-tree calculation. However, the benefit is that shortest-path trees can be assured to be loop free almost immediately after any link state changes occur and the information is flooded throughout the network. However, the network-wide flooding of state changes also limits the scalability of LS-based networks.

Table 1.3 lists some common IP IGPs, whether they are DV or LS, and mentions some notable characteristics.

Table 1.3   Some Common Interior Gateway Protocols

Name	Algorithm Class	Comments
Routing Information Protocol (RIP)	DV	Early IGP, single hop-count metric, longest path limited to 15 hops (small networks), simplistic notion of network/ subnet/endpoint hierarchy, second version (RIPv2) supported CIDR and variable subnets.
Open Shortest Path First (OSPF)	LS	Sophisticated replacement for RIP. Multiple simultaneous metrics, no inherent limit on path length within a network, recommended Internet standard.
IGRP	DV	Proprietary (Cisco systems) IGP, also Enhanced IGRP (EIGRP).
Intermediate System to Intermediate System (IS-IS)	LS	OSI-derived IGP, extended to operate on IP networks. Relative to OSPF, IS-IS has smaller metric precision and a limited number of link state records can be advertised per packet.

Exterior Gateway Protocols

The standard EGP in the Internet today is Border Gateway Protocol version 4 (BGP4). Its primary role is to distribute information between autonomous systems indicating where all the constituent networks are located. Every autonomous system has one or more routers that interface to a peer autonomous system—these are the *border routers* for the autonomous system. As its name suggests, BGP4 runs on these border routers and enables them to distribute to their neighboring autonomous systems information about the reachable networks within the local autonomous system.

Unlike IGPs, BGP4 is neither a distance vector nor a link state algorithm. Instead it is a path vector protocol, borrowing a number of key DV concepts.

A DV solution would try to use a single metric to express paths to destinations. However, because each autonomous system is free to utilize its own metrics with whatever meanings the autonomous system chooses, BGP cannot safely build inter-autonomous system forwarding paths with just the metrics reported by each autonomous system. A link state solution also requires common interpretation of link states and metrics across all autonomous systems for the solution to be safe. In addition, scaling problems are associated with keeping a global, inter-autonomous system, link state database synchronized across the hundreds of autonomous systems making up the Internet.

BGP advanced the basic DV model by introducing the idea of a path vector, whereby each border router advertises not only the existence of a path to particular networks (*reachability*) but also the list of autonomous systems through which the path passes. Any given border router can confirm that an advertisement for a given network is loop free if the border router's own autonomous system number does not already appear in the path vector. After an advertisement is accepted, the local border router inserts its own autonomous system number into the path vector before re-advertising the reachability information to its neighbors. BGP provides sophisticated mechanisms to control the scope of reachability advertisements, support relative priorities between different inter-autonomous system paths, and support policies that may restrict the autonomous systems through which certain traffic can be routed.

1.2.4 The Last Hop

IP endpoints do not advertise their existence by running an IP routing protocol. (To do so would violate the decoupling between the edge and core, because the core should take care of routing packets from one point to another itself). Every IP endpoint is connected to a router that is part of the network (by one of a variety of link level technologies). This router is typically configured to know the subnet prefixes that cover the locally attached IP endpoints, and it advertises these to the rest of the network. This router is the *last hop router* for packets arriving from elsewhere in the network.

When a packet arrives for a local endpoint, the router's forwarding table indicates only the interface through which the endpoint can be reached. Because the interface may be attached to a wide variety of link technologies, there are no generic mechanisms for determining how to forward the packet over this last hop. However, there is a generic requirement—the router must discover a link-specific identifier that will allow it to target the packet to the destination endpoint over that interface. If the router's interface connects to a shared Ethernet LAN, the router must be able to discover the Ethernet address of the IP endpoint. If the router's interface connects to an ATM network, there may be multiple virtual connections (VCs) to choose from and only one that leads to the IP endpoint. The interface may be a simple point-to-point link terminating in only a single endpoint, in which case there is a one-to-one mapping between the link and the terminating IP endpoint.

Every endpoint is configured with (or auto-discovers) the link address of their local router. Packet transmission from an endpoint also requires destination-based, longest-prefix match forwarding. This basically determines whether the target destination is on the local subnet (in the case of a subnet layered over a shared media such as Ethernet) or off the subnet (in which case, the packet is forwarded to the local router).

1.2.5 *Best Effort Forwarding*

Best Effort service is quite well suited to applications with lax demands for timely and predictable packet delivery. Such applications tend to generate their data in bursts, or at least can tolerate data being transferred in bursts. With TCP, the network can treat many applications as not only bursty but also as theoretically loss tolerant (because a lost packet is eventually retransmitted).

Shortest-path trees only establish connectivity. Even when the routing protocol's metric represents a meaningful characteristic such as nominal per-hop delay or available bandwidth, the network offers no guarantees about the actual availability of resources (for example, link bandwidth or router capacity) along a path at any given instant. Because of the decoupled edge/core model, IP routing protocols cannot react to the varying dynamic demands bursty end-to-end traffic flow(s) places on the network. In a typical IP network, the actual available bandwidth or latency on any given hop depends to a large degree on the dynamics of the traffic flowing through the network at the time. Because a network never has accurate a priori knowledge of an application's traffic characteristics, accurate bandwidth or latency based metrics are impossible to create.

A typical IP router reflects the simple service definition of the Best Effort IP network. As described in preceding sections, an IP router's basic job is to take a packet it has received over any interface, perform a forwarding table lookup on the packet's destination address, and forward the packet to the next-hop router thus discovered—and do the job as fast as possible for every packet it receives. But although the router worries about *where* to send packets, it rarely worries about *when* to send them. It is simply assumed that packets go out in the same order they arrived—first-in, first-out (FIFO) processing. When too many packets converge on a router in a short period of time and the outbound link cannot process packets fast enough, packets may be delayed or lost within the router. The router is said to be congested, and its behavior is acceptable because the network as a whole doesn't guarantee anything better.

It isn't too hard to figure out one simple solution to improving the bandwidth, end-to-end delay, and low packet loss figures—make the routers and links much faster than the offered end-to-end traffic loads. As the end-to-end traffic increases, add faster links and routers—no problem! However, such an engineering philosophy runs counter to a network operator's desire to keep costs down. "Faster" generally costs money. Sometimes faster links and routers are not affordable because the price points of the necessary technology are still too high for a particular network operator's needs. Also, many data networks are designed on the assumption that multiple sources of traffic can be *statistically multiplexed* together. Statistical multiplexing assumes that traffic sources are generally bursty and have some degree of delay and loss tolerance. Finite link and router capacity is multiplexed (shared) effectively when each traffic source's bursts are uncorrelated, allowing cheaper (slower) components to satisfy the overall demands of multiple end-to-end traffic flows.

However, a correlation exists between bursts belonging to different traffic flows, a standard Best Effort router simply allows the competing flows to interfere with each other. Two choices face a network operator—either foot the expense of faster links and routers or search for routers capable of controlling the interference between correlated traffic flows. The next generation of IP networks is starting to employ just these sorts of routers. The methods available to router and network designers to control traffic interactions within IP networks are a focal point of the rest of this book.

1.2.6 Real-World Considerations

Theoretical discussions about how IP routing works and how endpoints interact can sometimes miss additional complications introduced by technological and geopolitical realities. For example, there are many different types of inter-router link technologies. IP can run over just about anything capable of transmitting streams of bits or bytes with packet boundaries intact. ("IP on everything" has been a popular slogan in the Internet community.) Political realities within and between countries mean the Internet is actually made from multiple "backbones," interconnected at a limited number of geographically diverse points.

Link technologies have distinct characteristics such as available bandwidth and the predictability of their latency. Dial-up modem links tend to have low bandwidths in the tens of kilobits per second, and their jitter can increase by tens or hundreds of milliseconds when error correction is enabled. Ethernet LANs can see theoretical raw bit rates from 10Mbit/sec to 1Gbit/sec, but the available bandwidth depends on unpredictable sharing of multiple endpoints attached to the LAN. Wide area links can vary from T1 (1.5Mbit/sec) and E1 (2.048Mbit/sec) leased lines (or fractional versions) to OC-3/STM-1 (155Mbit/sec) and faster optical circuits. They typically have predictably low latency and minimal jitter, but are usually provisioned from a third party (sometimes resulting in relative inflexibility and high cost). High-speed access technologies such as Asymmetric Digital Subscriber Line (ADSL) are still evolving but have tended to focus on reliable high speeds rather than low latency or jitter. (An ADSL modem can introduce at least 20 milliseconds of latency under certain configurations.) Virtual links are also commonly used (for example, the Multicast Backbone (MBone), and the 6Bone IPv6 over IPv4 trial testbed), where IP packets are carried inside other IP packets—the bandwidth and latency characteristics depend on the underlying edge-to-edge IP path. The impact of various link level technologies will be discussed further in Chapter 6, "Link Layers Beneath IP," Chapter 7, "Low-Speed Link Technologies," and Chapter 8, "High-Speed Link Technologies."

Although there really was a single backbone in the earliest days of IP networking, today's Internet is made from a number of peer backbones. Some of these backbones exist because of political and geographical boundaries between countries, whereas others reflect commercial competitors who want to own their own backbone level infrastructure within the same country. The actual end-to-end path between any two sites on "the Internet" may be somewhat convoluted—simply because the source and destination are connected to different backbones. Two geographically close sites (for example, London and Paris, Sydney and Melbourne, or Los Angeles and San Francisco) might find themselves communicating over paths that loop through New York, Tokyo, or Amsterdam depending on their choice of backbone provider and where the backbone providers interconnect.

Top level backbones typically interconnect only at a few geographically diverse points—Network Access Points (NAPs) or Internet eXchanges—in order to ensure that any point on the Internet can connect to any other. Typically multiple points are used. This provides redundancy against failure, and it shortens many end-to-end paths.

1.3 Next-Generation Applications

Clearly, the Internet's existing techniques would not need to change if they were meeting current demands. Increases in raw packet carrying capacity would satisfy the growth in email traffic and probably most click-and-read Web surfing as well. But new applications have captured the public's imagination. Real-time services carrying video and audio content are coming into existence, and people want more reliable access to this content. Interactive services such as IP Telephony need predictable and low end-to-end delays. And commercial service providers are looking for ways to share their IP router infrastructure across multiple private customers while ensuring no one customer's network traffic affects the service rendered to another customer. All of these factors are driving a demand for a new IP network—a smarter core than before.

1.3.1 Voice and Video

Perhaps the most interesting next step in the Internet's evolution will be when it adequately supports real-time and interactive video and audio applications. Mapping the digital bit streams from video and audio codecs (coder/decoders) into and out of IP packets is not intrinsically difficult. The difficulty is in ensuring that the temporal ordering of these packets is retained as they cross an IP network—codecs typically like the bits to arrive close to the time that the corresponding video or audio content needs to be decoded. Because the Best Effort service definition makes no promises about timeliness or ordering, this approach is a gamble. However, whether motivated by the excitement of playing with new technology or the promise of communicating over a "free" Internet, many people have been willing to take the gamble of using Best Effort for voice and video.

Standalone applications such as CuSeeMe, VIC, and VAT were introduced to the IP world a number of years ago as experiments to see whether video and audio conferencing was possible over the Internet. Trials included regular broadcasts from select working group meetings of the Internet Engineering Task Force (IETF), proving that aside from the Internet's own unpredictability, nothing was stopping the viability of sophisticated audiovisual end-user applications. Look inside a Web browser today, and you're likely to find at least one plug-in designed to render streaming video and audio content on (or through) your PC. Standalone applications such as RealAudio and RealVideo are becoming almost de facto standards for delivering real-time content over Internet connections of highly variable quality, and everyone appears to be loving it!

Nevertheless, the Internet is definitely not a good medium for real-time and interactive applications. Everyone fascinated by audiovisual media over the Internet is also frustrated with the visual jerkiness and sound distortions that so easily and frequently infect a media stream from a distant Web site. But the frustration is forcing network providers—whether a local ISP, corporate enterprise, or wide area service provider—to improve the quality of the IP service their networks provide. Of course, there's little altruism here. As Best Effort IP service becomes a cheap commodity, providers are feeling the pressure to upgrade their offerings. Technologies that allow tiered levels of IP service quality also allow service providers to charge premium rates to access the higher tiers.

1.3.2 *Virtual Private Networks*

A number of network architectures have been given the label *virtual private network (VPN)* in the past few years. Although this section (or even this book) cannot discuss them all in detail, VPNs are causing IP service providers to seek additional mechanisms for controlling traffic interactions within their IP networks.

VPNs are the emulation of a private network over shared or public facilities. Most VPNs share a couple of key attributes:

- **Perception of privacy**—The customer has sole, isolated use of the network as it appears to him or her.

- **They are virtual**—What each customer sees is not necessarily the whole of the networking infrastructure put in place by the service provider.

The primary characteristic of a private network is that the customer's traffic is isolated from the underlying infrastructure and from other customers sharing that infrastructure. Such isolation has two critical aspects—the first is topological, and the second is temporal. *Topological isolation* means that customers can introduce whatever addressing space and routing they choose (one common use for private networks is a situation in which the IP addresses in use are not actually globally unique and would clash with someone else's use of the same addresses if they became visible on the Internet). Temporal isolation means that the private network's service in the face of bursty customer traffic depends solely on the characteristics of that customer's traffic.

Creating a *virtual* private network requires mechanisms that allow a common infrastructure (for example, a set of links and routers) to be shared while still making each customer believe that he or she has all the isolation of a private network (see Figure 1.7). Techniques such as IP tunneling across an IP backbone can support topological isolation, but they do not directly address the need for temporal isolation. The IP backbone still needs to be able to guarantee certain available bandwidth and end-to-end latencies to different IP tunnels.

To date, most IP VPNs have actually been built on top of connection-oriented wide area network (WAN) services such as Frame Relay (FR) or Asynchronous Transfer Mode (ATM). FR or ATM virtual connections (VCs) provide temporal isolation and are used to build private, independent IP networks for each customer. However, each private network requires its own parallel set of IP routers—the "virtual private" part of the service is provided by the underlying FR or ATM network. Many service providers are looking at ways of achieving the same thing at the IP router level to minimize the number of routers they have to replicate and manage. Such a service demands new temporal isolation capabilities from the next generation of IP routers and will be a true *IP VPN*.

Figure 1.7   A virtual private network must isolate customers topologically and temporally.

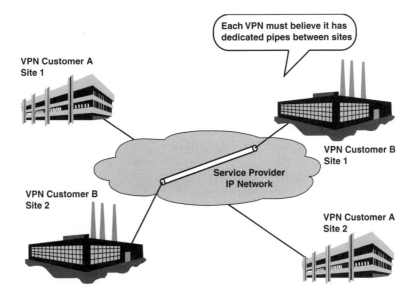

The Components of Network QoS

Regardless of the size and scope of an IP network, the observed end-to-end quality of service (QoS) is built from the concatenation of edge-to-edge QoS provided by each domain through which the traffic passes. Ultimately, the end-to-end QoS depends on the QoS characteristics of the individual hops along any given route. For example, in Figure 2.1 the QoS experienced by the intra-LAN phone application depends solely on the LAN, whereas the wide area phone application experiences QoS that depends on the LANs at either end, the Internet service providers (ISPs) at either end, and the IP backbone in the middle. A nonspecific PC-to-PC application depends on two LANs and the local ISP providing the LAN-to-LAN interconnect.

Figure 2.1   End-to-end QoS from a concatenation of segments.

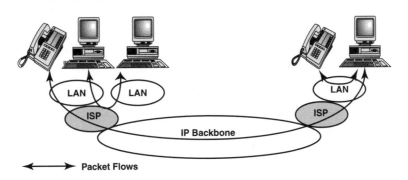

Not surprisingly, much of the unpredictable and undifferentiated packet loss and jitter in today's IP services is due to the manner in which traditional Best Effort routers cope with transient internal congestion. If a particular output port becomes the focal point for two or more inbound aggregate traffic streams, a Best Effort router simply uses first in, first out (FIFO) queuing of packets destined for transmission on the associated outbound link. Queuing introduces latency (delay) and the potential for packet loss if a queue overflows. When traffic patterns are bursty, the queuing-induced latency varies unpredictably from packet to packet—manifesting itself as jitter in the affected traffic streams.

IP networks (enterprise, access, and backbone) are being called upon to carry traffic belonging to a growing variety of customers with diverse requirements—for example, IP Telephony, IP virtual private networks (VPNs), bulk data transfer, and mission-critical e-commerce. Each customer makes unique demands for some level of service predictability, even in the presence of transient congestion due to other traffic traversing the network.

The demand for relative or absolute protection from other traffic on any particular network segment applies equally well to a high-speed LAN, a network based on T1 or E1 private links, a dial-up or ISDN access network, or a high-capacity backbone running at OC-48/STM-16 rates or higher.

This demand leads directly to three technical requirements:

- **Per-hop QoS**—The smallest controllable element in the network is the node (router or switch) joining two or more links. These nodes must be based on an architecture that allows sufficient differentiated queuing and scheduling to be applied at each hop and be able to appropriately utilize the QoS characteristics of inter-node links.

- **Routing and traffic engineering**—Where multiple parallel paths exist through a network, distributing traffic across these paths can reduce the average load and burstiness along any given path. This practice improves the network's apparent service quality because each router is less likely to drop or jitter packets. Mechanisms for discovering and imposing non-shortest-path forwarding are required.

- **Signaling and provisioning**—Controllable per-hop QoS and non-shortest-path forwarding is of little use if its not easily manageable. A practical solution requires some degree of automated distribution of QoS parameters and/or traffic engineering constraints to all the nodes (routers or switches) in the network. New information is distributed whenever a customer imposes or changes specific end-to-end (or edge-to-edge) QoS requirements.

These requirements are explored in more depth in the rest of this chapter.

2.1 A Hierarchy of Networks

Any network you might care to name is built from a hierarchy of components. Any path from one point to another is usually formed from the concatenation of shorter paths (hops) at the same level. A path at some level N becomes one hop in a path at level $N + 1$. Take the IP layer as the point of reference: It is made up of routers acting as switching points for IP packets and links that carry IP packets between routers. Each link is a single IP hop, yet the link itself might be made up of a number of its own *hops* and *nodes*.

The link can be a single Ethernet, a segment of a bridged Ethernet network, an IP tunnel, or an asynchronous transfer mode (ATM) virtual connection. In the case of a bridged Ethernet, one or more Ethernet switches may exist between the two routers. IP tunnels use one IP network to act as a link for another IP network (or sometimes the same IP network when certain types of traffic need to be hidden from sections of the network). An ATM virtual connection (VC) provides an end-to-end service between the ends of the VC, but in reality the VC may pass through many ATM switches along the way.

The IP-level QoS between two points depends on both the routers along the path and the QoS characteristics of each link's technology. Clearly the inter-router packet transport builds on the QoS capabilities of each link. If the link technology has no controllable QoS, the routers can do little to compensate because they rely on each link to provide predictable inter-router connectivity. However, in the presence of QoS-enabled link technologies, the router's behavior makes or breaks the availability of IP-level QoS.

Layering is recursive. For example, the QoS characteristics of an ATM VC depend on the predictability of the inter-switch links as much as on the ATM switches themselves. An ATM VC may span multiple ATM switches using Synchronous Optical Network (SONET) or Synchronous Digital Hierarchy (SDH) circuits for inter-switch cell transport. The SONET or SDH circuit itself is made up of one or more hops through various rings and multiplexors. Finally, the SONET or SDH circuits may have been multiplexed onto a single fiber along with totally unrelated circuits using different optical wavelengths—using wavelength-division multiplexing (WDM), an optical fiber multiplication technology that allows lots of virtual fibers to be provisioned within a single physical segment of fiber.

The Internet adds an extra wrinkle on the preceding model because many of the end-to-end paths used are not contained entirely within a single IP network—they are quite likely to span a number of independently administered IP networks (for example, LANs, service providers, and backbone operators as shown in Figure 2.2), each with its own routing policies and QoS characteristics.

Figure 2.2   One level's edge-to-edge network is another level's link.

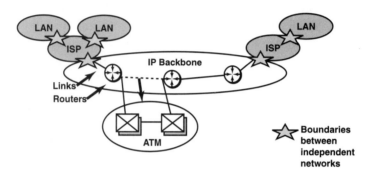

When only Best Effort is required or expected, you don't really need to care about the intermediate networks along the path, as long as their routing policy allows them to forward traffic. However, to support end-to-end QoS, you need to know more about the network's dynamic behavior. You do not need to know how each network achieves its QoS goals. It is enough to simply characterize each network in terms of the latency, jitter, and packet loss probabilities that may be imposed on the traffic.

Because one person's network is another person's link, the notion of end-to-end QoS must be generalized into one of edge-to-edge QoS. The QoS achieved from one end of a network to another is built from the concatenation of networks with their own edge-to-edge QoS capabilities, and each of these network's internal paths is built from links that may be networks in their own rights, again characterized by specific edge-to-edge QoS capabilities. The ability to characterize a network's edge-to-edge QoS behavior depends on the ability to characterize and control both the link and node behaviors at the network level.

2.2   Predictable Per-hop Behavior

The goal in a QoS-enabled environment is to enable predictable service delivery to certain classes or types of traffic regardless of what other traffic is flowing through the network at any given time. An alternative expression of this goal is the process of aiming to create a multiservice IP network solution where traditional bursty traffic may share the same infrastructure (routers, switches, and links) as traffic with more rigorous latency, jitter, bandwidth, and/or packet loss requirements. Regardless of whether you focus on enterprise, access, or backbone networks (or some combination of them all), the end-to-end path followed by a single user's packets is merely a sequence of links and routers. So, your attention must initially be drawn to the dynamics of a router's forwarding behavior.

Although a traditional router chiefly focuses on *where* to send packets (making forwarding decisions based on the destination address in each packet and locally held forwarding table information), routers for QoS-enabled IP networks must enable control of *when* to sends packets. You need to look more closely at those elements of a router that affect when packets are actually forwarded.

2.2.1 Transient Congestion, Latency, Jitter, and Loss

Each router is the smallest controllable convergence and divergence point for tens, hundreds, and thousands of unrelated flows of packets. In most data networks, traffic arrives in fluctuating bursts. On regular occasions, the simultaneous arrival of packet bursts from multiple links, which are all destined for the same output link (itself having only finite capacity), leave a router with more packets than it can immediately deliver. For example, traffic converging from multiple 100Mbit per second Ethernet links might easily exceed the capacity of a 155Mbit per second OC-3/STM-1 wide area circuit, or traffic from a number of T3/E3 links may simultaneously require forwarding out along a much smaller T1/E1 link. To cope with such occasions, all routers incorporate internal buffers (queues) within which they store excess packets until they can be sent onwards. Under these circumstances packets attempting to pass through the router experience additional delays. Such a router is said to be suffering from "transient congestion."

The end-to-end latency experienced by a packet is a combination of the transmission delays across each link and the processing delays experienced within each router. The delay contributed by link technologies such as SONET or SDH circuits, "leased line" circuits, or Constant Bit Rate (CBR) ATM virtual circuits is fairly predictable by design. However, the delay contributed by each router's congestion-induced buffering is not so predictable. It fluctuates with the changing congestion patterns, often varying from one moment to the next even for packets heading to the same destination. As you recall from Chapter 1, "The Internet Today," this randomly fluctuating component of the end-to-end latency is commonly referred to as "jitter."

Another issue is packet loss. Given that routers have only finite buffering (queuing) capacity, a sustained period of congestion may cause the buffer(s) to reach their capacity. When packets arrive to find buffer space exhausted, packets must be discarded until buffer space becomes available.

Clearly, you have a problem. The traditional router has, effectively, only a single queue for each internal congestion point (for example, in Figure 2.3 an output interface is draining the queue as fast as the interface speed allows) and no mechanism to isolate different classes or types of traffic from the effects of other traffic passing through it. The vagaries of the unrelated traffic passing through the shared queue at each internal congestion point is likely to have a heavy influence on each traffic stream's latency, jitter, and packet loss. Some types of traffic (for example, TCP connections carrying email) tolerate latency better than they tolerate packet loss, suggesting that long queues are ideal. However, other types of traffic—for example, User Datagram Protocol (UDP) carrying streaming video or audio—prefer that packets be discarded if held too long by the network, suggesting that shorter queues are better.

Figure 2.3   First-in, first-out queuing on a Best Effort router.

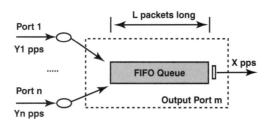

Consider the scenario in Figure 2.3. Packets arrive from each input port at a maximum rate of Y1 through to Yn packets per second (pps). The outbound link extracts packets from the queue at X pps. Take the total input rate as Y, the sum of (Y1 + Y2 + ... Yn). When Y is less than X, packets will not need to wait in the queue. However, it is more than likely that Y can burst well above X; in which case, the queue sees a net growth in size. The number of packets (P) in the queue after some interval (T) is expressed as P = T × (Y − X). A packet arriving at time T and finding the queue partially full experiences additional latency of X × P seconds (because the packet must wait for the queue to drain at X pps). If a packet arrives when the queue is full (P = L, the available queue space), the packet has nowhere to go and is dropped. Jitter comes from the fact that the components of Y are bursty and not correlated.

The preceding description also holds if you express the input and output rates in bits per second and the available queue space in bits (or bytes). If packets had a fixed length, a simple relationship would exist between the two forms of expression. However, in a typical IP environment packets are not of fixed length, adding further variability to the relationship between output link rate, the number of backlogged packets, and the latency experienced by backlogged packets.

Note

Latency can also be a function of the subnet technology—for example, the backoff scheme of Ethernet. However, backoff on Ethernet simply reveals itself as temporal unpredictability of the "link."

2.2.2 Classification, Queuing, and Scheduling

So what do you need to improve? The latency, jitter, and packet loss characteristics of any given IP network ultimately boil down to QoS characteristics of links and the dynamics of queue utilization and queue management within each router.

If network load exceeds service rate, a single queue at each internal congestion point is no longer sufficient. Instead, you need a queue for each identifiable class of traffic for which independent latency, jitter, and packet loss characteristics are required.

Each of these queues should have its own packet discard policies (for example, different thresholds beyond which packets are randomly or definitely discarded). Of course, the multiple queues per output interface are useless without a mechanism for assigning packets to the correct queues. A classification method is required over and above the router's traditional next-hop forwarding lookup. Finally, the queues must all share the finite capacity of the output link they feed into. This requirement implies the addition of a scheduling mechanism to interleave packets from each queue and, thus, mediate link access in a controllable and predictable manner.

For the purposes of this book, the preceding requirements can be captured as a statement that QoS-enabled networks require routers that can differentially Classify, Queue, and Schedule (CQS) all types of traffic as needed (see Figure 2.4). For the purposes of this book, such routers will be said to have a *CQS* architecture.

Figure 2.4   Per-hop Classify, Queue, and Schedule enables independent queuing and scheduling.

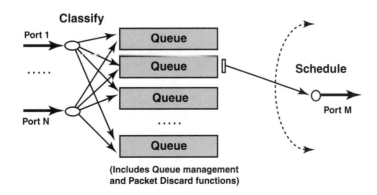

Later in this book, you look at various methods available for classifying traffic, comparing their relative complexities and the inherent granularity with which each scheme isolates different classes of traffic within an aggregate stream of packets. You also evaluate queuing schemes—the most important part of which is the queue's packet-dropping policy. These policies can range from simply dropping the most recently arrived packet when a queue reaches a hard limit (for example, it runs out of space) to making preemptive randomized drop decisions on the most recently arrived packet (based on how close the queue is to filling up and/or certain attributes carried within the packet itself). Finally, you consider the temporal effects of different scheduling algorithms on a network's capability to isolate different traffic classes from each other.

2.2.3 *Link-Level QoS*

Sometimes a router's scheduler must do more than simply interleave traffic at the IP packet level. The scheduler's capability to smoothly interleave traffic belonging to different queues depends on how quickly the outbound link can transmit each packet. For high-speed links (such as 155Mbit per second SONET or SDH circuits) a 1,500-byte IP packet takes less than 80 microseconds to transmit. This allows the scheduler to divide the link's bandwidth into slots up to 80 microseconds long—a very reasonable number, which drops to 20 microseconds on 622Mbit per second (OC-12 or STM-4) circuits. However, at the edges of the Internet many links are operating at 1Mbit per second or slower—in the 56 to 128Kbit per second range for Integrated Services Digital Network (ISDN) in North America and Europe and down to 28.8Kbit per second in the case of many dial-up modem connections.

A 1,500-byte IP packet takes around 94 milliseconds to transmit over a 128Kbit per second link, blocking the link completely during this time. Regardless of whether jitter-sensitive traffic has been classified into a different queue, those packets experience a 94-millisecond jitter when the scheduler pulls the 1,500-byte packet from another queue. Clearly, this poses some problems if QoS-sensitive applications are to be supported on the far side of typical low-speed access links.

The basic solution is to perform additional segmentation of the IP packets at the link level in a manner transparent to the IP layer itself. The CQS architecture is then applied at the link level by queuing segments rather than whole packets, thus allowing the scheduler to interleave on segment boundaries (see Figure 2.5). By choosing the smaller segment size appropriately, such an approach enables jitter-sensitive IP traffic to avoid being backlogged behind long IP packets. (However, nothing is gained for free—segmentation decreases overall transmission efficiency because each segment carries its own header to allow later re-combination of segments.)

Figure 2.5 Segmentation before scheduling improves interleaving on low speed links.

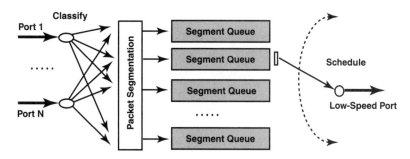

Although ATM was originally designed for high-speed links, its design reflects a similar concern with minimizing the interval over which traffic on a given class could hold the link. The ATM cell is short by design, and each ATM switch is an example of a CQS architecture. Arriving cells are queued for transmission according to the contents of their virtual path identifier (VPI) and virtual channel identifier (VCI) header fields. Taken together the VPI/VCI identify the VC to which the cell belongs, encoding both path information (where should the cell go next) and service-class information. Good ATM switches have queues for each traffic class on a per-port basis and have schedulers feeding cells out each port in accordance with the bandwidth guarantees given to each class.

2.2.4 Analogies

A real-world example of the CQS process is available from the airline industry. Airport check-in areas typically utilize a form of CQS architecture to provide different levels of service to different classes of passengers. The congestion point is represented by a set of check-in agents who are processing passengers as quickly as possible and at a moderately consistent rate (ignoring for a moment the variability of processing time caused by difficult passengers!). The link speed of this congestion point is represented by the aggregate passenger processing rate of the check-in agents. (The airline can add and remove agents to vary this speed.)

The arrival of passengers for check-in is a bursty process, typically peaking during the hour before a flight's scheduled departure time. Most of us are very familiar with the queues that build up during the sudden arrival of a group of passengers. If you've arrived along with many other passengers, your wait for check-in can be quite long. If you've arrived during a lull in activity, you may be checked-in quite soon after entering the check-in area.

The airlines typically like to provide expedited check-in service to their premium customers (for example, first-class passengers, or those in the higher frequent flyer club status levels). To do so, separate lines (queues) are established prior to the check-in agents. The classification of passengers into the appropriate queue can take a number of forms. Sometimes the airlines leave it to the passengers themselves to pick the appropriate queue; at other times an airline representative performs a perfunctory ticket check and directs people to the queue appropriate to their ticket or frequent-flyer class. It is worth noting here that classification doesn't need to take into account every piece of available information, only the relevant information. For example, although the passenger's identity (name) is important information during the check-in process, someone's name is largely irrelevant to the queue assignment at check-in.

The act of pulling a passenger from one of the queues represents a scheduling decision. Typically, check-in agents are dedicated to each queue (class of passenger), providing a minimum rate of service to that queue regardless of any blockages affecting other queues. To achieve efficient usage of agents, when a high-priority queue empties, the associated agents usually begin (temporarily) processing passengers from the lower-priority queues. By appropriate distribution of check-in agents, the premium class of customers experience faster (shorter lines and, thus, lower latency) and more predictable (lower jitter) check-in service than those in lower classes.

A related real-world example of queuing and scheduling can be seen in the designs of major highways and freeways. Consider exit ramps, which are a form of output buffering for cars. Exit ramps feeding onto smaller roads typically terminate at a controlled intersection. The lights controlling the flow of traffic from the off-ramp into the local road act as a coarse scheduler. When cars begin exiting the highway faster than they are being fed onto the local road, the exit ramp itself begins to fill up. During the morning and evening peak traffic hours, many cars may be consistently arriving that the exit ramp overflows, causing traffic chaos on the main highway itself. Fortunately for drivers, cars are not "dropped" when the exit ramp overflows (although drivers may choose to continue on and search for another exit).

Finally, an example of classification and scheduling can be found at the toll booths that are sometimes placed across major highways. Typically a multilane highway fans out to many more toll lanes, and a self-classification process ensues as cars approach the tollbooths and pick their preferred lane. Particular lanes may be set aside for trucks, or priority lanes restricted to cars holding special electronic passes—motorists are advised of the appropriate self-classification rules prior to arriving at the tollbooths. (This example does not have an equivalent to controlled scheduling because each lane processes cars independently of other lanes.)

As you will see in the following chapters, CQS router architectures may be implemented in a number of permutations, each with its own specific consequences for the QoS characteristics of the IP network as a whole. The fundamental task of each router hop now becomes

- To know *where* to send the packet (conventional forwarding)

- To know *when* to send it (the additional QoS requirement)

- To complete the preceding tasks independently of other traffic sharing the router

2.3 *Predictable Edge-to-Edge Behavior*

As noted earlier, any end-to-end service is constructed from both the concatenation and layering of edge-to-edge and per-hop behaviors. Network operators, focusing on the edge-to-edge capabilities of the networks under their control, have a range of possible per-hop behaviors to mix and match together. Over the years a number of solution spaces have emerged, each one reflecting a different set of assumptions and compromises with respect to the CQS and routing capabilities of routers within the network.

The first and most important observation is that network designers face a trade-off between the number of traffic classes carried by their networks and the number of traffic classes that their router's CQS architectures can handle. A number of solutions are based on distributed edge-and-core architectures, where the cores are fast routers with limited CQS capabilities and the edges are slower but with more advanced CQS capabilities.

A second observation is that the Internet's existing shortest-path routing algorithms are not necessarily optimal for different classes of traffic across an arbitrary mesh of routers and links. A single metric may not be appropriate for all traffic traversing a particular section of the network. In addition, the destination-based forwarding paradigm itself makes it difficult to force subsets of available traffic into following alternative, non-shortest paths across any given network topology.

2.3.1 *Edge-and-Core Models*

Whether in hardware or software, the design of a good CQS architecture is generally nontrivial. In many software implementations, tight processing budgets make classification, queue management, and scheduling difficult to introduce without affecting the overall peak performance of the box. Hardware implementations have only just started to become commonplace—and until recently the development of a CQS implementation for IP locked into hardware was too commercially risky.

The edge-and-core model allows core routers to leverage hardware implementations (for speed), while leaving complex (but slower) processing to software-based edge routers. The edge routers might be able to classify and independently queue hundreds or thousands of traffic classes, whereas the core routers are assumed to be limited to a handful of queues.

Limited numbers of queues in core routers leads to a new requirement that edge routers be able to smooth out the burstiness of traffic entering the network. In the preceding discussion of per-hop QoS control, individual traffic classes were permitted to be completely unpredictable on the assumption that you could accurately isolate and reschedule them at every potential congestion point. However, although a smart edge/dumb core model may have the requisite isolation granularity at the edges, it does not in the core. Multiple traffic classes will find themselves aggregated into shared queues within the core routers. The potential for unpredictable mutual interference is high unless the network imposes some level of predictability before the traffic reaches the core routers. The solution is for edge routers to manipulate the temporal characteristics of individual traffic classes (and, hence, the aggregate of those traffic classes) before they enter the core. The Internet Engineering Task Force (IETF) Differentiated Services model is one example, and it will be discussed in Chapter 4, "Edge-to-Edge Network Models."

Shaping and Policing

The primary focus of a CQS architecture is the protection of traffic in each queue from the burstiness of traffic in another queue. On a per-hop basis, it is clear that, given appropriate isolation of all QoS-sensitive traffic into distinct queues, a scheduler needs to guarantee only a certain worst-case servicing interval (or minimum bandwidth). If spare capacity is available, you might expect "good" scheduler behavior to allocate that capacity to any queues having packets waiting to be forwarded. However, this practice is not always desirable from a network-wide perspective.

Simply emptying a queue as fast as the line rate allows (in the absence of traffic in other queues) can increase the burstiness perceived by routers further downstream. As a result, a serious problem can develop if the downstream routers do not differentiate traffic with as much granularity as the local router does. In addition, service providers may wish to cap the maximum rate that a customer can send packets through the network. If the customer frequently gets significantly better bandwidth than the guaranteed minimum (perhaps because the network is new and/or under loaded), a perception issue surfaces: The customer begins to associate the typical performance with what he or she is paying for. If the spare capacity ever shrinks, the customer will receive edge-to-edge performance closer to the guaranteed minimum. However, the customer simply perceives the service to have degraded and is likely to complain loudly. Managing customer expectations is an important part of running a business, and in this case preemptive rate capping is one of the technology-based tools that may be employed.

Placing an upper bound on the maximum bandwidth (or minimum inter-packet interval) available to a traffic class is known as "traffic shaping." A shaping scheduler is configured to provide both a minimum service interval (the time between pulling packets from the same queue) and a maximum service interval (to guarantee the latency bound or minimum bandwidth). Packets arriving with a shorter inter-packet interval than allowed by the scheduler are queued until transmission—smoothing out the original burstiness. Figure 2.6 shows a scheduler that never samples the top queue more frequently than once every T seconds—no matter how closely bunched up the packets arrive, they are transmitted with at least T seconds between them. (A simple form of shaping scheduler is sometimes referred to as a "leaky bucket," because no matter how fast packets arrive they can only "leak out" at a fixed rate.)

Figure 2.6   Shaping requires a minimum scheduler time on certain queues.

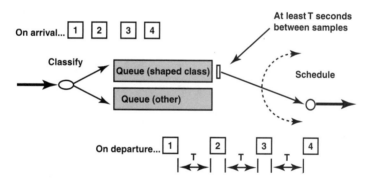

A real-world example of shaping can be seen in some freeway entrance ramps. In California, for example, some entrance ramps are equipped with stop/go lights that alternate every few seconds. The net effect is to allow cars onto the freeway with a known minimum time interval between them—regardless of how bursty the car arrival times may have been to the entrance ramp itself. This input traffic shaping improves the capability of cars already on the freeway to interleave with the new traffic.

Shaping is not a simple function to introduce into a Best Effort router because this function presumes the existence of an appropriate CQS architecture. Although not quite so elegant, an alternative solution has been to introduce a packet-dropping behavior that is sensitive to excess burstiness of a traffic class. When too many packets arrive in too short an interval, packets are simply dropped. This process is known as policing.

Policing can be implemented without queues or schedulers, although it typically needs some form of classification to differentiate between the policing rules imposed on different traffic classes. In its simplest form, each traffic class has an associated counter. The counter is incremented regularly every T seconds and decremented whenever a packet (belonging to the counter's class) is forwarded. If a packet arrives to be transmitted when the counter is zero, the packet is dropped instead. When no packets are being transmitted, the counter increments up to a fixed limit L. The net effect is that a packet stream arriving with an average inter-packet interval of T seconds (or greater) passes through untouched. However, if a burst of more than L packets arrive in less than T seconds, the counter reaches zero and extra packets are dropped. The value of L affects the burst tolerance of the policing function, and T sets the rate below which traffic is safe. This practice is a severe, yet effective, way to modify the burstiness of traffic downstream from the policing router!

The utility of policing is based on the assumption that most bursty traffic originates from applications using adaptive end-to-end transport protocols such as TCP. Packet loss is assumed to indicate transient congestion, and TCP reacts by slowing down the rate at which it injects packets into the network. Policing allows the network operator to fake the existence of transient congestion for a particular traffic class before it actually begins to occur further along the packet's path. Even if the traffic class is not using an adaptive end-to-end transport protocol, policing protects the rest of the network by continuing to drop packets that exceed the allowed parameters.

Both shaping and policing are extremely useful tools for network designers who face a trade-off between the number of traffic classes carried by their networks and the number of traffic classes their network's CQS architectures can handle. The basic issue is that individual traffic classes can be permitted to be unpredictable only if you can accurately isolate them at every potential congestion point. If you lack that isolation capability, you must attempt to impose some level of predictability prior to the potential congestion point. In the smart edge/dumb core model, the solution is for each edge router to preemptively shape and/or police the individual traffic classes before they enter the core to impose some overall order, smoothness, and predictability within each traffic class (and, hence, the aggregate of those traffic classes). Shaping may also be useful on the egress from a network in situations where the next network's aggressive policing would be otherwise detrimental.

Marking and Reordering

Although shaping can be a sophisticated solution to smoothing out bursty traffic, simple policing is a blunt instrument. A number of variations have been introduced to soften the effect of edge-router policing. A policing node may choose to only "mark" packets (rather than discarding them immediately) if they exceed a burstiness threshold. Routers further along the path recognize these marked packets as having a lower priority than unmarked packets. If transient congestion begins to fill the queues in a downstream core router, its queue management algorithm can begin dropping marked packets before it begins dropping unmarked packets.

As an additional refinement, the original policing node may implement a staggered set of burst thresholds—if a packet burst exceeds the lower threshold, subsequent packets are marked and transmitted; if the burst continues and exceeds a higher threshold, packets are dropped. Alternatively, the policing node might implement multiple levels of "allowed" average packet arrival rates—a lower rate below which packets are forwarded unmarked, an intermediate range of rates within which packets are marked and forwarded, and an upper threshold above which packets are dropped.

The impact on the core of the network is "softer" than would be achieved by a simple policing because many of the packets in the burst will have been marked instead of dropped. The advantage of such a scheme is that, in the absence of other network congestion in the core, this particular traffic class can utilize more of the available bandwidth.

Many algorithms can be invented to provide multiple marking levels and threshold calculations. However, network designers who plan on using edge marking of traffic also need to carefully choose their core routers. The main point of concern is potential *reordering* of marked packets relative to unmarked packets within a traffic class. This situation can happen if the core router uses two separate queues to differentiate between marked and unmarked packets in the same traffic class (see Figure 2.7). Because marked packets are of "lower priority," an implementation might choose to effect this relative priority by assigning more scheduler bandwidth to the queue of unmarked packets than for the queue of marked packets.

As a consequence a marked packet arriving *before* an unmarked packet in the same traffic class may find itself scheduled for transmission *after* the unmarked packet (or vice-versa). Assuming the marked packet makes it all the way to the other end, the receiving application perceives the traffic to contain out-of-order packets.

Although the IP specifications do not preclude packets being reordered by the network, this practice should be avoided because most end-to-end protocols do not handle this case efficiently. In networks where marking is intended to increase a packet's drop probability, the solution is not too difficult. Let the core router initially ignore the policing marker when classifying packets into queues, ensuring all packets in a traffic class are placed in one queue regardless of drop priority. Then modify the packet drop threshold for that queue on the basis of whether the packet is marked or not. The core router's packet-dropping algorithm, thus, activates more aggressively for marked packets, achieving the desired edge-to-edge behavior.

Figure 2.7   Separate queues for marked and unmarked packets can lead to reordering.

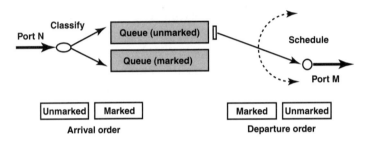

2.3.2 Edge-to-Edge Routing

No particular restrictions dictate how routers and links are interconnected to form an IP network. As discussed in Chapter 1, the Internet's shortest-path routing mechanisms are based on the assumption that a network's topology is rarely static and must be tracked dynamically. In any realistic network, each router may have more than one output interface over which it could send a packet—the role of routing protocols is to establish a single interface over which a packet should be sent. To make the calculations tractable, the choice of appropriate interface has largely been driven by algorithms using only a single metric to define the shortest path.

However, two general concerns have been raised with this approach when it comes to supporting QoS. First is the argument that a single metric may not be appropriate for all traffic traversing a particular section of the network. Second, the destination-based forwarding paradigm itself makes it difficult to force subsets of available traffic into following alternative, non-shortest paths across any given network topology.

QoS-Based Routing

QoS-based routing protocols attempt to take multiple metrics into account when building the network's forwarding tables. These protocols have been studied for years and often begin with an assumption that the network is built from conventional Best Effort IP routers. Starting from this assumption, single-metric routing is seen to have a number of limitations when attempting to meet the mixed QoS demands of a multiservice environment.

A metric can be considered a type of cost with each link (hop) having a cost associated with it. The routing protocols attempt to find paths with minimal total cost summed over all the links to possible destinations. However, this cost cannot represent the interests and needs of all traffic types. Should it represent the link's latency, its available bandwidth, its packet loss probability, or perhaps the actual expense of sending packets over the link? Pick one. You will end up with some traffic finding the choice appropriate, whereas for other traffic the choice is wasteful of resources.

For example, consider a network where latency is the metric. Certainly the shortest path now suits applications with tight real-time requirements. But they are not alone. The network is most likely also being used by traditional, bursty data applications that care significantly less about latency. The traffic from these other applications also follows the minimum latency shortest paths, adding to the load on the Best Effort routers along the path. An unfortunate side effect is that the bursty traffic consumes the same buffer space being used by the real-time traffic, increasing the jitter and average latencies experienced by all traffic through the routers. This approach also affects the accuracy of the latency costs that the routing protocols use to determine the shortest paths.

QoS-based routing creates multiple shortest-paths trees, covering the same actual topology of routers and links with each tree using different combinations of parameters as link metrics. The goal is to minimize unnecessary coexistence within routers of traffic with widely different QoS requirements. Packets with strict latency requirements are then forwarded by using the tree built with latency as a metric. Packet's with non-real-time requirements might have a different tree built (for example, to minimize the financial cost of the path). Several practical issues exist with implementation of QoS-based routing:

- Each router needs to have multiple forwarding tables (or their functional equivalent) on which to perform each packet's destination-based next-hop lookup, one for each type of shortest-path tree. Additional fields in the packet header are used to select one of the possible next hops associated with the packet's destination address. This situation complicates the design of the next-hop lookup engine.

- An increase in routing protocol overhead occurs because the router's CPU must support an instance of each protocol for each unique shortest-path tree. This requirement causes an increase in the time it takes for a network of such routers to converge after a transient in the network topology (for example, when links come or go or their costs somehow change). The convergence time increases further if the routing protocol is being asked to calculate trees based on multiple metrics simultaneously.

- Metrics such as latency or available bandwidth are highly dependent on the actual traffic flowing across the network. A shortest-path tree built with statically configured latency values could become outdated when traffic begins to flow across the network. The alternative, of updating each link's cost with regular real-time measurements, poses a real control-theory nightmare—every cost update would result in a recalculation of the associated shortest-path tree, leading to continual processing load on all the routers.

Interestingly, the development of routers with CQS architectures somewhat reduces the need for QoS-based routing. For example, consider the example that uses latency as a cost metric. Now consider that every router has at least two queues per output interface—one for latency sensitive traffic and the other for all remaining traffic. All traffic is routed along lowest-latency paths. Assuming the routers appropriately classify traffic into the two queues, the service received by latency-sensitive traffic is independent of the burstiness of all other traffic types. Arguably then, any conventional, single-metric IP routing protocol, when coupled with routers based on a CQS architecture, can support multiple levels of service differentiation. The main caveat here is that sufficient capacity exists along the single tree to provide adequate service to all participants.

Explicit Path Control

The internal topologies of many networks are such that multiple paths can be found between most points. A major limitation of conventional IP forwarding is that single-metric, shortest-path trees use only one of the possible paths toward any given destination. Because lightly loaded alternative paths are not utilized, routers that exist on the shortest-path trees for many different network destinations can be subjected to high-average load—they become *hot spots*, potentially limiting the capability of the network to provide adequate service differentiation even if the router itself has a CQS architecture.

As the average load on a hot-spot router rises, the probability of random packet losses and jitter increases. Although this observation is most evident for networks containing regular Best Effort routers, it also holds true (albeit to a lesser degree) when the network consists of multiple queue routers. To combat this problem, a network operator has two alternatives:

- Upgrade the routers and links to operate faster

- Utilize additional packet-forwarding mechanisms that allow the traffic to be split across alternative paths (some of which may be just as short as the "official" shortest path and others that may be longer according to the prevailing metric)

When the network itself is built from cheap, low- to middle-bandwidth technology, the former approach may be entirely suitable. This description is most likely going to apply to enterprise environments where traffic growth has outpaced the deployed technology and a successor technology is easily deployable (for example, a 10Mbit per second Ethernet environment, where the upgrade to 100Mbit per second or 1Gbit per second Ethernet solutions are available).

Simply upgrading equipment and/or links may not be an option when your network is already pushing the limits of available technology. High-performance IP backbones have this problem—their routers are usually pushed hard to support OC-12 and OC-48 rate interfaces, and to buy or provision such circuits across today's traditional carrier infrastructures presents a serious problem. In addition, although prices are dropping for OC-12 and OC-48 circuits, they remain an expensive resource.

A preferable alternative is to build the equivalent aggregate capacity through parallelism—an IP topology rich in routers and lower-speed links across which the aggregate load can be distributed. Overriding shortest-path routing to more optimally utilize the underlying infrastructure of routers and links is often referred to as traffic engineering. Figure 2.8 shows a simplistic example.

Figure 2.8   Overriding a shortest-path route to balance the load.

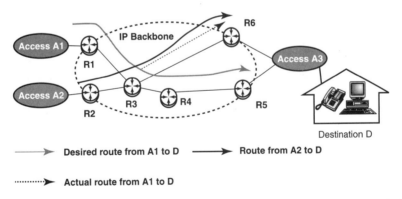

Access networks A1 and A2 both source traffic to destination D, which is reachable through Access network A3. A3 has two attachment points to the IP backbone, through R6 and R5. Conventional IP forwarding would cause packets from both A1 and A2 to converge to the same forwarding path at interior/core router R3, and be forwarded to R6 (because the path is shorter than R3[→]R4[→]R5). A good way to reduce the average load on R6 is to force some portion of the load (for example, the packets coming from network A1) to follow the R3[→]R4[→]R5 path instead. A network operator may also want to override shortest-path forwarding for policy reasons (for example, the external link between R6 and A3 may have been funded solely by A2 and A3, and therefore A1's traffic must not be allowed to traverse it).

Traffic engineering through explicit path control is an important part of any solution to providing QoS, although the main impact is on the overall efficiency of the network itself, rather than directly impinging on the end-users. This approach also raises an interesting routing question—having discarded the information being provided by the existing IP routing protocols, network operators need to supply an external source of information to control the traffic-engineered routing within their networks.

Explicit path control can be achieved in a variety of ways, either avoiding or permuting every router's conventional destination-based forwarding decision. The methods available at the IP level include

- Strict and loose source routing options

- Forwarding tables with lookup on the destination address and other fields in the IP packet header

- IP tunneling

- Multiprotocol Label Switching (MPLS)

In theory, an IP packet can have optional header fields added that specify (either explicitly or approximately) the sequence of routers through which the packet must pass on its way to the destination. However, most routers do not efficiently process packets carrying such optional header fields (the peak performance "fast path" through a router is typically optimized for packets having no additional headers). Packets with optional headers are processed in a parallel "slow path"—making this a poor choice if consistent QoS control is desired.

A slightly more feasible method is for the forwarding table to be constructed with regard not only for where the packet is going but also for where it has come. In this manner, it becomes possible to return different next-hop information for the same destination address just by taking the source address into account. However, this approach works only for a very constrained set of topologies and traffic-engineering scenarios. It is also expensive in terms of memory space in the forwarding tables.

Traffic Engineering with IP Tunnels

IP-IP tunneling forces the desired traffic patterns through the use of logical links. An IP packet is tunneled by placing it into the payload of another IP packet (the tunneling packet, as shown in Figure 2.9), which is then transmitted toward the desired tunnel endpoint. When the tunneling packet reaches its destination, the tunnel endpoint extracts the original IP packet and forwards it as though it had arrived over a regular interface.

Figure 2.9 Packet encapsulation for IP-IP tunneling.

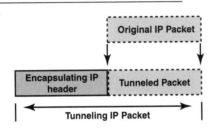

Taking the network example in Figure 2.8, R1 would be configured to encapsulate traffic for D inside tunneling packets addressed to R5, and R2 would be configured to encapsulate traffic for D inside tunneling packets addressed to R6. Figure 2.10 shows the effective topology resulting from this arrangement.

Figure 2.10 Traffic engineering with IP-IP tunneling.

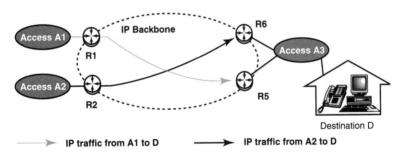

Several problems exist with this solution.

- Routers do not necessarily perform tunneling encapsulation and decapsulation in their "fast path"—this can be a major performance hit at the tunnel endpoints.

- The tunneling encapsulation (shown in Figure 2.9) adds overhead to each packet, reducing the Maximum Transmission Unit (MTU) that can be supported by the virtual link represented by the tunnel if fragmentation within the tunnel is to be avoided.

- The effective traffic engineering is very coarse—an IP-IP tunnel only allows control over the tunneled packet's final destination (the egress routers R5 or R6 in this example). The tunneling packet takes the shortest path across the backbone to R5 or R6 as appropriate.

Traffic Engineering with Label-Switched Paths

Multiprotocol Label Switching (MPLS) is discussed in some detail later in this book, but it is worth noting here that the primary role of MPLS for service providers is traffic engineering. MPLS is a connection-oriented form of IP networking—packets have labels added and are forwarded along preconstructed label-switched paths (LSPs) by routers modified to switch MPLS frames (label-switching routers, LSRs).

LSPs can mimic the IP-IP tunnels in Figure 2.10—one LSP between R1 and R5, and another LSP between R2 and R6. R1 would be configured to label all traffic for D with the label corresponding to the first hop of the LSP from R1 to R5. R2 would be configured to label all traffic for D with the label corresponding to the first hop of the LSP from R2 to R6.

The effective topology in Figure 2.11 between the edge LSRs is identical to that in Figure 2.10, but the solutions are different. First, the overhead per packet is reduced (an MPLS header is 4 bytes, compared to 20+ bytes for a complete encapsulating IP header). Second, the packet's actual hop-by-hop path within the backbone is under the control of the network operator when the LSP is established.

Figure 2.11   Traffic engineering with explicitly routed label-switched paths.

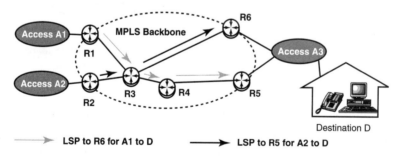

LSP to R6 for A1 to D   LSP to R5 for A2 to D

LSP and ATM VC are similar in many ways. Backbone operators who use ATM to transport their wide area IP traffic already utilize explicitly routed permanent virtual connections (PVCs) between the edges of their ATM networks and rely on the edge routers to map the correct traffic onto the appropriate PVCs. For many service providers, the move to MPLS is simply a generalization of ATM but with variable-length packets instead of fixed-length cells.

2.4 *Signaling*

Assuming that you can provide differentiated queuing and scheduling on a per-hop basis and have the appropriately controllable underlying link layers, the question becomes one of establishing and modifying the network's actual behavior. This matter requires coordination of the actual (rather than theoretical) behaviors along each path. A generic term for this process is *signaling*—the act of informing each hop along a path (or paths) how to recognize traffic for which a special processing behavior is required and the type of special processing required.

Signaling can be achieved in a number of ways with varying degrees of timeliness, flexibility, and human intervention (not all of which are conventionally considered signaling per se). At one extreme sits dynamic edge-to-edge signaling, where the network is informed each and every time a new class of traffic requires specific support.

The network itself responds on demand by internally establishing additional information (or modifying existing information) at each hop to achieve the requested edge-to-edge behavior. Examples of on-demand signaling include ATM's User Network Interface (UNI) and Network Node Interface (NNI) signaling protocols and the IETF's Resource Reservation Protocol (RSVP).

New network technologies frequently either do not have fully dynamic signaling protocols defined or have not matured to the point where reliable implementations of their signaling protocols exist. Under such circumstances the networks are usually provisioned for new services—often entailing human intervention to configure (or reconfigure) the controllers of the links and nodes along the affected paths. Provisioning is a form of signaling, even though the response time is usually orders of magnitude slower than dynamic signaling.

Because the number of links and nodes in a network can be quite large, many vendors are developing centralized controllers or servers where configuration or provisioning actually occurs. These controllers then automatically distribute the appropriate rules to the links and nodes in the network on behalf of the human operator. Designs that are more advanced allow these controllers to automatically react to changing network conditions in accordance with general policies that may be imposed by the human operator. Although such centralized schemes also constitute a dynamic mechanism, they differ from edge-to-edge signaling in that it is not user controlled.

The Internet has used a form of dynamic signaling for years—its routing protocols. Although most of us have been conditioned to think of signaling and routing as distinct activities, protocols such as Open Shortest Path First (OSPF) and Border Gateway Protocol (BGP) are the Internet's mechanisms for signaling topology changes. These mechanisms ensure the construction of up-to-date forwarding tables that reflect the best set of shortest paths across the network and adapt dynamically to changing topological conditions. Therefore, these mechanisms (that is, OSPF and BGP) qualify as signaling protocols. However, their focus is internal to the network itself, and their actions are generally not explicitly triggered by some user's request. Furthermore, their actions are designed primarily to effect the construction of paths, not the allocation of resources or priority processing for specific traffic along those paths.

Typically, signaling in the IP context is thought of as the additional actions required to establish a particular edge-to-edge QoS over and above the default Best Effort QoS. As previously noted this process can involve dynamic or provisioned behaviors (or some combination). In all cases, the process of establishing a desired edge-to-edge QoS requires careful balancing of existing per-hop resources and network-wide paths.

When a signaling request states a particular QoS goal, there are a number of variables to consider. In theory, both the path and the resources along the path are open to modification. For a given path, the signaling protocol should determine whether resources (for example, queuing space or share of link bandwidth) are available along that path. If the first path checked does not support the desired QoS, an ideal signaling protocol would find another path and try again. As an example, ATM's Private Network Node Interface (PNNI) signaling tries different paths until it finds one that can support the requested edge-to-edge QoS. Trying alternative paths presumes that the network has the capability to force traffic along the path that is discovered to be capable of supporting the desired QoS.

In conventional connectionless IP, however, traffic must follow the shortest-path trees established by the routing protocols (using whatever metric is specified by the network operator). As a consequence the IETF developed its RSVP signaling mechanism to simply follow (and adapt to) whatever routing exists in the network without attempting to discover alternative, non-shortest-path routes that might better support the requested QoS. Inherently a trade-off, RSVP avoids any reengineering of existing IP networks, doesn't reinvent or replicate the actions of the existing IP routing protocols, and can be introduced as a simple hardware or software upgrade to existing routers. However, if resources are exhausted along a particular shortest path, no simple way exists for RSVP to force traffic along a longer, but perhaps more lightly loaded path.

Another issue with signaling is the amount of additional state information the routers must carry. *State information* is anything that the router needs to characterize the special traffic—for example, IP header information on which to classify the packets—and to process the special traffic—for example, associated queue(s), packet-drop parameters, and scheduler priorities or weights. The routing and forwarding tables already held by each router represent topological state information—adding signaling for QoS only increases the number of tables consuming valuable memory in routers.

Any realistic QoS solution for IP networking must cope with the often conflicting demands that it be easy to implement, not send the amount of state information skyrocketing, optimize the use of network resources, adapt dynamically to routing changes, and work in a world where routing and signaling are decoupled.

2.5 Policies, Authentication, and Billing

If I offer you a first-class seat on the plane for the price of an economy-class seat, you would take it, right? At worst you might wonder what the catch is, but in the end nobody refuses better service if it costs no more than worse service—whether the comfort of an airplane's seating, the speed of package delivery from a shipping service, or Internet access from a local ISP is being discussed. Of course, a practical problem immediately arises if you're not being charged a premium price for the premium service—everybody else wants it, too.

Any networking technology that offers differentiation of service levels must also address the need to differentiate each user's *right to use* particular service levels. If everyone has a right to use the best service level at the same time, the resources would either run out, or the network would have to be engineered to cope. In general the network's resources are limited at various service levels, and so the task is one of allowing or disallowing particular users access to service levels based on their right to use. (If the network were engineered to handle everyone asking for premium service, without any differential impact on the cost of running the network, what would be the point of offering lesser service levels?) This right to use can be established in a number of ways—for example, payment of fees (financial cost) or administrative assignment (ranking of the user's importance). A commercial service provider would be inclined to utilize a fee basis—you get the service you pay for. A corporate enterprise network may determine service allocations based at least in part on the status of each user (or the user's department) within the company.

The whole issue of establishing and monitoring a user's right to use certain service levels opens up a can of worms that the Internet industry is only beginning to address. First are questions of policy (identifying the service classes that particular users are entitled to negotiate). Second is the problem of authentication (proving that the entity currently using the network is the claimed user, either during right-to-use negotiations or subsequent traffic transmission). Third is the question of billing (extracting the fee from the correct user) if fees are used to establish the right to use. Billing is even of interest to enterprise networks, where it may be used to provide additional granularity of usage control beyond the corporate status of a user or the user's department.

All three issues are also tightly coupled to the network's signaling because the network's signaling system must establish the requested edge-to-edge service levels and associate them with traffic coming from the user. If the users are utilizing dynamic, edge-to-edge signaling to negotiate their right to use, the signaling protocol itself must be tightly coupled with the policy, authentication, and billing mechanisms.

Human nature being what it is, the network must be capable of authenticating any user's request for, and use of, particular service levels. Users must not be billed for services they don't request, lest the operator finds itself in a court of law or being lambasted in the media (perhaps a worse fate for a service provider trying to garner the trust of the market place!). Of course, users must also be accurately billed for the service levels they do request. If the operator's fee structure is based in some part on the actual amount of usage, the consumption of services must also be tracked and authenticated.

If dynamic, edge-to-edge user-signaling protocols (such as RSVP) are to be used in fee-for-use environments, these protocols clearly need to incorporate sufficiently strong user authentication fields. (An operator might attempt to deduce a user's identity from physical attachment points on the network, but in an age of dial-up IP access and mobile nodes this approach is rarely effective.) In the absence of such capabilities, the user and service provider are forced to rely on more traditional or manual channels to negotiate service levels (the fax, phone, or postal service). Alternatively, the service provider can simply hope users don't go around impersonating each other when ordering service levels.

Enterprise environments are typically more structured and controlled, and in these environments authentication based solely on the node's topological position might be quite feasible. However, if the enterprise network includes mobile nodes or any likelihood that users will move around the network's topology, it will need to consider the same issues faced by a commercial service provider.

Two problems develop if the service provider decides to incorporate a usage-based component in the right-to-use fee. First, no clear industry consensus has emerged on what constitutes a realistic metric for use—is it simple packet counts, burstiness, peak or mean bandwidths, or some complex measurement of delivered latency and jitter?

Second, after you decide on a metric that you think the customers will understand, you face the problem of accurately measuring it in your network and reliably associating your measurements to particular users. Real-time measurement of traffic patterns is a major problem because it requires significant processing capabilities and needs to be undertaken for each and every instance of a distinct, user-defined traffic class.

This book cannot hope to cover the emerging solutions to policy management, user authentication, and billing models. However, you will be left with an understanding of the roles played by these important components of a total IP QoS solution and have the ability to assess whatever the industry offers.

CHAPTER 3

Per-hop Packet Processing

Chapter 2, "The Components of Network QoS," provides a broad overview of the issues facing providers and developers of quality of service (QoS) enabled Internet Protocol (IP) networks. Beyond simply forwarding packets through to their appropriate next hop, routers must now implement Classify, Queue, and Schedule (CQS) architectures to provide differentiated forwarding characteristics. In addition, links need to have their own predictable QoS characteristics to match the temporal control being supplied by routers. This chapter focuses on what it means for a router to be QoS enabled and to have a CQS architecture. The construction of actual *end-to-end services*, such as the Differentiated Services (DiffServ) and Integrated Services (IntServ) models, is discussed in Chapter 4, "Edge-to-Edge Network Models." In Chapter 6, "Link Layers Beneath IP," Chapter 7, "Low-Speed Link Technologies," and Chapter 8 "High-Speed Link Technologies," a range of link technologies are explored in more detail, with particular focus on their QoS characteristics.

3.1 A Generic Router

A generic router has only a few basic function blocks (see Figure 3.1).

- Multiple interfaces

- A forwarding engine

- A management engine

Input interfaces accept packets from other routers, and (based on each packet's IP destination address) the forwarding engine passes the packets to the appropriate output interfaces. Each interface then uses link-specific mechanisms for transmitting the packet to the next router (or host) along the path. When the router believes that localized congestion is increasing inappropriately, packets may also be dropped or marked as a means of indicating this state to the network around it. The forwarding engine's per-packet behavior (choice of output interface and congestion response) is ultimately controlled by the management engine.

Figure 3.1   A generic Best Effort IP router.

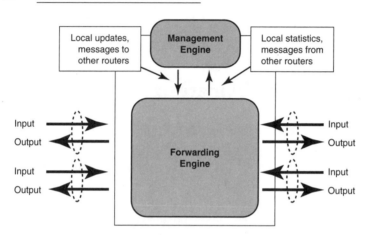

As briefly described in Chapter 1, "The Internet Today," a table known as the forwarding information base (FIB) drives a router's forwarding decision (*where* to send packets). For every possible IP destination address, a longest-prefix match search is performed across the FIB. If a match is found, the corresponding entry tells the forwarding engine which output interface should receive the packet; if no match is found, the packet is dropped. The FIB's contents reflect the current state of the IP topology surrounding the router, as determined by the IP routing protocol(s)—for example, Open Shortest Path First (OSPF) or Border Gateway Protocol version 4 (BGP4)—running on the management engine.

Note

Knowing the surrounding topology allows a FIB of next hops to be derived from the calculated shortest-path trees to all known destination(s)/prefixes.

Clearly Figure 3.1 is a highly abstract model. Early routers typically had a single central CPU handling all the management and packet-forwarding functions. Routers have since evolved toward more distributed architectures, all designed to remove or reduce performance bottlenecks. In high-performance backbone routers, the forwarding engine is distributed among the set of interface cards interconnected by a high-speed switch fabric or back plane [KLS98] [KESH98] [DSRTER]. Nevertheless, all such routers have a common sequence of steps that a packet must pass through while being processed.

Now that QoS is becoming important, the forwarding process is being redesigned to pay more attention to *when* routers send packets. Figure 3.2 provides an abstract view of the processing that occurs within the forwarding engine of Figure 3.1. In general, a packet passes through three major stages:

- Classification and FIB lookup (to establish the packet's identity and where it is going—its output interface)

- Policing and marking (to react if the packet has not arrived in an appropriate time frame)

- Queuing and scheduling (to forward the packet according to link-sharing or traffic-shaping rules or to drop it according to congestion-control rules)

The packet classification stage establishes the entire context for the packet's subsequent handling by the router. Although most of that context is used to establish temporal handling characteristics (policing, marking, queuing, and scheduling), some of the additional context may be used to modify the forwarding decision. For example, an advanced router might maintain multiple FIBs (representing shortest-path trees based on differing metrics) and choose between them by using other information in the packet's header (for example, the packet's source address). An equivalence, or at least a close relationship, often exists between a packet's context (as established through classification) and its "class" (as perceived on an end-to-end basis).

Note
A router might also take the derived next hop as part of the packet's context during latter processing, but this sort of detail is highly implementation dependent.

Figure 3.2 reflects a simplifying assumption that congestion occurs only at the output interfaces. A CQS architecture is required at all congestion points, whether within a network or within a router. Certain router architectures may also have internal congestion points (for example, at the input to the switch fabric or back plane) and must also provide differentiated queuing and scheduling at all these points.

Figure 3.2   Per-hop classification drives next hop, queuing, and scheduling.

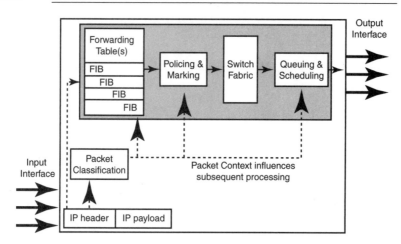

Router vendors differentiate their products based on cost versus performance. Early Best Effort routers found the FIB lookup stage to be their major bottleneck. However, in the past few years a number of exceedingly quick algorithms have been developed for FIB lookups—multimillion lookups per second are commonplace among the high-end router designs—so this concern is no longer a serious issue (for example, see "Scalable High Speed IP Routing Lookups" [FASTIP1] and "Small Forwarding Tables for Fast Routing Lookups" [FASTIP2]). The factor that is causing vendors to pause and rethink their architectures is the additional per packet processing required in a CQS architecture. As QoS capabilities are introduced into the market place, many routers will be differentiated by how (or even *if*) they implement the various functional components shown in Figure 3.2. Depending on the role a router is expected to play in the network's end-to-end service, some functions may not be implemented at all (such as multiple FIBs or policing and marking) or implemented in a limited fashion (such as classification or queuing).

The next few sections describe some classification, policing, marking, queuing, and scheduling schemes that have been (or are being) developed. (Shaping is dealt with as a form of scheduling.) FIB lookup algorithms are a well-understood area of router design, and this book does not describe specific approaches—it is sufficient to note that a QoS-capable router must have a FIB lookup algorithm with predictable temporal characteristics.

3.2 Classification

A router's packet classification mechanism directly influences the granularity with it can isolate different classes or types of IP traffic. In practice, a packet's context depends both on information carried within the packet itself and topological information derived from its arrival interface (and possibly its next-hop as determined from the FIB lookup). This section will focus on the component of the packet's context derived from the packet itself.

3.2.1 Keys and Rules

A common classification scheme is to pick some set of N bits in a packet header to differentiate up to 2^N types (or classes) of packets—this set is called the *classification key*. The act of classifying a packet involves matching the fields in the classification key against a set of *classification rules*. A classification rule must exist to cover every specific class of processing behavior required of a router—and rules specify the context that governs the routers subsequent processing of packets they match.

Classification schemes differ in the trade-off they make regarding the size of their classification key and their choice of which header bits make up the classification key. A key cannot be arbitrarily long—a router's memory limits constrain the amount of state information (rules) that can be kept to identify known classes. (However, preexisting semantics of the bits within the classification field may mean far fewer than 2^N permutations to deal with.) Per-packet processing time associated with the classification step also increases as the key gets longer (although not always in a linear fashion), which can hamper a router's throughput. On the other hand, a key cannot be too short—2^N must equal or exceed the minimum number of differentiable traffic classes required by the network being designed.

Regardless of which fields are being classified, the classification stage must be able to keep up with the peak packet arrival rate [KLS98]. Until a packet's context is established, differentiated queuing cannot be provided. When the classification stage is slower than the packet arrival rate, undifferentiated first-in, first-out (FIFO) queuing occurs before the classification stage.

The most complex classification schemes typically use a key covering multiple fields of the IP packet header, referred to as multifield (MF) classification. This may include some or all of the fields that usually define an IP *flow*—typically, the source and destination addresses, protocol field, and source and destination Transmission Control Protocol/User Datagram Protocol (TCP/UDP) port numbers. MF classification provides the greatest amount of context to the router's subsequent processing stages. However, when the network designer believes only a small number of traffic classes need to differentiated at any given hop, the usual solution is to assign a handful of bits at a fixed, known location within the packet header for classification. IPv4's type of service (ToS) octet, IPv6's Traffic Class (TC) octet, and the DiffServ field all fit into this category.

> **Note**
>
> By way of analogy, consider the airline scenario again. A whole range of information "classifies" you onto the correct flight during check-in, but smaller classification keys are used during the boarding process. When you pass through the boarding gate, the airline's gate staff expedites ticket inspection by focusing on your ticket's flight number and date. On the plane, flight attendants are typically interested in checking your seat number, on the assumption that the gate agents have performed the flight and time classification. In each case a subset of the information on the ticket was extracted by a mental "classification key" to optimize the decision-making process.

3.2.2 Type of Service (IPv4) and Traffic Class (IPv6)

IPv4 packet have always contained a single ToS octet to allow simple, per-hop packet classification. Figure 3.3 shows the RFC 1349 definition, in which three bits are assigned to represent the packet's precedence (relative priority) and four bits indicate the desired type of routing/forwarding service [RFC1349]. The last bit is reserved and set to zero.

Figure 3.3   IPv4 Type of Service.

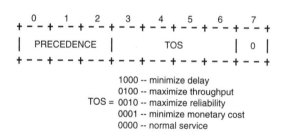

Classification based on the Precedence field indicates relative temporal priority between eight (2^3) precedence levels. Routers conforming to RFC 1812 are expected to use increasing numerical values from 0 to 7 to indicate progressively higher forwarding priority [RFC1812]. The four *ToS bits* were actually intended as a classification key for permuting the FIB lookup—different settings of the ToS bits request that the packet be routed along paths chosen for delay, throughput, reliability, or cost reasons. Figure 3.3 shows 5 of the 16 (2^4) ToS bit patterns and their specific interpretations. The remaining 11 possible values are currently undefined.

> **Note**
>
> An earlier specification, RFC 791, used three bits instead of four and treated each bit as a distinct flag requesting delay, throughput, or reliability to be the chosen routing metric.

In an analogous manner, RFC 2460 specifies that every IPv6 packet header should contain a single TC octet for simple traffic classification [RFC2460]. However, RFC 2460 defines no particular semantics for the TC octet, deferring instead to evolving work in the DiffServ area.

3.2.3 Differentiated Services Field

One problem with the RFC 1349 ToS octet is that it embodies a specific, limited model for differentiated traffic handling. The Precedence field allows only relative priorities to be encoded—packets of precedence 7 are transmitted before those of precedence 5, and so forth. In addition, the ToS subfield consumes 50 percent of the available bits for QoS-based routing—a feature that few routers support and one that has had very limited deployment within the Internet to date.

Recently the Internet Engineering Task Force (IETF) has revisited the model of providing QoS through the use of well-defined traffic classes and small, fixed, per packet classification keys. As part of the DiffServ architecture (described in Chapter 4), the IPv4 ToS octet has become the DiffServ field—allowing more variety in the type of packet queuing and scheduling rules that can be indicated. As shown in Figure 3.4, six bits of the old ToS octet make up a new *DiffServ Code Point* (DSCP), theoretically allowing up to 2^6 (64) different contexts, and hence per packet queuing and scheduling behaviors, to be indicated.

Figure 3.4   Differentiated Services field.

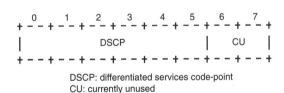

```
          0     1     2     3     4     5     6     7
       + - - + - - + - - + - - + - - + - - + - - + - - +
       |              DSCP             |     CU    |
       + - - + - - + - - + - - + - - + - - + - - + - - +
```

DSCP: differentiated services code-point
CU: currently unused

In a DiffServ network, the DiffServ field no longer provides route selection hints or any form of classification key for selection-specific FIB partitions. The IPv6 TC octet has been similarly redefined for use in DiffServ-based IPv6 networks—both redefinitions are covered in RFC 2474 [RFC2474].

3.2.4 Multifield Classification

Using only the DiffServ field for packet classification has a number of limitations. First, the number of traffic classes is at most 64 and frequently is far less. Second, such classification tells the router little about the packet's origins or its destination. An alternative approach is to use a classification key covering multiple fields in the IP packet header—or MF classification.

Typically a MF classifier is used to differentiate individual *application flows* from each other. This step requires a classification key covering the source and destination IP address fields (to identify the participating endpoints), the protocol field (indicating whether the payload is TCP, UDP, or some other protocol), and the TCP/UDP source and destination port numbers (indicating the application, assuming the payload is TCP or UDP).

Note
Although not strictly part of the IP header, the TCP/UDP port numbers always reside in the first 32-bit word after the end of the IPv4 header itself, making it easy for a MF classifier to locate them.

IPv4 Classification

Figure 3.5 shows the fields typically of interest in an IPv4 packet. Two areas of complexity must be addressed by a MF classifier. First, the Address, Protocol, and Port Number fields amount to 104 bits that must be checked for every packet passing through the router. Second, some classification rules apply to multiple application flows simultaneously and are typically expressed in terms of boundary conditions on subfields within the classification key. In some cases, boundary conditions may be expressed in terms of specific fields that are inspected and others than are not (masked out); then the router can get by with a simple *exact-match* classifier. However, if the requirement is for arbitrarily defined ranges (for example, match IP source addresses between 128.90.80.20 and 129.0.0.0 with a TCP source port between 1024 and 1090, and any values for the other fields) the router requires a *range-matching* MF classification stage.

Figure 3.5   Header fields of interest in IPv4 packets.

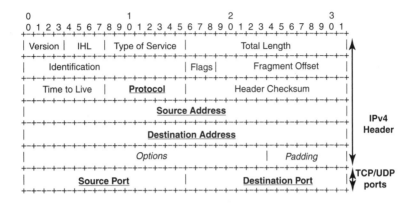

IHL=Internet Header Length

Although 104 bits are covered, the MF classifier usually finds itself dealing with far less than 2^{104} permutations because most of the subfields cannot assume arbitrary values. For example, the distribution of IP address values depends on where in the network the router exists—far fewer unique source and destination addresses are seen toward the edges of a network than toward the core. In addition, only a handful of the possible 256 protocols are likely to be seen. On the other hand, a good MF classifier must assume that the TCP/UDP port numbers can take on any value at all. Even allowing for these restrictions, the potential permutations number in the millions, especially in the core of the network (an issue for core routers attempting to provide flow-level service isolation and one of the justifications for the DiffServ model).

One limitation of MF classification is that fragmented IPv4 packets carry TCP/UDP port numbers in the first fragment only. Thus the MF classifier looking for specific TCP or UDP port numbers is quite likely to miss subsequent fragments of the same packet (unless the classifier correlates subsequent fragments with the first one carrying the port numbers). In contrast, the ToS/DiffServ byte is always carried in every fragment.

IPv6 Classification

MF classification is slightly different for IPv6 (see Figure 3.6). First, each address field now consumes 128 bits. An addresses + port numbers classification key is more than 288 bits long. Second, determining the TCP or UDP port numbers may require parsing along a list of header extension fields (following each Next Header flag) until the classifier either locates the beginning of the TCP or UDP payload or determines that the packet belongs to neither protocol.

Figure 3.6   Header fields of interest in IPv6 packets.

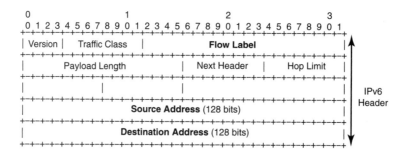

To assist in the implementation of MF classifiers, IPv6 added a 20-bit flow label to be interpreted with the packet's source address [RFC2460]. One possible use is for the packet's source to include a random, but unique, value in the Flow Label field of all packets requiring the same queuing and scheduling treatment by the network. By using a classification key covering only the Flow Label and Source Address fields (a total of 148 bits), routers along the path can isolate packets down to the flow level—without inspecting the Destination Address field and searching for TCP/UDP port numbers. Far fewer than 2^{128} source addresses exist in the IPv6 Internet, so a flow label + source address key sees far fewer than 2^{148} permutations. As with IPv4 MF classification, the number of permutations that a given router sees rises toward the network's core and drops toward its edges.

Interestingly, the use of the flow label plus the source address for classification limits the capability of the router to aggregate certain types of flows together. The source is responsible for assigning flow labels to packets and may choose to assign the same flow label to packets belonging to many different application flows. Because the flow label has no particular semantics (except "I am unique for packets requiring unique queuing and scheduling"), routers have a hard time deducing anything about the relationship between the application flows (or even if more than one flow exists) sharing a common flow label. (In contrast, because many applications use well known TCP or UDP port numbers, explicit classification on these port numbers would allow routers to recognize flows from related applications.)

Rule Precedence

A MF classifier must also be able to deal with having multiple rules that match the same packet. Whether exact or ranging matching is used, certain rules may be specified so that they are a subset or superset of other rules.

For example, consider two rules expressed in the following manner:

- **Rule1**—Match anything with IP source addresses between 192.0.0.0 and 192.1.0.0.

- **Rule2**—Match anything with IP source addresses between 192.0.0.0 and 192.1.0.0 and UDP port numbers between 128 and 255.

A packet from host 192.0.10.60 sending from UDP port 130 would match both of these rules. Which one has precedence? In general, a router's classification engine should allow the operator to assign specific precedence to rules that may be simultaneously matched.

In the preceding example you might be tempted to say that the "more exact" rule should have precedence (in this case Rule2), and that is certainly an option. However, overlapping rules are not always easily characterized as being more or less exact than each other. Consider the following two rules:

- **Rule1**—Match anything with IP source addresses between 192.0.0.0 and 192.1.0.0.

- **Rule2**—Match anything with TCP port numbers between 1024 and 2047.

Clearly, a packet on TCP port number 1100, coming from host 192.0.20.10, would match both rules. But which rule is more exact? Additional information must be configured into the router to guide the classification process as it attempts to determine which matching rule to use to define the packet's subsequent context.

Multifield Classification Can Include the Differentiated Services Field

Although the DiffServ field is typically used instead of MF classification, there is no reason why a MF classifier cannot also include the DiffServ field in its classification key. Alternatively, a router might employ a two-stage classification process in which initial MF classification establishes context within which to interpret the DiffServ field's contents (possibly creating virtual DiffServ domains having different DiffServ field semantics). Such choices are highly implementation dependent.

3.2.5 Security Issues

Packet classification aims to ensure that packets get the service level (and only that service level) to which they are entitled. You assume that packets arrive with legitimate values in the fields being used for classification. Two issues complicate the choice of appropriate classification schemes. First, the scheme should be secure against people attempting to obtain service to which they are not entitled. Second, the scheme should work in the presence of end-to-end payload encryption.

When a network uses the DiffServ field (or ToS/TC octet) to determine how much priority or bandwidth to give a particular stream packet, the network cannot simply allow end users to set their own DiffServ field values. Imagine that I've paid for low-throughput service and have been told to set DiffServ = X on all my transmitted packets. Imagine further that I know the network provides much higher bandwidth to packets marked with DiffServ = Y. It is very tempting for me to simply set DiffServ = Y on all my packets, knowing that my packets will get to their destination even though I'm using a service level for which I did not pay.

MF classification keys typically cover fields critical to the packet's correct delivery—any change to the address, protocol, or port numbers would be rather self-defeating. For this reason networks that internally utilize the DiffServ field for service differentiation should perform MF classification on user traffic on entry to the network. This classification determines the packet's correct DiffServ field value and should override any value placed there by the packet's source. Indeed, MF classification ought to be employed at all points in the network where external traffic may be injected by untrusted parties.

End-to-end payload encryption also poses an interesting challenge to MF classification (among other things). Packet encryption hides as much information from prying eyes as possible while leaving just enough information visible so that routers can correctly forward the packet. An inherent trade-off exists between the amount of information a MF classifier is allowed to see versus the number of fields encrypted. As a simple case, if the IP packet payload is encrypted, the TCP or UDP port numbers cannot be discerned. In a more complex situation, the application's IP packets may be entirely encrypted and then tunneled through the network. Routers in the core would find themselves classifying based on the tunneling packet's own header, which indicates little about the individual flows sharing the tunnel.

3.2.6 Line Rate Processing

The performance-limiting factor of most routers is the number of packet headers that can be processed per second, a limitation that can show up for traffic consisting of many smaller packets rather than fewer larger packets. When MF packet classification is added to the FIB lookup, the packet classification stage itself may become a bottleneck within the router. If the classification process cannot handle packets as fast as the inbound interface(s) can deliver them, a buffer (queue) is required before the classification stage. Incoming packets are arranged in a FIFO queue here without consideration to the class of which they may be a member and removed from this buffer only as fast as the classification stage operates (see Figure 3.7). This procedure adds an undifferentiated jitter element to all traffic passing through the classifier.

Figure 3.7   Buffering is required if classifier is slower than peak arrival rate.

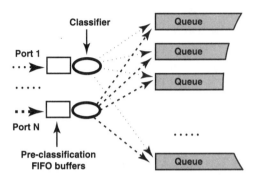

Preclassification buffering is rarely a problem for Best Effort routers but is important when considering a router's role in a QoS-enabled IP network. This buffering may even be tolerable if the classification stage operates at a sufficient percentage of the peak input rate (estimated by using the smallest size of IP packets a router is likely to see, rather than the mythical "average" IP packet size, around 250 to 350 bytes). Depending on the expected burstiness of small IP packet arrivals, the buffer may be small enough that the worst case jitter is tolerable.

Note
IP traffic shows multimedia size distributions with strong peaks around the 40-to-41-byte and mid-500-byte ranges. Emerging VoIP applications are likely to create new peaks in the sub-100-byte range.

For a router whose classification stage is always faster than the worst-case (peak) packet arrival rate, none of the above is a consideration.

3.3   Policing and Marking

Every traffic class has certain limits to its allowable temporal behavior—a limit on how fast packets may arrive or a limit on the number of packets that may arrive during some specified interval (sometimes referred to as a *traffic profile*). Policing and marking are closely related actions taken by a router when it determines a packet is outside the limits assigned to the traffic class of which the packet is a member (or *out of profile*). Policing is a heavy hammer—out-of-profile packets are simply dropped. Marking has a much softer touch—out-of-profile packets are "marked" by the modification of one or more header bits (rather than dropped) and passed to the router's output queuing and scheduling stage.

> **Note**
>
> The actual bits used to carry a mark depend on the specific packet classification scheme in use. Some examples are discussed in Chapter 4.

A related function is traffic *shaping*, which modifies the temporal characteristics of a traffic class by selectively delaying local packet forwarding. Shaping is covered in Section 3.5, "Scheduling."

3.3.1 Metering

Policing and marking share a common component—a metering function to determine whether each packet is in or out of profile. A simple example is the classic *token bucket* meter, which allows a small degree of burstiness within a particular traffic class while generally enforcing a lower long-term (average) rate limit. Tokens are added to a bucket at some fixed rate of X (tokens per second) and are removed from the bucket whenever a packet arrives (see Figure 3.8). A bucket also has a finite depth—it never contains more than Y tokens.

When a packet arrives and at least one token is available, the token is removed and the packet is considered to be in profile. If no tokens are in the bucket when a packet arrives, that packet is declared to be out of profile. The token replenishment rate X represents the long-term average rate limit if packets are to remain in profile. However, packets may arrive in short bursts and still be considered in profile—up to Y tokens may be available in the bucket, and therefore up to Y packets may arrive back to back in time and still get through. Judicious selection of X and Y allows a profile to enforce a desired long-term average packet rate while being tolerant of short bursts of packets arriving faster than X packets per second.

Figure 3.8 Token buckets provide a simple metering function.

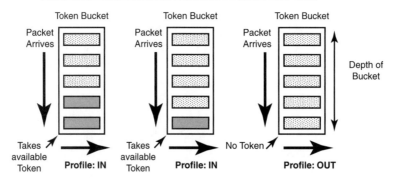

An alternative way of visualizing the token bucket's operation is shown in Figure 3.9. When the packet arrival rate R is less than X, the bucket fills up at (X – R) tokens per second, stopping when it reaches Y tokens. If R = X, the number of tokens in the bucket remains (on average) constant. When R begins to exceed X, the bucket drains at a rate of (R – X) tokens per second. As long as the bucket retains at least one token, packets are considered to be in profile. If R exceeds X for too long (exactly how long depends on R, X, and recent bucket depletion), the bucket empties and subsequent packets are considered out of profile. The out-of-profile state continues until R drops below X again (at which point the bucket begins to fill and regain a nonempty state). A token bucket can be seen as enforcing the rule that the total number of packets sent through the metering point over any time period T must be less than (T × X + Y).

Figure 3.9   Token buckets allow bursts above average rate.

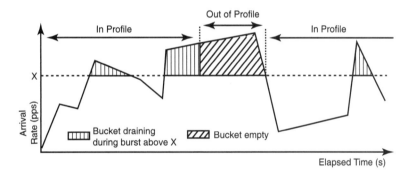

From an implementation perspective, token buckets are little more than a counter incremented X times per second to a maximum value Y and decremented toward zero each time a packet is received. If the counter is nonzero when a packet arrives, it is in profile; otherwise, it is out of profile. Multiple token buckets can be running simultaneously, established as a table of counters and associated X and Y parameters. When a packet arrives, its context (established by the preceding classification stage) selects which of the token buckets to use for metering (see Figure 3.10). Its context may also influence whether metering is followed by a policing action or a marking action (a router may be implemented to offer one or both of these actions).

Figure 3.10 Packet's context drives the choice of profile and action.

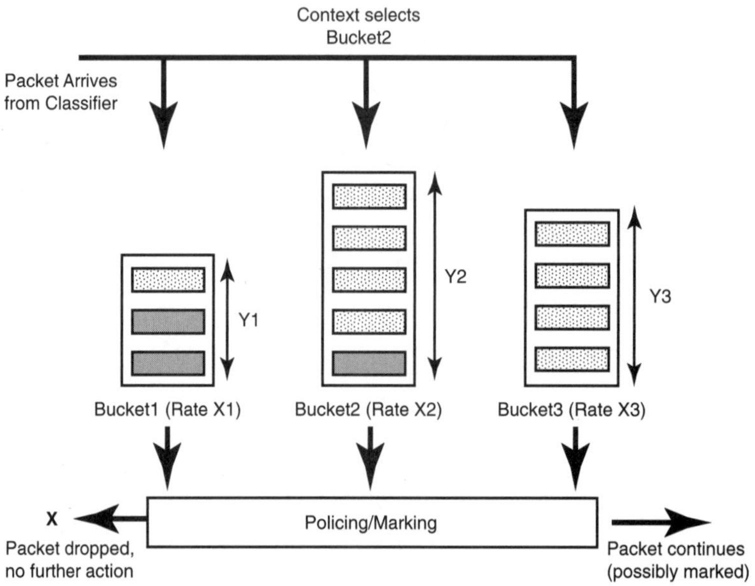

One final point to consider is whether the meter counts packets as atomic units or as the number of bytes that have passed the meter (in units of packets—a packet is in-profile whenever ever there are more tokens in the bucket than bytes in the packet). Given the variable nature of IP packet lengths, a simple relationship does not exist between the two metrics. Both packet per second and byte per second metering have their places.

3.3.2 Tiered Profiles

Tiered profiles are used when a single average rate and burst tolerance is insufficient to express the traffic's allowed temporal characteristics. Multiple levels (tiers) of profile checking allow multiple degrees of marking or a combination of marking and policing for the same packet contexts (classes).

For example, a tiered profile might specify that packets exceeding a certain rate X packets per second are simply marked, but if the excess packet rate exceeds a higher rate W packets per second, immediate policing is enforced. The appropriate metering function could be built by concatenating two or more token buckets. Consider two token buckets of depth Y; bucket 1 is replenished at rate X and bucket 2 at rate W, and X is slower than W. When a packet arrives, an attempt is made to remove a token from both buckets. Assume the following events occur:

- If tokens are available from both buckets, one token is extracted from each bucket and the packet is forwarded normally.

- If bucket 1 has no tokens, but bucket 2 does, then a token is extracted from bucket 2 and the packet is marked before forwarding normally.

- If both buckets are empty, the packet is dropped (policed).

Traffic arriving slower than X is always in profile. Up to Y packets may arrive faster than X (but less than W) and still be considered in profile, after which they are marked. If packets continue to arrive faster than X but below W, they are continuously marked (bucket 1 is empty, and bucket 2 remains full). Up to Y packets may arrive faster than W before they begin to be dropped (policed).

Policing and marking is critically important to the IETF's DiffServ effort—where marking is often referred to as "coloring." Two examples are described in the Internet drafts, "A Single Rate Three Color Marker" [SRTCM] and "A Two Rate Three Color Marker" [TRTCM]—three colors are used, corresponding to three levels of being in or out of profile.

3.3.3 *Protecting the Network*

Policing and marking are tools that protect the portions of the network downstream from the router at which the policing or marking activity occurs (often including the router's own switching fabric and output queuing and scheduling engines). Ultimately, you are trying to protect all subsequent queuing points in the downstream path from extreme, transient burstiness of a particular traffic class. Policing protects by simply removing packets from the data stream—no packet, nothing to queue. Marking protects by informing downstream routers that the marked packet can be treated as a second-class citizen if queue space is getting tight. How the queuing stage might use such marking is described in the next section. A related function, traffic *shaping*, is covered in Section 3.5, "Scheduling."

3.4 *Queue Management*

Chapter 2 introduced the basic truth that sharing a link's capacity in a controlled fashion requires competing traffic to be distributed across multiple queues at the output interface. Every class of traffic requiring distinct scheduling characteristics must be placed in its own queue with each packet directed to the appropriate queue using context information gathered through the preceding classification stage. Without distinct queues it is not possible for the following scheduler stage(s) to differentiate between the various classes of traffic competing for a single output link.

A *queue manager* function is responsible for establishing and maintaining queues and queuing behavior within the router. This function involves four basic activities:

- Adding a packet to the queue indicated by the packet's context (as established during the classification stage) if the queue is not full

- Dropping a packet if the queue is full

- Removing a packet when requested by the scheduler

- Optionally monitoring queue *occupancy* (the number of packets or bytes in each queue) and taking one of the following proactive steps to keep the occupancy levels low:

  - Removing a packet (or choosing not to add a packet) when a queue has (or is beginning to) become full

  - Marking a packet when a queue is beginning to become full

At some point every queue is declared full (even while space is available for other queues to grow) to ensure that no single class of traffic consumes all of the router's finite memory space used to create the queues.

However, merely ensuring that one queue doesn't starve other queues is not sufficient. In addition, any individual queue's average occupancy should be kept low. The term *active queue management* is often applied to methods for monitoring and controlling average queue occupancy. Low average occupancy has two benefits:

- Queues exist to absorb inevitable traffic bursts without loss. Operating with a high average occupancy reduces the space available to absorb bursts.

- The average latency experienced by traffic sharing a given queue increases as the average queue occupancy increases. Keeping the occupancy down helps keep end-to-end latency down.

Note
When a burst arrives while the queue occupancy is high, multiple packets may be discarded simultaneously. If the drops affect many TCP flows at one time, the congestion-avoidance behavior of all flows becomes synchronized and a severe drop occurs in average performance.

These observations hold even for routers having only a single FIFO queue on each output, so the benefits of active queue management are available even without having multiple queues and schedulers.

3.4.1 *Avoid Reordering*

Before diving into a discussion of individual queue management mechanisms, it is important to note how packet marking should not be used. Marking indicates that an upstream router found a packet to be out of profile, but not enough to justify immediate dropping. The intent is that downstream routers can treat marked packets as second-class citizens when local congestion becomes an issue.

However, there are two possible ways to treat packets as second-class citizens. One is to downgrade their forwarding priority by assigning them to different queues based on their marking. The other is to permute the algorithm a queue manager uses to keep queue occupancy low, being more restrictive about "allowed" occupancy for marked packets than for unmarked packets.

Unfortunately, the first approach can result in the *reordering* of marked packets relative to unmarked packets within a traffic class. Presumably, the queue into which marked packets are dumped is assigned a different scheduler priority relative to the queue assigned for "normal" packets within the same traffic class (see Figure 3.11). Reordering occurs when a marked packet, arriving *before* an unmarked packet in the same traffic class, finds itself scheduled for transmission *after* the unmarked packet. Assuming the marked packet makes it all the way to the other end, the receiving application perceives the traffic to contain out-of-order packets.

Figure 3.11   Separate queues for marked and unmarked packets can lead to reordering.

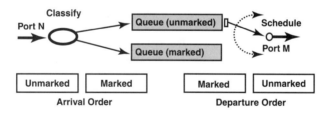

Although IP does not preclude packets being reordered by the network, most end-to-end protocols do not handle this case efficiently. The preferred approach is for profile-based packet marking to influence the active queue management applied to each packet—with a single queue serving all packets belonging to a given end-to-end class regardless of how they are marked.

3.4.2 Reducing Queue Occupancy

A queue's occupancy increases when the offered load (traffic arrival rate) exceeds the rate at which the scheduler is draining packets from the queue. Because the rate at which any particular queue is drained depends on how its scheduler reacts to traffic from other queues contending for access to the output link, occupancy can be considered to reflect the level of congestion currently being experienced at the queue's output interface.

Reducing a queue's occupancy requires some method of triggering congestion-avoidance behavior in the transport protocols generating the flows passing through the queue. Because a finite delay occurs before any transport protocol can begin to react to congestion within a router, queue management must accept two basic types of congestion:

- Transient congestion, occurring over time periods shorter than the reaction time of congestion-avoiding transport protocols

- Long-term (average) congestion, resulting from the approximately steady-state rates of all the flows passing through the queue

Transient congestion is caused by short, correlated bursts of traffic from one or more flows. In general a router does not want to drop packets from a burst unless absolutely necessary, and so vendors and operators select queue sizes to cover the burstiness they typically expect to see. However, there is always the chance that a burst will fill the queue, at which point packet drop is the only option available.

The average occupancy of a queue (measured over some recent time interval) is a significant issue when a queue is shared by multiple traffic flows because the average occupancy affects the latency experienced by all packets passing through that queue. A queue manager needs to continuously supply feedback to transport protocols to keep the long-term occupancy down—essentially a negative feedback control system in which the strength of the feedback is some function of queue occupancy. In principle you can apply feedback in two ways:

- In-band marking of packets

- Dropping of packets

In-band marking of packets requires the transport protocol to react to the receipt of marked packets by initiating congestion avoidance. In practice, packet dropping is the preferred approach in IP networks because TCP uses packet loss to trigger its congestion-avoidance behavior. Packet dropping also has a beneficial side effect of immediately reducing the downstream load.

Explicit Congestion Notification

Although packet dropping is currently the preferred way to apply feedback, nondestructive methods (that is, methods that do not involve packet discard) of signaling congestion are being designed and evaluated. Dropping packets essentially wastes the resources used to get the packet to the router seeing imminent congestion, so congestion indications that avoid this waste if at all possible are attractive.

One example is known as explicit congestion notification (ECN), which is described in RFC 2481 [RFC2481]. The two currently unused (CU) bits from the DiffServ field are redefined as the ECN Capable Transport (ECT) and Congestion Experienced (CE) bits. A transport protocol sender sets the ECT bit on outbound packets when it knows that both ends of the flow understand the meaning of the CE bit. If no congestion control feedback is required, the CE bit is ignored. When a router along the path wants to apply congestion control feedback, it has two options:

• If the ECT bit is set, set the CE bit.

• If the ECT is reset, drop the packet.

RFC 2481 also proposes modifications to TCP, enabling ECN-capable TCP clients to recognize each other during connection establishment and appropriately set the ECT bit on subsequent data packets.

At this writing, the preceding scheme is still an experimental proposal and operates only on long-term congestion levels within the network. (RFC 2481 explicitly warns against setting the CE bit based on transient queue occupancy levels.)

Drop from Front

Deciding to drop a packet leaves a question as to which one to drop. From an implementation perspective, dropping the packet that just arrived (drop from tail) is simple because that packet can be dropped simply by not inserting it into the queue. However, an alternative strategy is to drop the packet currently at the head of the queue—drop from front (DFF).

DFF expedites TCP's congestion-avoidance behavior—a "packet loss" event at the head of the queue is noticed sooner than one at the tail of a queue that may already have a serious level of backlogged packets [DFF96]. However, DFF is sometimes considered an unnecessary complexity, requiring explicit queue manipulation to remove an existing entry.

DFF has no particularly negative impact on nonflow-controlled traffic, and some slight benefit can be argued for real-time flows. A nonempty queue implies that every packet has been subject to delay, and the packet at the head of the queue has probably outlived its usefulness by the time it reaches its destination. DFF marginally increases the chance that the following packet reaches its destination in time to be useful.

When to Act

The most complex part of queue manager design is defining the control system itself that decides when (and how strongly) to apply feedback. Algorithms must take into account the granularity of packet context supplied by the packet classification stage. For example, if flow-granularity MF classification leads to separate queues for every application flow, each flow is, by definition, isolated from the aggressive or passive behaviors of other flows. The router can afford to apply a fairly simple full/not-full threshold decision process on each queue, accurately targeting individual flows causing transient congestion.

However, where routers are using ToS/DS-based classification, tens, hundreds, or even thousands of application flows may be mapped into the same queue. In this case the feedback scheme must work with *approximate* knowledge about which flows are actually causing the long-term congestion at any given time. A number of schemes have addressed this problem by introducing statistical feedback signals whose strength is derived from a combination of input variables such as the queue's average occupancy and markings previously applied to packets from upstream routers. A feedback mechanism known as random early detection (RED) is looked at more closely in the next section.

3.4.3 Random Early Detection

The Internet Research Task Force (IRTF) spent a number of years studying the problem of generating progressive negative feedback aimed at controlling the average occupancy of queues shared by many diverse flows. The group concluded that the best solution (taking existing router implementations into account) involves statistical, randomly distributed feedback signals whose strength (probability of occurrence) was an increasing function of average queue occupancy [RFC2309]. The particular example the IRTF uses to explain this behavior is known as random early detection (RED), which is sometimes erroneously referred to as random early discard, because the detection often leads to discard [RED].

RED uses the queue's average occupancy as a parameter to a random function that decides whether congestion-avoidance mechanisms ought to be triggered (for the purposes of the remaining discussion, assume that the trigger is "packet drop"). As the average occupancy increases, the probability of a packet-drop action increases. Figure 3.12 shows a sample probability function:

- For occupancy up to a lower threshold, min_{th}, packets pass through untouched (drop probability is zero).

- Above min_{th}, the probability of packet drop rises linearly toward a probability of max_p reached for an occupancy of max_{th}.

- At and above max_{th}, packets are guaranteed to be dropped.

These three phases are sometimes referred to as normal, congestion avoidance, and congestion control, respectively. The worst-case long-term queue size is limited to max_{th} (where the probability function jumps to 1). RED begins early in that it begins triggering congestion indications well before the queue becomes full.

Average occupancy is recalculated every time a packet arrives and is based on a low-pass filter, or exponentially weighted moving average (EWMA), of the instantaneous queue occupancy. The formula is

$$Q_{avg} = (1 - W_q) \times Q_{avg} + Q_{inst} \times W_q$$

Q_{avg} is the average occupancy, Q_{inst} is the instantaneous occupancy, and W_q is the weight for the moving-average function. W_q affects how closely the average occupancy parameter tracks the queue's instantaneous occupancy—higher values are more aggressive, and lower values are more conservative. The goal is to pick a value that allows RED to ignore short-term transients without inducing packet loss but to react to sustained levels of occupancy before everyone's latency is adversely affected or multiflow synchronization of TCP's congestion avoidance is felt.

A router may support different values for min_{th}, max_{th}, and max_p for different queues—balancing the total space available for queues, the number of queues required, and the latency/jitter bounds of the traffic class using each queue. In addition, W_q might well be different for each queue.

Figure 3.12   Drop probability varies with queue occupancy.

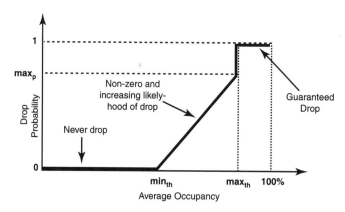

Statistical drop strategies have the following useful characteristics:

- They create a negative feedback mechanism for TCP whose intensity increases as a function of congestion level within the router.

Note

Imagine using a Geiger counter to detect how close you are to some radioactive source. Random ticks from the counter occur more frequently as you get closer to the source—normal humans react by backing away. RED is like a Geiger counter for TCP, indicating its closeness to outright congestion.

- Flows consuming a greater share of a queue's throughput (whose packets enter the queue more often) are subject to more intense feedback.

- Synchronization is minimized between the congestion-avoidance efforts of independent transport sessions sharing a particular queue.

Beginning random drops early (before the queue really has exhausted its allowed space) increases the likelihood of smoothing out the transient congestion before queue occupancy gets too high. Randomizing the drop distribution in the early stages reduces the chances of simultaneously subjecting multiple flows to packet drops.

Two key assumptions underlie drop-based active queue management:

- Many or most of the flows causing transient congestion are TCP-based and, therefore, respond to the negative feedback of early packet loss.

- The packets actually dropped belong to the TCP flow (or flows) causing the congestion.

The absence of per-flow classification and queuing means that these assumptions may not always be valid. Yet they are generally reasonable. More of the packets arriving during a congestion interval will belong to the aggressive flow than to other flows. It stands to reason that packet drops during the congestion interval are likely to hit a flow that is contributing to the congestion. Temporal characteristics of the congestion-causing flows allow RED and its variants to focus on relevant flows, even in the absence of explicit flow-level packet context.

Weighted Random Early Detection

Queue managers are not limited to providing a single type of behavior on any given queue. Additional information from the packet's context may select one of multiple packet discard functions. For example, a packet marked at some point upstream for exceeding a traffic profile (or perhaps on the input side to the router's own switch fabric) may find itself subject to a more aggressive discard policy compared to other packets classified in the same queue. (Marked packets still get through when the network is relatively congestion free. The intention is simply that a router jettison out-of-profile flows first when things get tight.) Or packets placed into different service classes at their source may have different associated discard functions.

In Figure 3.13 a queue manager selects one of two curves for a single queue based on, for example, a single bit in the ToS byte or DiffServ field. Unmarked packets are subject to RED with $min1_{th}$ as its lower threshold, $max1_{th}$ as its upper threshold, and max_p as the peak drop probability before the function jumps to 1. On the other hand, marked packets are subject to a more aggressive curve in which random drops begin at a lower average occupancy level of $min2_{th}$, increasing rapidly to 1 at $max2_{th}$.

Figure 3.13   Packet marking can modify drop function.

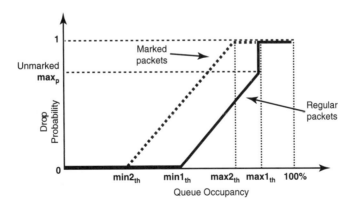

Modifying the probability function based on packet context is sometimes referred to as *weighting*. At least one major router vendor uses the IPv4 Precedence field to select up to eight min_{th}, max_{th}, and max_p parameters for its RED algorithm (although not the W_q parameter to the EWMA function)—referring to the scheme as Weighted RED (WRED).

Random Early Detection with In/Out

A relative of WRED is RED with an in/out bit (RIO), which also uses packet marking to modify the RED algorithm on a packet-by-packet basis [RIO]. RIO assumes that packets have already passed through an upstream marker, and a single bit in the packet header indicates whether the marker found the packet to be in or out of profile. RIO differs from WRED in that it modifies the EWMA function on the basis of packet markings.

RIO's goal is to discriminate against out packets during times of congestion. It does so by running two EWMA occupancy algorithms in parallel on the same queue—Q_{avgIN} for in packets and Q_{avgOUT} for out packets. Similar to Figure 4.13, two sets of min_{th}, max_{th}, and max_p are present—one for in and one for out packets. Typically min_{th} and max_{th} are lower for out packets than for in, whereas max_p is higher for out packets than for in.

Where the processing differs is in the use of two distinct moving-average queue occupancy values. When calculating a drop probability for in packets, the queue occupancy is taken from Q_{avgIN}, whereas for out packets the queue occupancy is taken from Q_{avgOUT}. Q_{avgIN} is based on the average queue occupancy of in packets alone, whereas Q_{avgOUT} is based on the average total queue occupancy (of both in and out packets).

A consequence of this design is not only that the probability curve for out packets is more aggressive but also that the moving average for out packets drives up the curve in response to *both* in and out traffic entering the queue. However, the number of out packets passing through the queue does not affect the drop probability for in packets. This factor goes some way to prevent sustained bursts of out packets from triggering unnecessary congestion avoidance on flows whose packets are remaining in profile.

Adaptive Random Early Detection

Basic RED requires careful adjustment of its parameters to operate effectively—it ought to drop just enough packets to achieve its goals and no more. Unfortunately, parameter settings depend on the nature and burstiness of traffic passing through a RED-based queue. For example, W_q affects how rapidly Q_{avg} tracks instantaneous queue occupancy and should be picked so that RED ignores transient burstiness yet reacts in time to dampen long-term congestion buildup. Yet the speed at which long-term congestion arises depends in part on how many TCP flows are simultaneously being mapped into the queue.

In the presence of a few TCP flows, congestion is likely to build relatively slowly, and W_q should be low. However, using this same value of W_q in the presence of many TCP flows results in the RED congestion-avoidance phase not kicking in early enough or aggressively enough. Conversely, picking W_q to enable sufficiently fast RED behavior with many TCP flows can result in overly aggressive drop behaviors when only a few flows are passing through the queue.

Adaptive RED (ARED) attempts to address this limitation by allowing RED to modify its parameters based on recent congestion history [ARED]. It is noted in ARED that for N connections sharing a queue, the effect of any given RED-induced packet drop is to reduce the offered load by a factor of $(1 - 1 / (2 \times N))$. In other words, as N rises, RED needs to become more aggressive to achieve constant effectiveness.

To address this problem, ARED dynamically adjusts max_p based on recent movements of Q_{avg} (see Figure 3.14). If Q_{avg} drops below min_{th}, a more conservative value of max_p is calculated. If Q_{avg} rises above max_{th}, a more aggressive max_p is calculated. If Q_{avg} oscillates around min_{th}, Adaptive RED continually reduces max_p (because the packet-drop behavior is doing its job and could probably be softened). If Q_{avg} oscillates around max_{th}, max_p is continually increased (because the packet-drop behavior is not having sufficient impact).

Figure 3.14   Adaptive random early detection varies max_p.

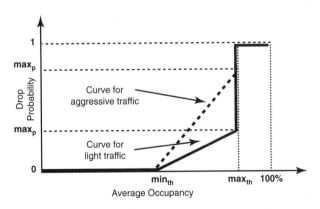

As a consequence, the ARED algorithm tracks changing loads on the queue that may be due to increases or decreases in the number of TCP flows passing through it at any time. The algorithm works without requiring any explicit or externally derived knowledge of the number of flows.

Flow Random Early Detection

Flow RED (FRED) represents yet another refinement of the RED algorithm [FRED97]. The solution addresses RED's tendency to be unfair when the queue is being shared between flows having widely differing reactions to early congestion notification. The following characterization is given in "Dynamics of Random Early Detection" [FRED97]:

- Nonadaptive flows—Transport protocols that ignore packet drops

- Robust flows—TCP connections with short round trip times (RTTs) that, therefore, recover quickly from packet drops

- Fragile flows—TCP connections with long RTTs that, therefore, recover slowly from packet drops

When a mixture of these flows passes through a RED-managed queue, the behavior of a nonadaptive flow can push Q_{avg} above min_{th} and cause nonzero packet loss to all other flows even if those other flows are generally behaving. Likewise, robust flows are affected less by any individual packet loss than are fragile flows simply because TCP's recovery rate depends on a flow's RTT. The overall effect is that congestion notification affects different types of flows in an unbalanced manner.

FRED handles this condition by adjusting the per packet-drop behavior on the basis of short-term per flow state (but only about flows that have packets in the queue at any given time). Two variables, min_q and max_q, represent the lower and upper number of packets any given flow ought to have queued at a given time. The variable Avg_{cq} represents the estimated average number of packets each flow currently has in the queue.

When Q_{avg} is less than max_{th}, FRED always accepts packets belonging to flows with less than min_q packets already in the queue. Setting min_q between two and four ensures some minimum queue space to fragile flows. If the flow has more than max_q packets currently in the queue, FRED drops the new packet regardless of Q_{avg}. This practice constrains nonadaptive flows. Where a flow has between min_q and max_q packets in the queue, FRED uses regular RED to determine whether a new packet ought to be accepted or dropped.

Even though FRED does not require per-flow queuing, it does require the router to establish per-flow context, adding some classification complexity relative to previous variants of RED.

3.5 Scheduling

Scheduling dictates the temporal characteristics of packet departures from each queue—typically at the output interface toward the next router or host, but potentially at other queuing points within a router. Traditional routers have only a single queue per output link interface. So, the scheduling task is simple—pull packets out of the queue as fast as the underlying link can transmit them. In routers having CQS architectures, each interface has a scheduler stage that shares the output link's capacity among the queues associated with the interface. Link sharing is achieved by appropriately scheduling when, and how frequently, packets are pulled from each queue and transmitted.

Because a packet's context (or traffic class) dictates which queue it is placed in, the scheduler is the ultimate enforcer of relative priority, latency bounds, or bandwidth allocation between different classes of traffic. A scheduler can establish minimum available bandwidths for a particular class by ensuring that packets are regularly pulled from the queue associated with that class (that is, ensuring that the queue is regularly serviced). A scheduler can also provide *rate shaping* (imposing a maximum allowed bandwidth for a particular class) by limiting the frequency with which the class's queue is serviced. Depending on a scheduler's design, it might impose both upper and lower bandwidth bounds on each queue or impose upper bounds on some queues and lower bounds on others.

Scheduling algorithms are usually a compromise between implementation simplicity and desirable temporal characteristics. Every scheduler design has its own particular *service discipline*—the manner in which it chooses to service queues. The simplest schedulers focus on servicing queues in some predictable sequence (whether fixed or configurable), focusing on regulating the service intervals rather than the resulting throughput. More advanced schedulers allow relative or absolute bandwidth goals to be set for each queue, and they continuously adapt their servicing discipline to ensure the average bandwidth or latency achieved by each queue is within configured bounds.

The mathematics behind many schedulers is beyond the scope of this book, and so the focus is more on their general characteristics rather than proofs of their operation.

3.5.1 Rate Shaping

Like policing or marking, rate shaping is used to bound or constrain the unpredictability of a certain traffic class. Unlike policing or marking, rate shaping requires queues, queue management, and scheduling—regardless of whether the shaping function is built into a scheduler feeding a shared link or operates independently on a FIFO queue into a single link or switch port. Rate shaping modifies the temporal characteristics within a class.

Why Do It?

A system that allows queues to be emptied as fast as possible (limited by an output's line rate or a switch fabric's transmission rate) sees an increase in the downstream burstiness of traffic passing through that queue. Even if the original traffic source was transmitting packets at a relatively smooth rate, aggregation of many slightly bursty sources through a fast-as-possible queuing point results in increased burstiness. This additional burstiness can lead to unnecessary policing, aggressive active queue management, or outright queue over-flow further downstream.

Shaping can also help to balance customer expectations. If the customer frequently gets significantly better bandwidth than the guaranteed minimum (perhaps because the net-work is new and/or underloaded), a perception issue surfaces—the customer begins to associate the typical performance to be what he or she is paying for. If the spare capacity ever shrinks, the customer will receive edge-to-edge performance closer to the guaranteed rate and is likely to perceive this change as a degradation. Preemptive rate shaping from the time the customer connects helps to shape expectations of the service's long-term capabilities.

Schedulers and Leaky Buckets

Rate shaping is achieved by limiting the frequency with which a queue is serviced even when the scheduler has nothing else to do. If packets arrive with a shorter interpacket interval than allowed by the scheduler, they are queued—smoothing out the original burstiness. Figure 3.15 shows a scheduler that never samples the top queue more frequently than once every T seconds—no matter how closely bunched up the packets arrive, they depart with at least T seconds between them.

Figure 3.15   Shaping requires a minimum scheduler time on certain queues.

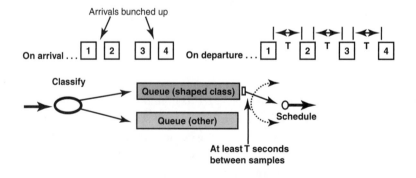

Although Figure 3.15 implies an unknown number of "other" queues, shaping is not constrained to general link-sharing schedulers. Shaping can also be applied to a single queue (perhaps one feeding an internal switch port), independently of other queues in the system. Such a scenario is often referred to as a *leaky bucket* (not to be confused with a token bucket metering stage in which no queuing or shaping of the packet stream occurs), as packets leak out of the queue at a fixed rate.

In general a shaping stage that fixes its packet emission rate results in variable effective bit rate (because IP packets vary in size from one to the next). If the motivation for shaping is to avoid overloading a later processing stage that is packet per second limited, this approach may be acceptable. However, if shaping is intended to constrain the average bit rate through the queue, the service interval needs to be dynamically variable—taking into account the number of bytes recently transmitted, the length of the next packet in the queue, and the target average bit rate.

3.5.2 Simple Scheduling

The simplest schedulers focus on servicing queues in some predictable sequence (whether fixed or configurable). They aim to regulate their service intervals rather than the throughput subsequently received by the traffic passing through them.

Strict Priority

One approach to scheduling involves ordering queues by descending priority and servicing a queue at a given priority level only if all queues of higher priority levels are empty. The scheduler is said to operate on a *strict priority* scheme. Imagine that in Figure 3.16 the scheduler considers queue 1 to have a higher priority than queue 2, queue 2 is higher than queue 3, and queue 3 is higher than queue 4. Queue 1 is serviced as fast as the link can transmit packets as long that queue has packets waiting. Only when queue 1 is empty does the scheduler consider queue 2, which is similarly serviced at the link's transmission rate while it has packets ready to go and queue 1 remains empty. Similarly, queue 3 is serviced at link rate when queues 1 and 2 are empty, and queue 4 is serviced at link rate when queues 1, 2, and 3 are empty.

However, this service discipline allows higher priority queues to starve lower priority queues of bandwidth. For example, if the traffic class being mapped into queue 1 were to arrive at 100 percent of the output link's capacity for a sustained period, the scheduler would never get around to servicing queues 2, 3, or 4. Avoiding starvation requires careful provisioning of upstream network elements—in particular, upstream policing or rate shaping must be introduced to ensure that the traffic class mapped into queue 1 is never allowed to exceed some fraction of the local output link's capacity. This behavior ensures that queue 1 is empty every so often, allowing the scheduler to spend some time servicing the lower priority queues.

Figure 3.16   Many queues feed a scheduler.

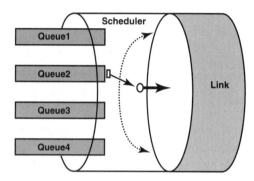

Priority scheduling is extremely useful in the provisioning of a low-latency traffic class. Assume that class X requires low end-to-end latency, is mapped into the highest priority queue at every hop, and has been rate shaped or otherwise limited to not starve the other queues. Consider what happens if a packet from class X arrives. If the scheduler is idle, the highest priority queue is serviced immediately. If the scheduler is busy transmitting a packet from another queue, the highest priority queue waits only as long as it takes to transmit that packet. Worst-case latency depends on the speed of the link (which is generally known) and the maximum size of the packet, or the Maximum Transmission Unit (MTU) for the link.

Round-Robin

An alternative algorithm, often termed *round-robin (RR)* scheduling, avoids local queue starvation by cycling through the queues one after the other, transmitting one packet before moving on to the next queue (for example, see "On Packet Switches with Infinite Storage" [RFC970] or "Round Robin Scheduling for Fair Flow Control in Data Communications Networks" [HAHN86]). Empty queues are skipped—the scheduler always moving to the next queue in the sequence that has a packet to transmit. Using Figure 4.16 as an example, a simple sequence might cycle through queues in numerical order: 1, 2, 3, 4, 1, 2, 3, 4,... continuously. If each queue has packets to send, the transmission schedule matches the queue service sequence. If some queues are empty, the remaining queues are serviced more frequently—in the extreme case, an individual class may receive all the link's bandwidth if the other queues are empty (for example, the scheduler pulls packets from queue 3 as fast as the link allows if queues 1, 2, and 4 are not seeing any traffic). Yet starvation is avoided—when a packet arrives at an empty queue, that queue is serviced during the scheduler's next cycle.

The downside to RR scheduling is that latency bounds are hard to enforce. Unlike priority scheduling, it is not possible to assign one queue for low-latency traffic. Every queue's service interval depends entirely on how many other queues have packets in them at any instant and the length of those packets. Consider an interface with N queues, a link speed of L_{rate}, and an MTU of P_{len}. The time it takes to transmit one MTU-sized packet (the longest packet that can be carried) is P_{len} / L_{rate}. So in the worst case, a packet may arrive at an empty queue that has just been skipped and have to wait $(N - 1) \times (P_{len} / L_{rate})$ seconds until the scheduler comes back around. Both of those variables are difficult to predict from one instant to the next, and so RR scheduling tends to be a good source of jitter.

It is possible to bias the service sequence by returning to certain queues more frequently (for example, using a sequence 1, 2, 3, 2, 4, 2, 1, 2,...), which provides more transmission opportunities to certain queues. However, random packet size distributions still cause problems for jitter and long-term bandwidth regulation.

3.5.3 Adaptive Schedulers

From a service provisioning perspective, having a router that can maintain bandwidth allocations to traffic classes sharing each outbound link is often extremely useful. Neither strict priority nor RR schedulers take into account the number of bits transmitted each time a queue is serviced. Given that IP packet sizes tend to vary randomly from one instant to the next, these scheduling schemes cannot be used to regulate the relative average throughputs achieved by any given queue's traffic class.

Maintaining bandwidth goals requires a scheduler whose service discipline dynamically adapts to the number of *bits* recently transmitted from each queue. It may support requirements for minimum bandwidth guarantees, maximum bandwidth enforcement (rate shaping), or both. In practice, interleaving is constrained to occur on variable-length packet boundaries. As a consequence, adaptive algorithms can only approximate the target bit rates over a period of many packets.

A number of scheduling algorithms have been developed to meet this need—for example, Deficit Round Robin (DRR), Fair Queuing (FQ), and Weighted Fair Queuing (WFQ). These algorithms are usually not simple, and so general descriptions rather than analyses of the underlying mathematics are used.

Deficit Round Robin

DRR is an extension to the original round-robin service discipline [DRR95]. DRR tracks how many *bytes* have been sent from a given queue, compares the number to how many bytes ought to have been sent, and considers the difference a "deficit." The deficit for any given queue is used to modify that queue's service interval, thereby regulating the long-term bit rate achieved by each queue.

DRR assigns each queue a constant Q_N (its *quantum*) and a variable D_N (its *deficit*). The quantum Q_N reflects the long-term average number of bytes per cycle you want the queue to send. D_N is initially zero for all queues and is reset to zero whenever a queue is emptied. When the scheduler steps to a new queue, it resets a counter B_{sent}, reflecting the number of bytes transmitted from the current queue in this round. Packets are transmitted from the current queue N while the following two conditions hold:

- The queue has packets to send.

- $(Q_N + D_N)$ is greater than or equal to (B_{sent} + the bytes in the next packet on the queue).

If the queue is emptied, D_N is reset to zero. However, if the scheduler stops before emptying the queue, a deficit exists between the number of bytes it hoped to send $(Q_N + D_N)$ and the number of bytes sent (B_{sent}). The queue's deficit D_N is reset to $(Q_N + D_N - B_{sent})$, and the scheduler moves on to the next queue in the sequence.

For each queue the value $(Q_N + D_N)$ represents the maximum number of bytes that can be transmitted during a service interval. Recalculating D_N at the end of a service interval compensates the queue next time with more bytes to send if it was short-changed this time.

Assuming packets are never larger than P_{len} (the MTU of the link), D_N is never larger than P_{len} at any instant. Over a long period of time, after the scheduler has cycled through all N queues K times, the expected number of bytes sent by queue N is $K \times Q_N$. This value never exceeds the actual number of bytes sent by more than P_{len}. Each queue may be assigned different values for Q_N, leading to different long-term relative bandwidth allocations. If less than N queues have packets to send, the link's bandwidth is divided according to the Q_N parameters of the queues with packets.

Weighted Round Robin (WRR) is closely related to DRR. A similar concept of quantum and deficit is used, but the algorithm is slightly different (see Appendix A.2 of "Link-Sharing and Resource Management Models for Packet Networks" [FLOYD95]). In WRR, the queue is serviced until a packet is sent that puts the number of bytes sent (B_{sent}) *over* the allowed limit for the queue (which is still $Q_N + D_N$). However, the deficit is now a negative value (reflecting then the amount sent in excess of $Q_N + D_N$) and acts to decrease the number of bytes the queue may transmit the next time around. As with DRR, the quantum for each queue can be used to establish proportional bandwidth sharing.

Neither scheme provides significantly better control over jitter than RR does because each queue's service intervals still fluctuate with the number of other queues having packets to send. Although not part of the basic RR definition, vendors can implement DRR/WRR to provide maximum rate bounds (for rate shaping) on each queue in addition to guaranteed minimum bounds.

Fair Queuing and Weighted Fair Queuing

Another variation of RR scheduling involves continuously recalculating the scheduling sequence so that the next queue to be serviced is the one that "needs" to be serviced to meet its long-term average bandwidth target. WFQ is a specific approach to determining a queue's need for service and evolved from two closely related approaches appearing around the same time—*Fair Queuing* (sometimes referred to as bit-wise RR scheduling) [DKS89] and *virtual clock* [ZHANG89, ZHANG91].

Fair Queuing (FQ) and virtual clock attempt to approximate the even link sharing that would result if packets from each flow (queue) were being evenly interleaved on a bit-by-bit basis—much as a TDM system multiplexes multiple serial data streams onto a single high-speed channel. A hypothetical time division multiplexing (TDM) scheduler would RR poll the queues, pulling one bit from each queue during a single cycle. As a consequence, this "ideal" service discipline ensures that whenever N queues with data to send are present, each queue is serviced at one N^{th} of the link's rate. A packet is fully transmitted when its last bit has been removed from its queue.

Because it slices time at the bit level, sharing between queues is fair (and assuming every queue has a packet to send, sharing between the flows entering the queues is also fair). However, in real life this result can only be approximated because interleaving occurs on packet rather than bit boundaries. FQ sequences packet transmissions in the order in which they *would have* arrived at the other end of the link had ideal TDM been used. Over multiple packets, this scheme shifts data from each queue at approximately the same rate as it would have been transmitted by using a pure TDM link.

Two limitations exist with plain FQ scheduling. First, the scheduler must time stamp packets as they arrive in their queues and calculate predicted ideal departure time to sequence the transmission. Because time calculations can be extremely time-consuming, approximate clocks are used, triggered by packet arrivals and departures. If a queue goes empty, the time-stamping (clocking) scheme can be skewed for that queue, resulting in temporary deviance from ideal transmission scheduling when the queue starts to receive packets again—and short-term unfairness even if the scheduler is fair in the long term. Second, FQ is designed for per-flow queues to provide flow-level isolation. FQ does not lend itself to the more common networking problem of enforcing arbitrary relative weights to bandwidth sharing by aggregated traffic classes (that is, *controlled unfairness*).

WFQ [DKS89] is also known in earlier literature as packet generalized processor sharing (PGPS) [PGPS]. WFQ is a more general version of FQ and is significantly more useful because it allows different weights to be applied to individual queues. Whenever N queues with data to send are present, each queue M is serviced to give it a fraction W_M of the link's rate (where $W_1 + W_2 + ... W_N = 1$). When some of the queues are empty, excess link capacity can generally be distributed among the remaining queues according to their relative weights. Although not part of the basic WFQ definition, vendors can implement WFQ to provide maximum rate bounds (for rate shaping) on each queue in addition to guaranteed minimum bounds.

3.6 *Hierarchical Link Sharing*

In real networks the requirements for link sharing are often too complex for a single type of scheduler. Traffic flows having hierarchical relationships to each other often share links, and this condition requires routers with hierarchical scheduling capabilities. A detailed introduction to hierarchical link sharing is provided in "Link-Sharing and Resource Management Models for Packet Networks" [FLOYD95].

For example, consider a link being shared by traffic belonging to a number of companies. Each company may have purchased (or otherwise negotiated) the right to a certain minimum share of the link's bandwidth. This situation could be achieved by assigning traffic to queues on a per company basis and using a single scheduler. However, each company may also have specific rules governing the relative treatment of individual flows within their aggregate during periods of congestion. Enforcing this additional level of traffic differentiation at the same node as the underlying link sharing requires a hierarchical queuing and scheduling solution.

Figure 3.17 shows a simple case. Companies A and B have purchased unequal shares (30 percent and 70 percent) of an expensive 2Mbit per second shared long-distance link, and their local access links are each 10Mbits per second. When both companies are sending at or above their guaranteed share, the access router is required to enforce the 30:70 sharing ratio (using appropriate queuing to absorb transient bursts above 0.6Mbits per second and 1.4Mbits per second, respectively).

However, the sharing agreement may also include a requirement that if one company doesn't use its share the excess capacity be available to the other company. So, when Company A is using less than 0.6Mbits per second (its 30 percent share), Company B is allowed to burst above 70 percent (1.4Mbits per second). Conversely, Company A is allowed to burst higher than 30 percent of the link when Company B is sending less than 1.4Mbits per second.

Figure 3.17 Traffic may have a hierarchy of internal relationships.

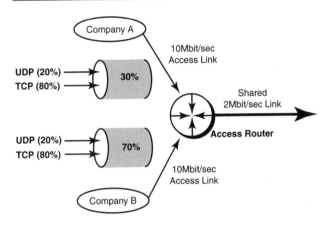

In addition, each company's aggregate traffic is made up of individual flows belonging to different TCP and UDP applications. During times of congestion at the access router, each company wants UDP flows to receive 20 percent and TCP flows to receive 80 percent of their respective aggregates. Assume further that TCP should be allowed to use whatever capacity UDP traffic is not using (within each company's aggregates), and vice versa. For example, if both companies are consuming their shares, Company A's UDP traffic would receive 0.12Mbits per second and its TCP traffic would receive 0.48Mbits per second. However, if Company A's UDP traffic drops to 0.05Mbits per second, the company's TCP traffic is allowed to expand to 0.55Mbits per second—without giving up any capacity to Company B.

One of the additional consequences of hierarchical link sharing is that if Company B drops its aggregate bandwidth consumption to 0.5Mbits per second, Company A may be allowed to expand and consume 1.5Mbits per second—with its UDP and TCP dividing this 1.5Mbits per second according to the 20:80 rule.

The service desired in Figure 3.17 requires a two-stage scheduler hierarchy as shown in Figure 3.18. This example has four queues, two groups of two—one group for each company and one queue within each group to isolate UDP and TCP packets. (Figure 3.18 does not show the matching classification stage, which must have sufficient information to differentiate packets both in terms of company and protocol type.) Logically, one can view the link sharing as being enforced by concatenated schedulers—one scheduler feeds the link, pulling packets from each group to meet the 30:70 sharing requirement at the company level. Each group has its own scheduler offering packets to the link scheduler in accordance with the 20:80 UDP versus TCP sharing requirement.

Figure 3.18   A scheduler hierarchy is required.

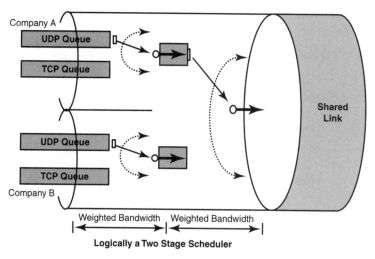

Floyd and Jacobson's "Link-Sharing and Resource Management Models for Packet Networks" has a specific focus on the use of *class-based queuing (CBQ)* to implement this sort of hierarchical link sharing—a single scheduler (based on weighted round-robin and priority scheduling) whose service discipline across all the queues implements the functional equivalent of Figure 3.18 [FLOYD95]. Hierarchical link-sharing schemes have also been developed that use WFQ schedulers.

3.7   Virtual Queues

Earlier in this chapter it was asserted that a distinct queue is required for every class of traffic requiring distinct scheduling treatment. This statement is often taken to mean that per-flow scheduling requires tens or hundreds of thousands of queues (to match the number of transport flows visible at many points in the network, especially in the core). However, the number of queues required actually depends on the nature of the per-flow service being delivered.

At least one reasonable service goal is for a router to *equally share* a link's bandwidth among the transport flows contending for access. For a link supporting W bits per second, each M flow should receive W/M bits per second on average. A simple design might attempt to establish M queues, assigning one to each flow expected to pass through the router. However, a number of researchers noted the following about bandwidth-sharing schedulers [SUTER98]:

- They act only on queues that actually have packets backlogged and waiting for transmission.

- They typically keep a history about a queue's utilization only for a short period after a queue empties (T seconds).

- If a queue is empty longer than T seconds, that queue might as well not exist at all.

Noting that most transport flows are bursty leads to the additional observation: Of M active long-term flows, only N flows have packets queued in the router during any given interval T, and N is less than M. Combining these observations leads to the conclusion that only N queues are required, assuming that the router can dynamically reassign these queues to whichever of the M flows have packets in the router at any given instant. During any given interval T, the scheduler is tasked with evenly dividing the link bandwidth among N queues—over the long term this practice will succeed in dividing the link evenly among all M flows. (A similar observation was made to justify the FRED algorithm—per flow state was needed only for flows whose packets were currently in the RED-managed queue [FRED97].)

At least one router architecture has been developed along these lines [KLS98]. The solution tightly couples a "learning" MF classification stage with a high-speed queue manager stage capable of creating and deleting queues at line rate. Whenever the classification stage receives a packet whose header doesn't match any known MF classification rules, a new matching rule is created and associated with a free queue. Subsequent packets belonging to that flow are matched and sent to the assigned queue. If all queues are attached to previously learned MF classification rules, the least recently used queue and classification rule are released and reassigned to the newly arrived packet. The design value N can be predicted from the known arrival rates (limited by the interfaces, for example, OC-3c or OC-12c ports) and the scheduler's interval T. In the case of "Beyond Best Effort: Router Architectures for the Differentiated Services of Tomorrow's Internet" [KLS98], the designers reported the ability to maintain fair-link sharing across hundreds of thousands of flows at OC-12c rates using only 64K on-demand queues.

3.8   References

[ARED]   Feng, W., D. Kandlur, D. Saha, and K. Shin. "A Self-Configuring RED Gateway." *INFOCOM 99.* (March 1999).

[DFF96]   Lakshman, T. V., A. Neidhardt, and T. J. Ott. "The Drop from Front Strategy in TCP over ATM and Its Interworking with Other Control Features." Proceedings from *INFOCOM 96.* (1996): 1242–1250.

[DKS89]   Demers, A., S. Keshav, and S. Shenker. "Analysis and Simulation of a Fair Queueing Algorithm." Proceedings from Symposium on Communication Architectures and Protocols, *ACM SIGCOMM 89.* (September 1989). (Also in *Journal of Internetworking Research and Experience*, October 1990).

[DRR95]   Shreedhar, M., and G. Varghese. "Efficient Fair Queuing Using Deficit Round Robin." Proceedings from *ACM SIGCOMM 95.* (October 1995). (Also in *Computer Communication Review* 25, no. 4, October 1995).

[DSRTER]   Bernet, Y., A. Smith, and S. Blake. "A Conceptual Model for DiffServ Routers." Internet Draft (work in progress) draft-ietf-diffserv-model-00.txt. (June 1999).

[FASTIP1]   Waldvogel, M., G. Varghese, J. Turner, and B. Plattner. "Scalable High Speed IP Routing Lookups." *ACM SIGCOMM Computer Communication Review* 27, no. 4 (October 1997).

[FASTIP2]   Degermark, M., A. Brodnik, S. Carlsson, and S. Pink. "Small Forwarding Tables for Fast Routing Lookups." *ACM SIGCOMM Computer Communication Review* 27, no. 4 (October 1997).

[FLOYD95]   Floyd, S., and V. Jacobson. "Link-Sharing and Resource Management Models for Packet Networks." *IEEE/ACM Transactions on Networking* 3, no. 4 (August 1995).

[FRED97]   Lin, D., and R. Morris. "Dynamics of Random Early Detection." Proceedings from *ACM SIGCOMM 97*. Cannes, France. (October 1997): 127–137.

[HAHN86]   Hahne, E., and R. Gallager. "Round Robin Scheduling for Fair Flow Control in Data Communications Networks." *IEEE International Conference on Communications.* (June 1986).

[KESH98]   Keshav, S., and R. Sharma. "Issues and Trends in Router Design." *IEEE Communications Magazine.* (May 1998).

[KLS98]   Kumar, V., T. Lakshman, and D. Stiliadis. "Beyond Best Effort: Router Architectures for the Differentiated Services of Tomorrow's Internet." *IEEE Communications Magazine.* (May 1998).

[PGPS]   Parekh, A. "A Generalized Processor Sharing Approach to Flow Control in Integrated Services Networks." Ph.D. dissertation. Massachusetts Institute of Technology. (February 1992).

[RED]   Floyd, S., and V. Jacobson. "Random Early Detection Gateways for Congestion Avoidance." *IEEE/ACM Transactions on Networking* 1, no. 4 (August 1993): 397–413.

[RFC970]   Nagle, J. "On Packet Switches with Infinite Storage." RFC 970. (December 1985).

[RFC1349]   Almquist, P. "Type of Service in the Internet Protocol Suite." RFC 1349. (July 1992).

[RFC1812]   Baker, F. (ed). "Requirements for IP Version 4 Routers." RFC 1812. (June 1995).

[RFC2309]   Braden, B., D. Clark, J. Crowcroft, B. Davie, S. Deering, D. Estrin, S. Floyd, V. Jacobson, G. Minshall, C. Partridge, L. Peterson, K. Ramakrishnan, S. Shenker, J. Wroclawski, and L. Zhang. "Recommendations on Queue Management and Congestion Avoidance in the Internet." RFC 2309. (April 1998).

[RFC2460]   Deering, S., and R. Hinden. "Internet Protocol, Version 6 (IPv6) Specification." RFC 2460. (December 1998).

[RFC2474]   Nichols, K., S. Blake, F. Baker, and D. Black. "Definition of the Differentiated Services Field (DS Field) in the IPv4 and IPv6 Headers." RFC 2474. (December 1998).

[RFC2481]   Ramakrishnan, K., and S. Floyd. "A Proposal to Add Explicit Congestion Notification (ECN) to IP." RFC 2481. (January 1999).

[RIO]   Clark, D., and W. Fang. "Explicit Allocation of Best Effort Packet Delivery Service." *IEEE/ACM Transactions on Networking* 6, no. 4 (1998): 362–373.

[SRTCM]   Heinanen, J., and R. Guerin. "A Single Rate Three Color Marker." Internet Draft (work in progress) <draft-heinanen-diffserv-srtcm-01.txt>. (May 1999).

[SUTER98]   Suter, B., T. V. Lakshman, D. Stiliadis, and A. K. Choudhury. "Buffer Management Schemes for Supporting TCP in Gigabit Routers with Per-Flow Queueing." *IEEE Journal on Selected Areas in Communications* 17, no. 6 (June 1999).

[TRTCM]   Heinanen, J., and R. Guerin. "A Two Rate Three Color Marker." Internet Draft (work in progress) <draft-heinanen-diffserv-trtcm-01.txt>. (May 1999).

[ZHANG89]   Zhang, L. "A New Architecture for Packet Switching Network Protocols." MIT Technical Report TR-455. (August 1989).

[ZHANG91]   Zhang, L. "VirtualClock: A New Traffic Control Algorithm for Packet-Switched Networks." *ACM Transactions on Computer Systems* 9, no. 2 (1991): 101–121.

Edge-to-Edge Network Models

So far we've focused on the details of how individual routers can differentiate traffic, provide predictable bandwidth sharing, and use packet drops or marking to keep average localized congestion under control. But this information doesn't mean too much without a networkwide model of how these mechanisms ought to be used. This chapter explores three network models—*Integrated Services (IntServ, or IS)*, *Differentiated Services (DiffServ, or DS)*, and *Multiprotocol Label Switching (MPLS)*.

IntServ, the first attempt of the Internet Engineering Task Force (IETF) at a service model that supports per-flow quality of service (QoS) guarantees, requires relatively complex Classify, Queue, and Schedule (CQS) architectures along any edge-to-edge path. DiffServ can be viewed as a minimalist counterpoint to IntServ, throwing out everything that isn't essential to the provision of two or three aggregate service levels. MPLS is included because it can build on the CQS architectures developed for IntServ or DiffServ and adds support for explicitly constructed, non-shortest-path routing of traffic.

A number of concepts are common to each approach:

- A network is characterized as having Edge and Core routers.

- Edge routers accept customer traffic (that is, packets from any source outside the network) into the network.

- Core routers provide transit packet forwarding service between other Core routers and/or Edge routers.

- Edge routers characterize, police, and/or mark customer traffic being admitted to the network.

- Edge routers may decline requests signaled by outside sources (for example, customer networks); this process is called *admission control*.

- Core routers differentiate traffic insofar as necessary to cope with transient congestion within the network itself.

- Statistical multiplexing must be utilized wherever appropriate to maximize utilization of core resources. The approaches differ in the details of what their Edge and Core routers are expected to do and how their actions are coordinated to generate desirable edge-to-edge services while optimally utilizing internal network resources.

Much of the following discussion assumes that the reader is familiar with the classification, metering, policing, marking, queuing, and scheduling concepts described in Chapter 3, "Per-hop Packet Processing."

4.1 Integrated Services

The underlying principles behind the IETF's IntServ, or IS, model are documented in RFC 1633 [RFC1633]. IntServ's goal was to augment the existing Best Effort Internet with a range of end-to-end services tailored for a new breed of real-time-streaming and interactive applications. Motivated in part by the MBone experiments with distributed conferencing and limited "broadcasts" of IETF meetings in the early 1990s, a number of researchers began to define the set of end-to-end services an IP network should provide to such applications. To date, IntServ has developed support for two broad classes of applications:

- Real-time applications with strict bandwidth and latency requirements, whose users could not get what they sought from Best Effort IP networks

- Traditional applications, whose users wanted performance equivalent to a lightly loaded Best Effort network—regardless of how much load the network was really under

The first came to be known as *Guaranteed Service (GS)* [RFC2212], and the second came to be known as *Controlled Load (CL)* [RFC2211].

With a focus on supporting individual applications, IntServ developed an architecture requiring per-flow traffic handling at every hop along an application's end-to-end path and explicit a priori signaling of each flow's requirements. The Resource Reservation Protocol (RSVP), which is discussed in Chapter 5, "Establishing Edge-to-Edge IP QoS," was concurrently developed to fulfil the role of signaling protocol for IntServ [RFC2205, RFC2210].

An IntServ *flow* is defined as any identifiable (classifiable) set of packets from a source to one or more receivers for which a common QoS treatment has been requested. A stream of packets having the same source address, destination address (whether unicast or multicast), protocol, and port numbers is one example of an IntServ flow. An IntServ flow is simplex—it goes in one direction only. For example, a multiparty videoconference between N users will need N flows (assuming one flow from each source being multicast to the other participants).

4.1.1   Network Model

IntServ's basic model is built from a concatenation of network elements (NEs) [RFC2216] that provide transit service between a traffic source and its receiver(s) (see Figure 4.1). A NE can be a host, a router, or an underlying link—anything that participates in the delivery of a requested IntServ service. There are three types of NEs:

- A QoS-enabled NE can actively deliver per-flow behaviors in support of one or more IntServ services.

- A QoS-aware NE understands enough to indicate what it cannot support. (For example, it may support RSVP in order to recognize and deny service requests.)

- A non-QoS NE has no IntServ capabilities and no ability to interact meaningfully with the IntServ NEs around it.

While the IntServ working group developed the basic service definitions and router models required to support them, a related Integrated Services over Specific Link Layers (ISSLL) working group began specifying how a number of known link layer technologies are used as *QoS-aware NEs*.

Before a new flow is allowed to use a network's resources, it is subject to admission control by each NE along the proposed path—a local, per-hop decision closely coupled with the signaling protocol used by the end applications. A flow is admitted only when each NE along the path indicates it can support the request.

Admission is based in part on the source application's own characterization of its traffic profile. After a flow is admitted, NEs on the edge (and sometimes through the core) of the network impose policing (and possibly rate shaping) functions on the flow. These functions limit an application's capability to inject traffic in excess of its negotiated traffic profile.

Figure 4.1 IntServ assumes per-flow traffic handling by all network elements.

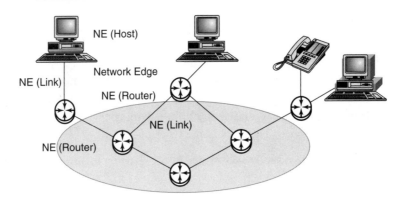

4.1.2 Traffic Characterization

The IntServ working group broadly classified typical applications into two categories—*Real Time* and *Elastic*. The Real Time category was then further subdivided into *Tolerant* and *Intolerant* subcategories. Although these categories do not necessarily cover every possible permutation of application-generated flows, they provided a useful framework within which to design the CL and GS services. The differences between each category boil down to differences in how applications react to packet transport delay.

Real Time Applications

Real Time covers situations in which packets must reach the destination(s) within some bounded period of time after the previous packet; otherwise, the packet's contents are wasted—a distinct notion of timeliness is associated with packet delivery.

Tolerance of total end-to-end delay varies widely among Real Time applications. For example, a streaming audio/video application (such as a Web-based broadcast) is essentially one-way information transfer, and the audiences are not overly concerned if they see and hear events milliseconds or even seconds after they really occurred. At the other extreme is interactive audio- or videoconferencing with tighter bounds imposed by the needs of natural human interaction. Human conversational styles typically assume rapid (a few hundred milliseconds or less) transit of our words and gestures, so interactive applications must work within those limits.

Note

Synchronizing the delays experienced by related audio and video streams is an application issue and outside the domain of IntServ.

Another element is *jitter*—packets may sometimes arrive spaced more closely together than necessary or further spaced apart than required. Both interactive and streaming media applications use local buffering at the receiver to smooth out variability in packet arrival times—referred to as *play-out buffering*. A first-in, first-out (FIFO) queue is fed with packets arriving from the network and serviced when the codec needs another packet to process. When packets arrive more quickly than required, the queue grows. When packets arrive more slowly than required, the queue shrinks.

To minimize the chances of the queue shrinking to zero, applications typically pre-fill the queue with some number of packets before starting the codec. The queue's average occupancy then remains around this level (given that the source's packet transmission rate matches the receiver's packet consumption rate). This average backlog of packets constitutes a buffer against jitter but also adds to the average end-to-end latency experienced by the application—although the buffer can be made relatively large for streaming-media applications, it must be kept small as possible for interactive applications.

Two types of Real Time applications are described in RFC 1633:

- **Tolerant**—The codecs can handle infrequent emptying of the play-out buffer by fabricating "filler" packets that approximate the audio or video signal in progress.

- **Intolerant**—The play-out buffer must never empty because packet loss is catastrophic to the receiving process.

Tolerant applications can afford to approximately guess "typical" jitter bounds and perhaps use less play-out buffering—achieving lower end-to-end latency at the expense of infrequent sound or image degradation. Intolerant applications must establish their play-out buffers to cope with worst-case network jitter (in other words, the worst-case end-to-end latency the network could impose).

RFC 1633 observes that Intolerant Real Time applications require some way of knowing or strictly bounding the worst-case end-to-end latency delivered by the network. Tolerant Real Time applications can cope with the latency occasionally varying outside a defined limit.

Elastic Applications

Elastic encompasses applications that don't much care when their packets arrive but will process them immediately whenever they do. Elastic applications impose requirements on interpacket delays only when the application seems to "work better" if the typical delays are kept low. (Of course, there is always some point at which delay becomes "too long," but for Elastic traffic its measured in tens of seconds or minutes.)

Examples of Elastic applications include email, IP-based fax, File Transfer Protocol (FTP), and domain name system (DNS). Applications based on either Transmission Control Protocol (TCP) or User Datagram Protocol (UDP) can be Elastic—although TCP-based applications are almost always Elastic simply because TCP does not lend itself to nonelastic (real time) applications.

The general belief in RFC 1633 is that Elastic applications care more about the average end-to-end latency and are relatively tolerant of infrequent instances of severe jitter. This belief leads to a notion that the best service for Elastic applications is as-soon-as-possible delivery, which can be alternatively described as "give me generally low delay whenever you can."

4.1.3 Service Models

Intserv defined only two service models, after observing that Tolerant Real-time and Elastic applications have similar jitter tolerance. GS provides strict end-to-end latency bounds, for Intolerant Real Time traffic [RFC2212], whereas CL supports nominal end-to-end latency bounds (with some likelihood of moderate to extreme jitter), for Tolerant Real Time and Elastic traffic [RFC2211].

Controlled Load

CL's essential definition is given in RFC 2211 as follows:

> The end-to-end behavior provided to an application by a series of network elements providing controlled-load service tightly approximates the behavior visible to applications receiving Best Effort service *under unloaded conditions* from the same series of network elements.

In this context *unloaded conditions* means "not heavily loaded or congested" rather than "no other traffic whatsoever." Thus CL provides only the nominal "pretty good" service of a relatively uncongested Best Effort path. RFC 2211 goes on to observe that

- A very high percentage of transmitted packets will be successfully delivered by the network to the receiving end-nodes. (The percentage of packets not successfully delivered must closely approximate the basic packet error rate of the transmission medium).

- The transit delay experienced by a very high percentage of the delivered packets will not greatly exceed the minimum transmit delay experienced by any successfully delivered packet. (This minimum transit delay includes speed-of-light delay plus the fixed processing time in routers and other communications devices along the path.)

So when a flow requests CL service, that flow expects to see an emulated Best Effort service as though the network were unloaded, regardless of what other traffic the network is trying to carry at the same time. In a sense, CL service can be considered a private Best Effort network service and is extremely useful for allowing different application flows to share a network while constraining their degree of mutual interference. Because CL allows some uncertainty in its worst-case performance the network can statistically multiplex resources allocated internally for CL service.

Guaranteed Service

GS's essential definition is given in RFC 2212 as follows:

> Guaranteed service provides firm (mathematically provable) bounds on end-to-end datagram queuing delays. This service makes it possible to provide a service that guarantees both delay and bandwidth...

> Guaranteed service guarantees that datagrams will arrive within the guaranteed delivery time and will not be discarded due to queue overflows, provided the flow's traffic stays within its specified traffic parameters. This service is intended for applications which need a firm guarantee that a datagram will arrive no later than a certain time after it was transmitted by its source.

An application provides a characterization of its expected traffic profile, and the network calculates and returns an indication of the resulting end-to-end latency it can guarantee. If this latency is within the limits desired by the application, it can go ahead and be assured the path will deliver packets within this calculated latency bound. Otherwise, the application can modify its traffic characterization and request the network to recalculate the end-to-end latency it is able to guarantee.

GS requires an application's self-characterization to be given in terms of a rate and burst size (the parameters of a token bucket). The end-to-end delay is made up of intrinsic path delays (transmission delays due to the speed of light, packet serialization, and so on) and queuing delays through every NE. Although intrinsic path delays cannot be varied, each NE's queuing delay depends on the token bucket parameters provided by the application. The network calculates the worst-case latency it can guarantee by summing the queuing and intrinsic delays of every NE, given the application's token bucket parameters and the load on the network due to existing reservations.

GS does not attempt to bound or quantify the minimum latency, average latency, or nominal jitter—only the worst-case latency bound is guaranteed. GS is most suitable for Intolerant Real Time applications that supply their own play-out buffers to deal with jitter. Bounding the worst-case latency bounds the worst-case jitter (and, hence, play-out buffer size). Compared to CL, GS allows less latitude for statistical multiplexing within the network.

4.1.4   Signaling and Admission Control

Every application is presumed to use some form of signaling to negotiate service with an IntServ-capable network. IntServ signaling has two primary functions:

- **Negotiation**—When the network decides whether it can support the application's requested service (also referred to as *admission control*)

- **Configuration**—When the network configures NEs along the path to support the negotiated flow characteristics

In theory, signaling can take the form of preprovisioning or SNMP-based management, but in practice applications are likely to use RSVP [RFC2205]. •

Using RSVP

The use of RSVP in support of IntServ is provided in RFC 2210 [RFC2210]. RSVP itself is discussed in Chapter 5—for the time being, it is sufficient to note the following general characteristics:

- **Sources emit regular PATH messages downstream toward the receiver(s)**—Two message objects relevant to IntServ are carried in PATH messages: SENDER_TSPEC (describing the traffic) and ADSPEC (modified at each hop to reflect network characteristics between source and receiver).

- **Receiver(s) respond with RESV messages upstream toward the sender**—One message object relevant to IntServ is carried in RESV messages: FLOWSPEC (describing the receiver's desired QoS service to be applied to the source's traffic).

To initiate a reservation, a flow's source constructs appropriate SENDER_TSPEC and ADSPEC elements and begins sending them in PATH messages towards the receiver. The ADSPEC informs the receiver which service classes (CL, GS, or both) are appropriate for the traffic. Along the way, IntServ-capable NEs may modify the ADSPEC element to reflect restrictions or modifications required by the network. At the receiver the SENDER_TSPEC and (possibly modified) ADSPEC are used to determine which parameters to send back upstream in a

FLOWSPEC element. The FLOWSPEC selects either CL or GS and carries parameters required by NEs along the upstream path to determine whether the request can be honored (admission control).

One of the most important pieces of information the ADSPEC conveys is whether any NEs along the path support only limited (or no) IntServ capabilities. This information is carried in "break bits." A global break bit is set if a hop somewhere along the path cannot support any IntServ service, and service-specific break bits indicate whether CL or GS service cannot be supported at some hop along the path [RFC2215]. (For the case where the non-IntServ NE also doesn't understand RSVP, the break bit is likely to be set by a neighboring NE (upstream or downstream) aware of the disconnect in the path.) The existence of a set CL or GS break bit implies that the receiver cannot meaningfully negotiate that service. If the global break bit is set, the path is unable to support any IntServ service.

A source characterizes itself with the following SENDER_TSPEC parameters:

- Token bucket rate r and size b (measured in bytes per second and bytes, respectively)

- Peak data rate p

- Minimum policed unit m

- Maximum packet size M

Token bucket parameters reflect the source's perspective on its traffic rate and burstiness. (Only IP-level bytes are counted. Link-layer overhead is derived on a hop-by-hop basis.) If the true peak rate is known, it can be reflected in p; otherwise this parameter is set to the source's link interface speed (or infinity if no other information is available to the source application). Rates may be expressed from 1 byte per second to 40 terabytes per second. Bucket depth may be expressed from 1 byte to 250 gigabytes.

Packets smaller than m are treated as though they are size m for the purposes of token-bucket metering. This practice also allows NEs along the path to compute the maximum bandwidth overhead needed to carry a flow's packets (adding link-specific overhead at each hop to m). Smaller values of m increase the link-level bandwidth required to support a given IP level bandwidth target (since link-level overhead becomes a higher fraction of total bytes transmitted per-hop) and so increase the chance of a flow being denied service. If an application knows it will send few really small packets, it might advertise a larger value of m—increasing the likelihood that a request for CL or GS service will be admitted.

Another important parameter for both CL and GS services is the maximum packet size emitted by the source. SENDER_TSPEC informs receivers of the largest packets an application *could* emit, whereas the ADSPEC object collects information on the smallest per-hop Maximum Transmission Unit (MTU) seen along the path from source to receiver. The receiver then uses this smallest MTU size to specify (in the FLOWSPEC) the largest packet the receiver wants the source to transmit. The source must (if the flow is accepted) abide by the smaller limit even if it could transmit larger packets.

Controlled Load Parameters

A receiver can request CL service only for flows where the associated ADSPEC object indicates that CL service is available. If so, the receiver returns a FLOWSPEC with the same range of parameters as advertised in the source's SENDER_TSPEC above. The token bucket parameters reflect what the receiver expects to see, and the maximum packet size M is the smallest MTU along the path (as reported by the ADSPEC object arriving in each PATH message). Setting m higher than reported by the source application increases the chances the reservation will succeed but also increases the chances that bursts of packets smaller than m will be unexpectedly policed or shaped.

A flow is accepted for CL service on the understanding that it will conform to the parameters in the FLOWSPEC advertised by the receiver. Every NE along the path is expected to perform local metering, followed by policing or shaping, to enforce the advertised and agreed-to bounds. If the source begins sending traffic outside those bounds, it will be considered nonconformant and either dropped or forwarded as regular Best Effort traffic. Additionally, packets larger than the agreed maximum packet size will also be considered nonconformant.

CL service allows for statistical multiplexing to be used within the network itself, and so admission control (when evaluating the FLOWSPEC at each upstream NE) can be relatively liberal in what it accepts relative to existing CL commitments.

Guaranteed Service Parameters

A receiver can request GS service only for flows where the associated ADSPEC object indicates that GS service is available. If so, the ADSPEC object carries a number of GS-specific parameters from which the receiver can construct an appropriate FLOWSPEC to return upstream. In addition to the r, b, p, m, and M parameters also used for CL service, GS service is characterized by R (rate) and S (slack term) parameters.

The rate R is measured in the same units as r, and must be equal to or more than r. R reflects the theoretical service rate that, at each NE, will result in a desirable delay bound. S is measured in microseconds and reflects how far each NE is allowed to deviate from the ideal delay bound. Larger values for R and smaller values for S represent stricter delay bounds.

Appropriate values for R and S are determined from the network's estimates of how much intrinsic per-hop delay D and rate-dependent per-hop delay C is introduced along the path. D_{tot} and C_{tot} are carried by the downstream ADSPEC object when GS service is available and are incremented by the D and C contributions of each NE along the path. The relationship is

$$S = D_{req} - (b/R + C_{tot}/R + D_{tot})$$

where D_{req} is the application's desired delay bound and b is the token bucket parameter advertised by the source.

As the RESV message propagates back up toward the source, every NE performs local admission control by calculating how much delay it will add (given the receiver's choice of R) and possibly taking some of the available slack term. The NE will accept the request if it can support the desired service rate R or if some combination of a lesser service rate and the slack term can be used to meet the desired delay bound. The S and R terms in the FLOWSPEC may be adjusted accordingly before continuing to propagate the RESV message further upstream. The overall result is that a GS service request will succeed only if every NE along the path accepts the RESV presented to it from its downstream neighbor (adjusted in accordance with the delay already added by the NEs close to the receiver).

Route Selection

One notable characteristic of the IntServ model is that it does not mandate the use of QoS-based routing. Resources are either available or not available along whatever shortest-path route is currently in place. This simplification is driven by two observations:

- Without modifying the next-hop-forwarding paradigm, it is not possible to force packets to follow non-shortest paths.

- QoS-based routing protocols for inter-domain traffic are still not well understood, nor are they widely deployed.

Clearly, had IntServ been tied to the development of QoS-based, non-shortest-path packet forwarding technologies, IntServ's development would have been significantly more unwieldy. Fortunately, the IETF recognized that the addition of traffic classification and differential queuing and scheduling capabilities would add significant benefit to IP networking even in the absence of QoS-based routing. In the current IntServ architecture RSVP allows resource reservations to track changes in the underlying shortest-path routing (described further in Chapter 5).

Interestingly, the emergence of MPLS (discussed later in this chapter) actually provides a solution to non-shortest-path routing. However, whether MPLS path control will ever be folded into a next generation of IntServ remains to be seen.

4.1.5 Router Requirements

IntServ makes use of all the per-hop capabilities described in Chapter 3. Multifield classification is presumed in order to establish per-flow context for each and every accepted flow. This context is then used to drive token-bucket metering, which may result in packet dropping or re-marking of nonconformant traffic. Multiple queues are a given, uniquely assigned to each accepted flow (with at least one queue for Best Effort and nonconforming traffic).

IntServ also requires a sophisticated control plane to perform signaling. In the case of RSVP, this requirement implies a distinct layer of management software to participate in RSVP message exchanges; calculate IntServ object parameters; and appropriately configure the router's underlying classification, metering, queuing, and scheduling components.

Because IntServ fundamentally assumes that each flow has its own queue, congestion control schemes based on statistical, preemptive packet drop (for example, Random Early Detection, or RED) are rarely mentioned. Such schemes are intended for situations in which a multitude of flows share a queue and some need to be protected from the vagaries of others. With per-flow queue assignment, an IntServ router can be quite precise in its queue sizing—the use of hard limits affects only one flow at a time.

4.2 Differentiated Services

It would be fair to observe that the IETF's DiffServ architecture [RFC2475] arose as a counterpoint to the relative complexity and end-to-end nature of the IntServ architecture. A number of people argued successfully that what the Internet needed was incremental improvements on its Best Effort service model and that IntServ was attempting to jump too far all at once. Something just a little better than Best Effort would, presumably, be fine.

This simplification is shown in Figure 4.2—complex decision making (for example, multi-field classification) is pushed to the edges, and useful edge-to-edge services are built from a restricted set of behaviors in Core routers. Initially focused on the backbone service provider space (where router performance is at a premium and transport flows number in the hundreds of thousands), two key benefits are expected from this approach:

- Faster core routers (by limiting their classification and queuing stage complexity)

- Less state to signal, process, and store (cross-core QoS characteristics can be expressed in terms of only a few aggregate behaviors)

Core routers establish packet context, and hence their packet-handling behavior, solely from the *DiffServ Code Point (DSCP)* carried in every packet. As described in Chapter 3, the DSCP is carried within the DS field (the old IPv4 ToS byte). Multifield (MF) classification and marking at the network's edge allow a wide variety of traffic to be mapped into a smaller subset of behaviors provided by the network's core. Edge routers may also be expected to provide policing or rate shaping—smoothing out the temporal characteristics of traffic classes entering the core. For further information see "A Conceptual Model for DiffServ Routers" [DSRTER].

Figure 4.2   DiffServ aims to simplify core router complexity.

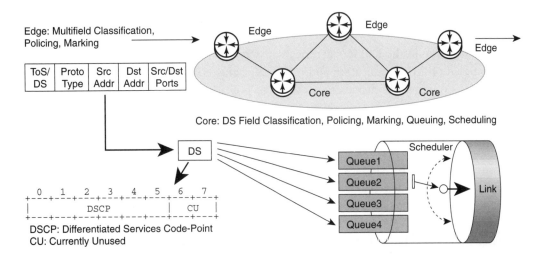

Standardizing particular edge-to-edge service models has been considered outside the scope of the IETF's DiffServ working group, which focuses instead on specific per-hop queuing and scheduling behaviors (known as *per-hop behaviors*, or *PHBs*). PHBs are seen as building blocks from which a number of edge-to-edge services might be built with the task of building such services left to the network operators. Two PHBs have been published so far—Expedited Forwarding (EF) [RFC2598] and Assured Forwarding (AF) [RFC2597]. Each document gives a hint at the sort of edge-to-edge service models its authors have in mind. In addition, the working group has defined a set of Class Selector PHBs that emulate the services selected by the original IPv4 Precedence bits.

4.2.1 Terminology

No new architecture is complete without its own set of terminology. RFC 2475 provides some new terms that are briefly covered here. A network using particular edge-mapping rules and DiffServ mechanisms to provide edge-to-edge QoS is referred to as a *DiffServ Domain*, or *DS Domain*. Neighboring DS Domains are not constrained to use the same PHBs and edge-mapping rules. Where an end-to-end path involves the concatenation of DS Domains (a *DS Region*) it is up to the network operator(s) to ensure each DS Domain acts in a way that supports the end-to-end QoS goals. Edge routers surrounding a DS Domain are known as *DS Boundary nodes* with traffic entering a DS Domain at *DS Ingress nodes* and exiting at *DS Egress nodes*. Core routers providing transit service are known as *DS Interior nodes*.

A critical function in the DiffServ architecture is *traffic conditioning*—setting the DSCP of packets based on MF classification and temporal characteristics (*marking*), and the possible modification of temporal characteristics through policing (dropping) or rate shaping. *Traffic conditioner* functionality is typically located at DS Ingress nodes. The rules a particular traffic conditioner uses to control its actions are known as a *traffic conditioning agreement (TCA)*.

Individual application-to-application flows (unique Src/Dst address, protocol type, and TCP/UDP port numbers) are referred to as *microflows*. Within a DS Domain many microflows will share a given DSCP—the collection of packets sharing a DSCP is referred to as a DS Behavior Aggregate (BA). The main premise of DiffServ is that Core routers (interior nodes) need to concern themselves only with BAs, rather than with microflows.

4.2.2 Per-hop Behaviors and Codepoints

PHBs specify externally visible queuing, queue management (for example, packet drop), and scheduling characteristics. This approach is intended to allow implementers some freedom in their choice of algorithms—for example, Weighted Fair Queuing (WFQ), Weighted Round Robin (WRR), and so on—to achieve the desired behavior. Some PHBs are defined with closely related behaviors and are referred to as *PHB Groups* (for example, a set of PHBs that specify the same basic queuing and scheduling behavior but indicate different drop probabilities to the queue manager).

PHBs are indicated by specific values in the DSCP. Although each PHB's definition also provides a "recommended" DSCP value, DiffServ allows multiple DSCP values to map to the same PHB (whether in the same or different DS Domains). PHB Groups have multiple DSCP values—typically one for each specific PHB within the group. RFC 2474 provides broad guidelines for allocating particular DSCP values [RFC2474], as shown in Table 4.1.

Table 4.1   DSCP Allocation Table.

Pool	DSCP*	Usage
1	xxxxx0	Assigned by IANA**
2	xxxx11	Experimental/local use
3	xxxx01	Experimental/local/IANA

* Bits marked "x" are either 1 or 0.

** Internet Assigned Numbers Authority; typically assigns numbers at the request of IETF working groups for IETF-developed protocols.

Pool 1 is reserved for PHBs that have well-defined meanings (typically those standardized or under standardization by the DiffServ working group). Pool 2 is available for local use (nonstandard or experimental PHBs within specific DS Domains or Regions). Pool 3 is similar to Pool 2 except that if Pool 1 values are ever exhausted, Pool 3 values may be assigned to specific PHBs developed by the DiffServ working group.

Traditional Best Effort behavior is referred to as the "default PHB," which has a recommended DSCP value of `000000`. Core routers also select the default PHB when they encounter an unknown DSCP.

4.2.3 Class Selector Per-hop Behaviors

Limited backward compatibility with the old IPv4 ToS field's Precedence classes [RFC1812] is achieved by reserving part of Pool 1 for *Class Selector* PHBs. RFC 2474 defines the Class Selector PHBs as those that closely approximate the packet handling of various IPv4 Precedence levels. The associated *Class Selector Codepoints* are DSCP values in the range 000000 to 111000 (represented as xxx000)—the lower three bits of the DSCP corresponding to the three bits of the original Precedence field. (A "precedence" of 000 results in the default PHB DSCP—they are semantically and syntactically equivalent with both indicating Best Effort forwarding behavior.) A router implementing Class Selector PHBs must implement at least two, and it may implement up to eight distinct PHBs. Multiple Class Selector Codepoints may map to a single Class Selector PHB.

RFC 2474 has the following to say about the handling rules for Class Selector PHBs:

- PHBs selected by a Class Selector Codepoint SHOULD give packets a probability of timely forwarding that is not lower than that given to packets marked with a Class Selector Codepoint of lower relative order, under reasonable operating conditions and traffic loads.

- PHBs selected by codepoints 11x000 MUST give packets a preferential forwarding treatment by comparison to the PHB selected by codepoint 000000 to preserve the common usage of IP Precedence values 110 and 111 for routing traffic.

- PHBs selected by distinct Class Selector Codepoints SHOULD be independently forwarded; that is, packets marked with different Class Selector Codepoints MAY be re-ordered.

Various queuing and scheduling algorithms (WFQ, WRR, CBQ, Priority, and so on) meet these requirements. It is sufficient that a router is configured to properly map a packet arriving with any given Class Selector Codepoint onto a PHB that meets the preceding requirements (including PHBs implemented for other services and to which other non-Class Selector DSCP values also map).

4.2.4 Expedited Forwarding

RFC 2598 [RFC2598] defines the very simple EF PHB and its associated service model. An EF PHB requests every router along the path to always service EF packets (packets arriving with a DSCP which is locally mapped to the EF PHB) at least as fast (if not faster) than the rate at which EF packets arrive. This situation leads to three subsequent requirements:

- Rate shape or police EF traffic on entry to the DS Domain, to cap the rates at which EF traffic may enter the network core.

- Configure the EF packet-servicing interval at every Core router to exceed the expected aggregate arrival rate of EF traffic.

- EF packet-servicing intervals must be unaffected by the amount of non-EF traffic waiting to be scheduled at any given instant.

RFC 2598 notes that it is possible to meet the scheduling requirements with various scheduling algorithms, but does not mandate any particular approach. Jitter characteristics are the main sources of difference (for example, mapping EF to the highest queue of a priority scheduler provides lower jitter than does mapping EF to an appropriately weighted queue of a WRR scheduler).

Although in practice EF packets will be sent to a specific queue for appropriate scheduling (see Figure 4.3), the definition of EF service is such that on average this queue ought to be small or empty. As a consequence, the EF PHB is a suitable building block for low-loss, low-latency, and low-jitter edge-to-edge services. RFC 2598 notes that EF can be used to build "virtual lease line" services (low latency/loss paths characterized by a peak bandwidth parameter) because it carves out a guaranteed slice of edge-to-edge bandwidth protected against all other users of the DS Domain.

Figure 4.3   Expedited Forwarding encodes a single queue selection.

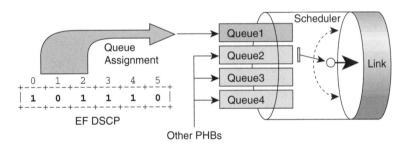

By definition packet drops within the network are meant to be rare for EF service. Individual traffic flows using EF service are rate shaped or aggressively policed on entry to the DS Domain. So, correctly configured Core routers should never see EF traffic arriving with an aggregate rate exceeding their configured service intervals. As such, progressive or statistical drop mechanisms such as RED are not part of the EF PHB definition.

A single DSCP of 101110 is recommended to indicate EF PHB. It is worth noting that although the PHB is easy to define, an actual service based on EF requires careful coordination of policing, shaping, and scheduler service intervals along any path EF traffic is likely to take.

4.2.5 *Assured Forwarding*

Defined in RFC 2597, AF is actually a PHB Group for edge-to-edge services specified in terms of relative bandwidth availability and multitiered packet drop characteristics [RFC2597]. Whereas EF supports services with "hard" bandwidth and jitter characteristics, the AF group allows more flexible and dynamic sharing of network resources—supporting the "soft" bandwidth and loss guarantees appropriate for bursty traffic. RFC 2597 actually defines four PHB Groups, each independently supporting AF behavior.

Two distinct classification contexts are encoded within the DSCP—a packet's *service class* and its *drop precedence*. The service class provides context with which to select an appropriate queue (and, hence, a particular bandwidth share from the scheduler). The drop precedence provides context to weight RED-like behavior [RED] expected from the queue manager—making it more or less aggressive depending on whether a packet's drop precedence is high or low. AF requires active queue management with independent RED-like behavior on each queue to keep long-term congestion down while allowing short-term burstiness.

We can consider the DSCP to be laid out as nnnmm0 with nnn encoding the service class (queue selection) and mm encoding the drop precedence (Figure 4.4). RFC 2597 currently defines four service classes and three levels of drop precedence. A shorthand notion exists for referring to a particular AF PHB—AF**xy** refers to AF service class x with drop precedence y. Table 4.2 gives the DSCP values associated with each combination of service class and drop precedence.

Figure 4.4   Assured Forwarding encodes service class and drop precedence.

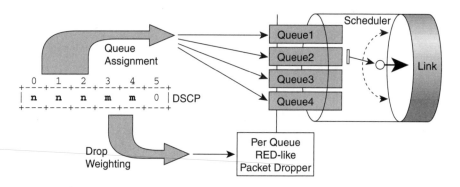

Table 4.2   DSCP Values for each AF PHB Group.

	Class 1	Class 2	Class 3	Class 4
Drop precedence 1 (low)	001010	010010	011010	100010
Drop precedence 2 (medium)	001100	010100	011100	100100
Drop precedence 3 (high)	001110	010110	011110	100110

Although an AF DSCP identifies one of four queues (classes), it does not specify a queue's maximum size or the scheduler service interval associated with each queue. The network operator configures these parameters on a case-by-case basis (depending on the edge-to-edge service desired from each AF class at the time). Each service class is distinguished by the level of forwarding resources (bandwidth and queue space) it receives at each hop, independent of the other three (implying the use of WFQ, WRR, or similar schedulers). To prevent possible re-ordering of packets belonging to application flows within a service class, an AF-compliant router must not map different service classes into the same queue and is not allowed to distribute packets belonging to a single service class across multiple queues.

Specific drop probabilities for each precedence level are assigned by the network operator to meet the desired packet-loss characteristics for each class. The only requirements are that drop precedence 3 must have a more aggressive drop probability than precedence 2 has and that precedence 2 must be more aggressive than precedence 1 has. In addition, the probability functions are per-class—packets marked AF12 (service class 1, drop precedence 2) may be subject to an entirely different drop probability function than packets marked AF22 (service class 2, drop precedence 2). Although RFC 2597 defines three drop precedence levels, a minimal AF implementation may get by with only two distinct drop probability functions. In this case, both precedence 2 and 3 are mapped to the function returning the higher drop probability. As with EF, actual edge-to-edge service based on an AF PHB Group requires coordination between Edge routers (to limit the type of traffic mapped to each AF class and drop precedence) and the Core routers (to ensure that appropriate resources and behaviors are provided to each class and drop precedence).

4.2.6 Traffic Conditioning

Any traffic allowed to enter a DS Domain must first be subject to traffic conditioning. This process typically occurs at the DS Ingress node—the Edge router that sits between a DS Domain and a non-DiffServ network, or between two DS Domains.

A traffic conditioner utilizes most of the classification, metering, marking, and dropping characteristics discussed in Chapter 3. Some form of MF classification is typically applied to establish a packet's context, and from this context the traffic conditioner knows which metering profile to apply, which DSCP to assign, and whether to police or rate shape the packet. The classification rules and associated actions are specified by one or more TCAs.

Implementations are not required to be arbitrarily flexible—for example, EF service only requires a DS Ingress node's metering stage to drop packets that are outside a profile represented by a single-stage token bucket. However, such traffic conditioning is not sufficient for AF service, which requires the Ingress node to assign DSCP values based on both the MF classification (which determines the AF service class) and the output from its metering stage (which determines the drop precedence). For example, a single-stage meter might mark in-profile packets as AFx1 and out-of-profile packets as AFx2 (or AFx3), instead of dropping them. A multistage meter could differentiate between AFx1, AFx2, AFx3, or local drop (policing) (for example, see "A Single Rate Three Color Marker" [SRTCM] and "A Two Rate Three Color Marker" [TRTCM]).

DiffServ has its own form of "uncertainty principle"—the less context a Core router has about individual packets, the less tolerant the system is to burstiness of microflows within a behavior aggregate. Because Core routers no longer see individual microflows, these routers are unable to mediate between aggressive and nonaggressive microflows making up a given behavior aggregate. Ingress rate shaping bounds the interference between microflows making up a behavior aggregate and smoothes the burstiness of any given behavior aggregate—compensating for the lack of packet context available to Core routers.

In principle a DS Domain might reach an agreement with its upstream traffic sources such that the packets arrived with their DSCP already appropriately set. However, even with such an agreement in place, traffic conditioning is still recommended on ingress to the local DS Domain—at the very least, policing and shaping ought to be applied to guard against accidental or deliberate attempts to inject traffic outside the allowed profiles.

4.2.7 Deployment Considerations

DiffServ's architectural simplicity is attractive, but actual deployment of edge-to-edge services requires filling in a lot of unspecified parameter values—and there are few guidelines for network operators to follow. Mapping hundreds or thousands of mostly unrelated microflows to a limited set of PHBs requires a careful balancing act—an act that is as much dependent on the network's topology at any point in time as it is on the ingress traffic conditioning and interior queuing and scheduling.

Relative to IntServ, a DiffServ network is far less tolerant of individuality among the microflows being carried. Two approaches arc available to ensure that individual edge-to-edge services survive being aggregated as they pass through the core:

- Aggressively rate shape or police at the edges

- Overprovision the core

In the first case, the network as a whole appears fairly intolerant from the perspective of the external traffic sources. In the second case, the network will, on average, be under-utilized. These conditions represent the two competing issues facing network designers—balancing service flexibility against network efficiency. (The intermediate stance of metering and marking of progressive drop precedence levels counts as tolerable but hardly tolerant because it bumps up the probable packet-loss rates during traffic bursts.) More discussion can be found in "A Framework for Differentiated Services" [DSFWK].

Another issue relates to backward compatibility with existing use of the IPv4 ToS field. One problem during early DS trials in 1999 was that some existing TCP implementations closed any connections where the IPv4 Precedence bits changed after the connection was established. This behavior is entirely compliant with RFC 793, and so the "fault" could not necessarily be attributed to the TCP implementations. However, the IPv4 Precedence bits are the lowest three bits of the DS field. Any DS-based transit network between two TCP peers might well modify the DSCP so that the TCP peers perceive the precedence to have changed—triggering a shut down of the connection. At the time of writing, discussions were underway to update RFC 793 to say that TCP implementations should ignore the precedence fields, removing the problem [TCP99]. However, this response reflects an interesting problem for designers of DS networks—do the users require transparent transport of their initial ToS octets from ingress to egress, and how do you achieve it if they do?

4.2.8 IntServ over DiffServ

Although they may seem quite distinct, IntServ and DiffServ can work together to create an overall end-to-end solution. At least one proposal [ISDS99] has recognized that an IntServ network can be built around DiffServ networks by treating a DiffServ network as a virtual link NE—rather as one would use an Asynchronous Transfer Mode (ATM) network to provide a link (Figure 4.5).

Figure 4.5 IntServ can treat a DiffServ transit network as another NE.

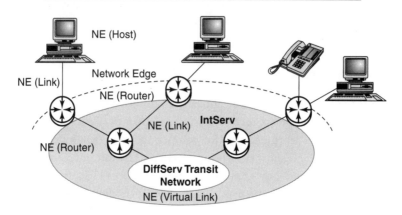

For example, EF service could be used to create protected bandwidth pipes (virtual leased lines) between the IntServ routers surrounding a DiffServ network. Because the pipe's QoS characteristics are known, the surrounding routers can map their individual IntServ flows onto the EF-based pipe in much the same way they would map many flows onto a real leased line.

Clearly, the DiffServ network doesn't need to understand or participate in the end user's per-flow RSVP signaling—the IntServ routers surrounding the DiffServ transit network handle this process. End-user RSVP signaling is passed transparently through the DiffServ network.

Such a hierarchy ensures that state information is only tracked out toward the edges of the IntServ network, where presumably the density of end-user flows is low enough to be supported by practical routers. As you head closer to the core of the network, the IntServ/DiffServ boundary routers aggregate their IntServ flows so that a DiffServ-only provider can support connectivity. This approach is likely to be deployed as a means to allow distributed enterprise sites to form a cohesive, IntServ-capable network even when their wide area IP service provider delivers only DiffServ service.

4.3 *Multiprotocol Label Switching*

Although not primarily a QoS mechanism, MPLS can be an important tool for backbone service providers. It can leverage the different per-hop capabilities discussed in Chapter 3 in many of the same ways that the IntServ and DiffServ models propose while allowing traffic engineering of non-shortest-path routes within a network. As such, it is worth exploring in some further detail.

MPLS represents the convergence of connection-oriented forwarding techniques and the Internet's routing protocols [MARCH]. The most prominent prestandard incarnations of MPLS (Ipsilon's IP Switching [IPSW], IBM's ARIS [ARIS], Cisco's early TAG Switching [RFC2105], and Toshiba's Cell Switch Router architectures [RFC2098]) leveraged the high-performance cell-switching capabilities of ATM switch hardware and melded them together into a network using existing IP routing protocols. As standardization progressed, packet-based MPLS also emerged to simplify the mechanics of packet processing within Core routers, replacing full or partial header classification and longest-prefix-match lookups with simple index label lookups.

MPLS offers one powerful tool unavailable to solutions based on conventional IP routers—the capability to forward packets over arbitrary non-shortest paths and emulate high-speed tunnels between non-label-switched domains. Such traffic-engineering capabilities enable service providers to optimize the distribution of QoS-sensitive and Best Effort traffic around their network. Additionally, MPLS can support metering, policing, marking, queuing, and scheduling behaviors ranging from the fine granularity of IntServ to the aggregated granularity of DiffServ—and offer them simultaneously on a single network.

4.3.1 *Multiprotocol Label Switching Overview*

The earliest motivation for developing MPLS lay in the desire to simplify wide area, high-performance IP backbone architectures. During the mid-90s the only pragmatic solution was to use ATM. Use of the orthogonal addressing schemes used by IP and ATM led to logically decoupled overlays of IP routers on top of ATM networks with ATM merely providing wide area, link-level connectivity. In theory an IP/ATM network consisted of logical IP subnets (LIS) interconnected by routers (analogous to the use of subnets in conventional LAN-based IP networks) [RFC2225]. Inter-LIS traffic traveled through routers even when a direct ATM path existed from source to destination. However, IP routers were significantly slower than ATM switches. Whenever possible, operators minimized IP/ATM router hops by placing all their routers into one LIS.

This single-LIS approach has two serious scaling problems—the number of virtual connection (VCs) and the number of Interior Gateway Protocol (IGP) peers. In practice a single LIS backbone would result in each router having a VC open to every other router—resulting in a VC mesh. A mesh of IGP peering relationships would also be created among the routers in the LIS. With a small number of routers, meshes might be considered reasonable. However, as service providers started to see their LIS sizes heading towards 10s and 100s of routers, the number of IGP peers grew prohibitive. Adding each new router became an ATM-level problem too, as the $(N + 1)^{th}$ router resulted in N new VCs being added across the ATM network.

MPLS solves the IGP mesh-scaling problem by making every interior ATM switch an IGP peer with its neighbors—other directly attached ATM switches or the directly attached IP routers originally surrounding the single LIS. ATM switches become IGP peers by replacing their ATM control plane with an IP control plane running an instance of the network's IGP. With the addition of a Label Distribution Protocol (LDP) [LDP99], each ATM switch becomes a Core (or Interior) label-switching router (LSR), and each participating IP router becomes an Edge LSR (or Label Edge Router, LER). Core LSRs provide transit service in the middle of the network, and Edge LSRs provide the interface between external networks and the internal ATM switched paths. The demands on the IGP drop dramatically, as each node now has only as many peers as it has directly ATM-attached neighbors.

The MPLS working group gives the name Forwarding Equivalence Class (FEC) to each set of packet flows with common cross-core forwarding path requirements—packets whose shortest-path routes coincide as they cross a given network. LDP dynamically establishes a shortest-path VC (now known as a label-switched path, or LSP) trees between all the Edge LSRs for each identifiable FEC. This mode of operation is referred to as *topology-driven* MPLS—the close coupling of IP routing protocols and LDP ensures that the LSP mesh continuously tracks topology changes. (Several topology-driven LDP schemes exist, but in the end they create the same LSP mesh of shortest paths under steady-state conditions.)

The label (virtual path identifier/virtual channel identifier, or VPI/VCI) at each hop provides per-hop processing context, indicating the next-hop and QoS requirements for cells carrying the packets belonging to each FEC. VC utilization is no worse than the single LIS case and, with the introduction of VC-merge-capable, ATM-based LSRs can be much more efficient. (At merge points along a multipoint-to-point sink tree, the ATM cells are carefully interleaved so as to retain the boundaries of the packets being transported toward the Edge LSR. Only a single VPI/VCI is required downstream of the merge point, regardless of the number of VCs coming in from upstream.)

Pure packet-based MPLS networks are a trivial generalization of the ATM model—simply replace the ATM-based Core LSRs with IP router-based Core LSRs and use suitable packet-based transport technologies to link the LSRs. As the performance of packet-based core routers is heading into the OC-12c, OC-48c, and higher ranges, some operators are considering pure packet-based MPLS for their backbones. (ATM-based MPLS becomes difficult at such high speeds because OC-48c and faster segmentation and reassembly engines—required by LERs—are proving difficult to produce.)

Figure 4.6 shows a basic MPLS network as it might be deployed by a service provider connecting multiple customer sites. On each physical link, a LSP is represented by a particular label, specific within the context of that link. The same LSP may be represented by different labels on other links along the LSP's route—the association between actual label values and LSP at any hop is created on-demand by the LDP. Because the number of labels required on any one link is small (bounded by the number of FECs that might pass through a particular link), MPLS can utilize a small bit field (relative to the number of bits in a full IP header) to carry the label.

Figure 4.6   MPLS consists of Edge, Core, and Label Switched Paths.

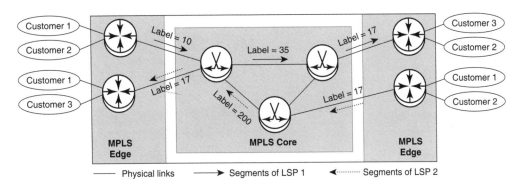

4.3.2   *Label-Switched Paths and Per-hop Processing*

Simply replacing connectionless shortest-path forwarding with label-switched shortest-path forwarding is not a major win. However, an LSP need not follow the shortest path between any two Edge LSRs. Although conventional IP routing protocols typically do not generate non-shortest-path routes, external routing algorithms can be used to determine new routes for LSPs that result in more optimal distribution of loads around a network. This feature is a major advantage of MPLS over IntServ or DiffServ alone.

From a QoS perspective, MPLS labels simplify the Core LSR's classification phase of determining per-hop behavior. LSRs may make use of all the metering, policing, marking, queuing, and scheduling techniques described in Chapter 3 for regular IP routers. However, instead of classifying packets based on their IP header contents, the MPLS label itself provides all the necessary context (possibly in conjunction with the identity of the arrival interface) to determine a packet's (or cell's) next hop and the associated metering, policing/marking, queuing, and scheduling rules (Figure 4.7). The switching table contains one (or more, if per-interface label spaces are supported) Label Information Base(s) (LIB) containing next-hop information for labels the LSR knows about, including a new label to apply when the packet (or cell) is forwarded. Each entry may optionally contain processing behavior rules to apply to packets (or cells) arriving with a particular label value.

Figure 4.7   Simplified Core LSR forwarding engine.

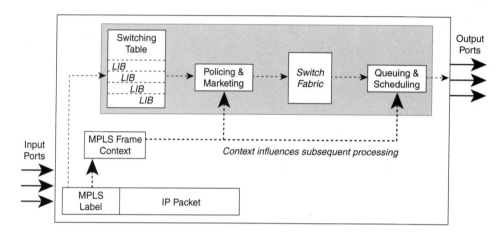

Just like the generic IP router in Chapter 3, an LSR can be broken into a management and forwarding engine. Although Figure 4.7 focuses on the forwarding engine, a management engine is responsible for populating the switching table with appropriate next-hop label, output port, queuing, and scheduling rules for all current MPLS label values. Switching table entries are modified whenever a new label needs to be activated or an old label needs to be removed.

Generic Multiprotocol Label Switching Label Encoding

Figure 4.8 shows the structure of the generic MPLS Frame [MENCAPS]. A MPLS Label Stack of one or more 32-bit entries precedes the original IP packet. Each entry contains a 20-bit label (indicating the LSP to which the packet belongs) and a 3-bit Experimental field (for example, to indicate additional queuing and scheduling disciplines independent of the LSP). An 8-bit Time to Live (TTL) field is defined to assist in the detection and discard of looping MPLS packets. The S bit is set to 1 to indicate the final (and possibly only) stack entry before the original packet—a LSR that pops a stack entry with S set to 1 must be prepared to deal with the original packet in its native format.

Figure 4.8   MPLS Label Stack encoding for packet-oriented transport.

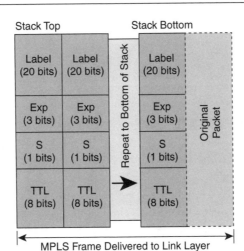

Encoding Labels on Specific Links

MPLS forwarding is defined for a range of link-layer technologies, some of which are inherently label switching—for example, ATM and Frame Relay (FR)—and others that are not—for example, Packet over SONET/SDH (POS) and Ethernet. Although switching logically occurs on the label in the top (and possibly only) stack entry, ATM and FR switch their native data units (cells and frames respectively) based on a link layer copy of the top stack entry.

> **Note**
>
> The stacking scheme allows for LSPs to be tunneled through other LSPs. The action of putting a packet onto a LSP constitutes a "push" of a MPLS Label Stack entry. The action of reaching the end of a LSP results in the top stack entry being removed (or "popped").

For packet-based link layers, the MPLS Frame is simply placed within the link's native frame format—Figure 4.9 shows the example when running over Point-to-Point Protocol (PPP) links. Unique PPP codepoints identify the PPP frame's contents as a MPLS Frame. A similar encapsulation scheme is used when transmitting over Ethernet with unique EtherTypes identifying the payload as a MPLS Frame.

Figure 4.9   MPLS encoding for PPP over SONET/SDH links.

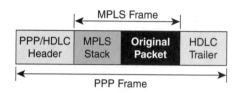

LSPs may also be partially or wholly based on cell switching technology (for example, ATM, which is discussed further in Chapter 6, "Link Layers Beneath IP"). When ATM is used, Core LSRs leverage ATM switch fabrics and hybrid packet/cell LSRs originate and terminate the LSPs—segmenting MPLS Frames at the ingress to an ATM LSP segment and reassembling the MPLS Frames at the egress (Figure 4.10). Packet-to-cell (and vice versa) conversions may occur in Edge LSRs or at Core LSRs where a LSP passes from an ATM-based link to a POS-based or Frame-based link.

Figure 4.10   MPLS encoding for ATM links.

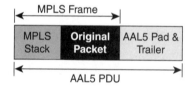

The top-level label may be carried in three ways across MPLS-ATM links [LDPVC, VCID]—in the VPI/VCI, in the VCI alone (limiting the label space to 16 bits), or indirectly associated with a VC (using a VC identifier—VCID) crossing some non-MPLS ATM network elements. (VPI/VCI, VCI, and VC are discussed further in Chapter 6.) In all cases, the MPLS Frame still carries a placeholder label stack entry representing the top label—simplifying the design of packet-based LSRs that terminate ATM-based LSP segments. (Because it is never actually interpreted for switching, the label field of this placeholder is set to zero. However, the existence of the stack entry makes it easy to build Core LSRs that reassemble an ATM-based MPLS Frame on one interface and then switch it to a POS interface simply by writing the outbound label value into the preexisting top-label stack entry.)

When Frame Relay switches are utilized as LSRs, the MPLS Frame is mapped directly into the FR Frame, and the value of the top MPLS label is copied into the data link connection identifier (DLCI, which may support 10, 17, or 23 bits of label space, depending on the specifics of each FR switch) [MFR].

Driving Per-hop Behavior

By definition a particular LSP is associated with a particular FEC. For Best Effort services, the FEC is derived solely from topological considerations. However, three slightly different solutions exist when additional edge-to-edge QoS requirements are taken into account:

- Each distinct queuing and scheduling behavior may be encoded as a new FEC (LSP), ignoring the Experimental field.

- The Experimental field encodes up to eight queuing and scheduling behaviors *for the same* FEC (LSP).

- The Experimental field encodes up to eight queuing and scheduling behaviors *independent of* FEC (LSP).

As shown in Figure 4.11, the Label field can provide context from which per-hop queuing and scheduling parameters are determined. With this approach up to 2^{20} combinations of path and per-hop behavior are possible. However, per-hop behavior is intimately associated with a specific LSP because the entire Label field is also being used to determine a packet's next hop (its path context). Distinct service classes (such as DiffServ's AF) require distinct LSPs if the Experimental field is not being used. Likewise, distinct drop precedence levels require distinct LSPs. Whereas a network may have thousands of LSPs active simply to cover the topological requirements, having to multiply the number of LSPs by the number of distinct service classes and drop precedence levels between Edge nodes is not always an enticing prospect.

Figure 4.11   The Label alone can provide per-hop behavior context.

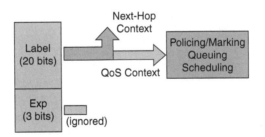

If the Experimental bits are allowed to provide additional classification context, up to eight (2^3) additional permutations of service class and drop precedence are possible. These permutations may be determined within the context of particular LSPs (using both the Label and Experimental fields to derive context—see Figure 4.12) or completely independent of the LSP (ignoring the Label field and using just the Experimental field for context—see

Figure 4.13). These approaches can significantly reduce the number of Label field values required to encode multiple service classes and drop precedence levels across a MPLS network.

Figure 4.12   The Label and Experimental bits together provide per-hop behavior context.

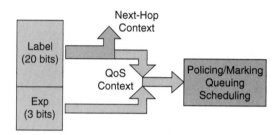

Some possible approaches include

- Using the Label field to select a queue (service class), and using one or two Experimental bits to encode different drop precedence levels.

- Using the Label field to select a group of four queues, using two bits from the Experimental field to select one of those four queues, and using the remaining bit from the Experimental field to encode drop precedence.

- Ignoring the Label field, and using four shared queues per output interface. Two bits from the Experimental field select one of those four queues, and the remaining bit from the Experimental field encodes drop precedence.

- Using the Label field to select a group of N queues ($N \leq 8$), and using the Experimental field to select one of eight permutations of queue assignment and drop precedence.

Although the first approach allows multiple drop precedence levels per LSP, it does require a distinct LSP for each service class (queue). If the goal is to conserve switching-table space, the second approach allows a limited number of service classes to be associated with every LSP. Because the queue assignment involves service classes within the context of a particular LSP, this approach is well suited to LSRs having hierarchical queuing and scheduling capabilities. Each LSP's service classes can be independently configured relative to the service classes associated with any other LSP. The third option is very similar to DiffServ's AF service—path information is ignored when making service class and drop precedence selection, and all LSPs are forced to share one of four global service classes and two per-class drop precedence levels at every hop.

The fourth option is similar to the second and third, but it is included to remind us that the Experimental field need not be divided on bit boundaries. It is entirely possible to define up to eight combinations of queue assignment and drop precedence. (Some queues may have only one precedence, and another queue may have multiple.) Indeed, in the latter half of 1999 the MPLS working group was beginning to develop a proposal along these lines to map part of the DiffServ AF PHB group onto a set of Experimental field values.

Figure 4.13   Experimental bits alone provide per-hop behavior context.

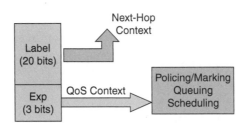

Compared to whether path information is used or not used to provide additional context, the actual method of encoding service classes and drop precedence clearly has less impact on MPLS scaling. As with DiffServ, a MPLS network must provide appropriate policing and shaping of traffic around the edges when the core LSRs are queuing and scheduling on limited information. A MPLS network that takes path information (the Label value) as part of the packet's context can have more finely grained control over per-hop resource sharing than a regular DiffServ network can have. This outcome should not be too surprising—the MPLS Label value is essentially a compressed version of the information derived from MF classification at the ingress to the MPLS network. If the Edge LSRs classify individual flows onto their own LSPs, the Label value at any hop allows a Core LSR to "know" enough context to differentiate packets at the flow level. The benefit is that a Core LSR does not need to understand the semantics of the fields making up the Edge LSR's MF classification—the former can focus solely on providing per-LSP, per-hop behaviors.

Proposals also exist for carrying end-to-end congestion indications in the Experimental field, indicating the presence of congestion within the core without necessarily influencing a packet's drop precedence further downstream. Because the Experimental field contains only three bits, innovative LSR designers may need to interpret the Experimental field on a per-LSP basis—some LSPs ignore it, some require the field to be interpreted as service class and drop precedence, and so on.

Label-Switched Path Merging and Quality of Service

One way of reducing the amount of label space consumed within a given MPLS network involves the use of LSP merging. (LSP merging is sometimes called "VC merging" because its origins lie in the desire to conserve VPI/VCI space in ATM-based MPLS.) LSP merging involves having two or more incoming labels map to a single downstream label at a core LSR. In essence traffic belonging to the same FEC but originating from different Ingress LSRs is merged onto a single LSP at some point in the middle of the network. From the merge point onward, a single LSP replaces two or more LSPs that would otherwise have independently converged on the same Egress LSR for the same FEC. Naturally, this technique reduces label consumption on all links downstream of the merge point.

When the FEC encodes only topological information, many cross-core paths can possibly benefit from LSP merging. Although originally proposed for Best Effort MPLS, LSP merging can equally be applied when aggregating LSPs whose per-hop behaviors are being determined solely by the Experimental bits. In these cases, the downstream queuing and scheduling behaviors are already assumed to represent (and be provisioned for) the aggregate of all traffic flowing through a given LSR port, regardless of whether the path information is itself aggregated or distinct.

However, LSP merging becomes more complex if the LSP itself also encodes QoS characteristics. For example, if an edge-to-edge service relies on the network providing per-LSP queuing and scheduling, aggregating two or more LSPs onto a single downstream LSP (and, hence, single service class) may not be appropriate, even though they may be heading for the same Egress LSR and belong to the same (topologically speaking) FEC. The same concerns apply when the Experimental bits are interpreted within a LSP-established context.

4.3.3 Edge Behaviors

At the edge of a MPLS network sits the Label Edge Router (LER). A LER terminates and/or originates LSPs and performs both label-based forwarding and conventional IP routing functions. On ingress to a MPLS domain, a LER accepts unlabeled packets and creates an initial MPLS Frame by prepending (pushing) one or more MPLS Label entries. On egress the LER terminates a LSP by popping the top MPLS stack entry and forwarding the remaining packet based on rules indicated by the popped label (for example, that the payload represents an IPv4 packet and should be processed according to regular IP routing rules).

Figure 4.14 shows a LER labeling an IP packet for transmission out a MPLS interface. Conventional IP packet processing determines the FEC and, hence, the contents of a new packet's initial MPLS Label Stack (and its outbound queuing and scheduling service). Once labeled, packets are transmitted into the Core along the chosen LSP.

Figure 4.14   Ingress Label Edge Router.

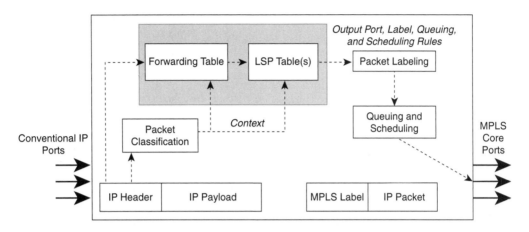

Note

The MPLS output technology can be either packet or cell based; the approach doesn't materially affect this simplified model. When cell based, the MPLS frame is further segmented, and the VPI/VCI is set to the value of the top label in the MPLS Label Stack.

Hybrid LSRs may originate/terminate some LSPs while acting as a transit point for other LSPs (an Edge for some traffic, a Core for others). LSRs may even do both simultaneously when it supports the tunneling of one LSP within another. At the ingress to such a tunnel, the LSR pushes a new Label Stack entry based on the ingress packet's existing top label. At the egress from the LSP tunnel, the top-level label is popped, and the LSR then switches the remaining MPLS Frame based on the new top label. (Tunneling of LSPs within LSPs is likely to occur when an MPLS network is used as a single hop for an overlying MPLS network—for example, a virtual private MPLS network running over another MPLS network.)

LERs are also responsible for traffic conditioning—which, borrowing from the DiffServ definition, covers both classifying packets onto particular LSPs and rate shaping (or policing) the traffic going onto particular LSPs to maintain overall service goals.

As noted earlier, a LER classifies incoming IP packets, using as much header information as necessary to map packets to the correct LSP and to correctly set the Experimental bits (if appropriate). Packets that end up being mapped to the same per-hop behaviors at core

LSRs can be referred to as a MPLS Behavior Aggregate. A MPLS Behavior Aggregate may be defined by the 20-bit Label field (per-LSP), the 3-bit Experimental field (analogous to DSCP classification), or some combination of Label and Experimental fields. Unlike DiffServ, a MPLS Behavior Aggregate's granularity can range from very coarse to microflow.

As with DiffServ, ingress rate shaping is required on traffic that is destined to be combined with other traffic to form a behavior aggregate further downstream. For behavior aggregates encompassing multiple microflows, core LSRs are unable to mediate between aggressive and nonaggressive microflows within the behavior aggregate. Ingress rate shaping bounds the interference between microflows making up a behavior aggregate. It is worth noting that where the network supports per-LSP per hop behaviors from edge-to-edge and at all core LSRs, rate shaping becomes less important for protecting the core queues (because each LSP has its own queue) and more important for bounding individual customer expectations.

Finally, if the notion of being in or out of profile is supported across the MPLS network, the LER must meter the packets entering the network and set appropriate drop precedence levels.

4.3.4 Traffic Engineering

Topology-driven MPLS may be combined with the PHBs described in the preceding sections to create a network capable of supporting specific edge-to-edge service levels. However, it doesn't assist the network operator in balancing the load around the nodes and links making up the network's core. Load balancing requires explicitly defining the cross-core routes each LSP takes in order to optimize the average and peak traffic loads on the various paths that may exist between any two LERs. Such explicit management of LSPs is often referred to as traffic engineering [TE99].

Constraint Routed Label-Switched Paths

Figure 4.15 shows a scenario that can benefit from traffic engineering. Access networks A1 and A2 are sending traffic to destination D, reachable through Access network A3. A3 has two attachment points to the MPLS backbone, through routers R6 and R5. Classical shortest-path routing asserts that network A1 reaches D through R6 and so does network A2. The shortest path converges at router R3 and takes a single hop to R6 regardless of whether traffic comes in through routers R1 or R2 (because in either case this path is shorter than R3→R4→R5).

Topology-driven MPLS will establish two LSPs matching the shortest-path topology for reaching D—one from R1 to R6 and the other from R2 to R6. The problem is that the convergence at interior/core router R3 creates a higher average load on R6 (as well as along the link between R3 and R6) than is really necessary while leaving the path R3→R4→R5 underutilized.

Figure 4.15   Explicitly routed LSPs allow selective non-shortest-path routing.

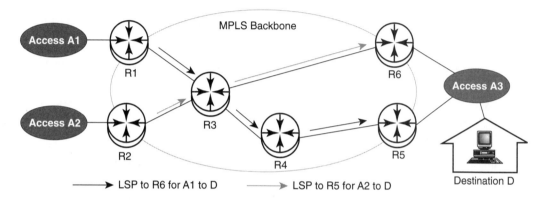

Forcing some portion of the load to follow the R3→R4→R5 path has two benefits:

- It reduces the average load on R6, thereby reducing the average sizes of shared queues and improving the router's burst tolerance.

- It increases the available bandwidth on the R3→R6 link for traffic remaining on that path.

Except in the most trivial cases, achieving general non-shortest-path routing is difficult or impossible when using connectionless forwarding. However, with MPLS it is easy to install a LSP with a path that follows R1→R3→R4→R5 for traffic from A1 to D while simultaneously supporting another cross-core path R2→R3→R6 for traffic from A2 to D.

Such traffic-engineered LSPs are conventionally referred to as Constraint Routed LSPs (CR-LSPs) because they represent the path that satisfies additional constraints beyond simply being the "shortest." The MPLS working group is developing two solutions for signaling such LSPs.

Explicit Signaling for CR-LSPs

One solution borrows from existing RSVP (MPLS RSVP, or M-RSVP [MRSVP]), and the other adds functionality to the base LDP (CR-LDP [CRLDP]). At an abstract level the functions of M-RSVP and CR-LDP are somewhat similar. Both enable a LER to

- Trigger and control the establishment of a LSP between itself and a remote LER

- Strictly or loosely specify the route to be taken by the LSP

- Specify queuing and scheduling parameters to be associated with this LSP at every hop

A strict route specifies every Core LSR through which the LSP must transit. Routes may also be loosely defined—some of the transit LSRs are specified, and hops between each specified LSR are discovered by using conventional IP routing. The major difference between the M-RSVP and CR-LDP protocols is the specific mechanism used to pass their signaling messages from LSR to LSR across the MPLS network.

M-RSVP borrows RSVP's refreshed-soft-state model of regular PATH and RESV messages—defining it for use between two LERs. The exchange of PATH and RESV messages between any two LSRs establishes a label association with specific forwarding requirements. The concatenation of these label associations creates the desired edge-to-edge LSP. CR-LDP defines a hard-state signaling protocol, extending the control messages inherent in the basic LDP to enable a per-hop label association function similar to that achieved by M-RSVP.

The relative merits or demerits of these two schemes are beyond the scope of this book. It is sufficient to note that manageable traffic engineering and QoS control cannot be realized unless one of these protocols is deployed. Both solutions are likely to move to the standards track within the MPLS working group.

4.4   References

[ARIS]   Viswanathan, A., N. Feldman, and R. Boivie. "ARIS: Aggregate Route-Based IP Switching." IBM Technical Report TR29.2353. (February 1998).

[CRLDP]   Jamoussi, B. et al. "Constraint-Based LSP Setup Using LDP." Internet Draft (work in progress) draft-ietf-mpls-cr-ldp-02.txt. (August 1999).

[DSFWK]   Bernet, Y. et al. "A Framework for Differentiated Services." Internet Draft (work in progress) draft-ietf-diffserv-framework-02.txt. (February 1999).

[DSRTER]   Bernet, Y., A. Smith, and S. Blake. "A Conceptual Model for DiffServ Routers." Internet Draft (work in progress) draft-ietf-diffserv-model-00.txt. (June 1999).

[IPSW]   Newman, P., T. Lyon, and G. Minshall. "Flow Labeled IP: ATM Under IP." Proceedings from *INFOCOM 96*, San Francisco. (March 1996): 1251–1260.

[ISDS99]   Bernet, Y., R. Yavatkar, P. Ford, F. Baker, L. Zhang, M. Speer, R. Braden, and B. Davie. "Integrated Services Operation over DiffServ Networks." Internet Draft (work in progress) draft-ietf-issll-diffserv-rsvp-02.txt. (June 1999).

[LDP99]   Andersson, L., P. Doolan, N. Feldman, A. Fredette, and B. Thomas. "LDP Specification." Internet Draft (work in progress) draft-ietf-mpls-ldp-05.txt. (June 1999).

[LDPVC]   Davie, B., J. Lawrence, K. McCloghrie, Y. Rekhter, E. Rosen, G. Swallow, and P. Doolan. "MPLS Using LDP and ATM VC Switching." Internet Draft (work in progress) draft-ietf-mpls-atm-02.txt. (April 1999).

[MARCH]   Rosen, E., A. Viswanathan, and R. Callon. "A Proposed Architecture for MPLS." Internet Draft (work in progress) draft-ietf-mpls-arch-06.txt. (August 1999).

[MENCAPS]   Farinacci, D., Y. Rekhter, E. Rosen, G.Fedorkow, D. Tappan, T. Li, and A. Conta. "MPLS Label Stack Encoding." Internet Draft (work in progress) draft-ietf-mpls-label-encaps-07.txt. (September 1999).

[MFR]   Conta, A., P. Doolan, and A. Malis. "Use of Label Switching on Frame Relay Networks Specification." Internet Draft (work in progress) draft-ietf-mpls-fr-03.txt. (November 1998).

[MRSVP]   Awduche, D., L. Berger, D. Gan, T. Li, G. Swallow, and V. Srinivasan. "Extensions to RSVP for LSP Tunnels." Internet Draft (work in progress) draft-ietf-mpls-rsvp-lsp-tunnel-03.txt. (September 1999).

[RED]   Floyd, S. and V. Jacobson. "Random Early Detection Gateways for Congestion Avoidance." *IEEE/ACM Transactions on Networking* 1, no. 4 (August 1993): 397–413.

[RFC1633]   Braden, R., D. Clark, and S. Shenker. "Integrated Services in the Internet Architecture: An Overview." RFC 1633. (June 1994).

[RFC1812]   Baker, F. (ed.). "Requirements for IP Version 4 Routers." RFC 1812. (June 1995).

[RFC2098]   Katsube, Y., K. Nagami, and H. Esaki. "Toshiba's Router Architecture Extensions for ATM: Overview." RFC 2098. (February 1997).

[RFC2105]   Rekhter, Y., B. Davie, D. Katz, E. Rosen, G. Swallow. "Cisco System's Tag Switching Overview." IETF RFC 2105. (February 1997).

[RFC2205]   Braden, B. (ed.) et al. "Resource Reservation Protocol (RSVP)—Version 1 Functional Specification." RFC 2205. (September 1997).

[RFC2210]   Wroclawski, J. "The Use of RSVP with IETF Integrated Services." RFC 2210. (September 1997).

[RFC2211]   Wroclawski, J. "Specification of the Controlled-Load Network Element Service." RFC 2211. (September 1997).

[RFC2212]   Shenker, S., C. Partridge, and R. Guerin. "Specification of Guaranteed Quality of Service." RFC 2212. (September 1997).

[RFC2215]   Shenker, S., and J. Wroclawski. "General Characterization Parameters for Integrated Service Network Elements." RFC 2215. (September 1997).

[RFC2216]   Shenker, S., and J. Wroclawski. "Network Element Service Specification Template." RFC 2216. (September 1997).

[RFC2225]   Laubach, M., and J. Halpern. "Classical IP and ARP over ATM." RFC 2225. (April 1998).

[RFC2474]   Nichols, K., S. Blake, F. Baker, and D. Black. "Definition of the Differentiated Services Field (DS Field) in the IPv4 and IPv6 Headers." RFC 2474. (December 1998).

[RFC2475]   Blake, S., D. Black, M. Carlson, E. Davies, Z. Wang, and W. Weiss. "An Architecture for Differentiated Services." RFC 2475. (December 1998).

[RFC2597]   Heinanen, J., F. Baker, W. Weiss, and J. Wroclawski. "Assured Forwarding PHB Group." RFC 2597. (June 1999).

[RFC2598]   Jacobson, V., K. Nichols, and K. Poduri. "An Expedited Forwarding PHB." RFC 2598. (June 1999).

[SRTCM]   Heinanen, J., and R. Guerin. "A Single Rate Three Color Marker." Internet Draft (work in progress) draft-heinanen-diffserv-srtcm-01.txt. (May 1999).

[TCP99]   Xiao, X., E. Crabbe, A. Hannan, and V. Paxson. "TCP Processing of the IP Precedence Field." Internet Draft (work in progress) draft-xiao-tcp-prec-00.txt. (September 1999).

[TE99]   Awduche, D., J. Malcolm, J. Agogbua, M. O'Dell, and J. McManus. "Requirements for Traffic Engineering over MPLS." Internet Draft (work in progress) draft-ietf-mpls-traffic-eng-01.txt. (June 1999).

[TRTCM]   Heinanen, J., and R. Guerin. "A Two Rate Three Color Marker." Internet Draft (work in progress) draft-heinanen-diffserv-trtcm-01.txt. (May 1999).

[VCID]   Nagami, K., N. Demizu H. Esaki, Y. Katsube, and P. Doolan. "VCID Notification over ATM link." Internet Draft (work in progress) draft-ietf-mpls-vcid-atm-04.txt. (July 1999).

CHAPTER 5

Establishing Edge-to-Edge IP QoS

So far the primary focus has been on the techniques and components available to network designers who need to support Internet Protocol (IP) quality of service (QoS). This chapter looks in detail at the mechanisms that control and configure these network components. Chapter 2, "The Components of Network QoS," introduced these mechanisms as signaling, policy, authentication, and billing.

Signaling can be considered the act of informing each hop along a path (or paths) how to recognize traffic for which a special processing behavior is required and indicating the type of special processing required. (Provisioning is a subset of signaling, normally implying that the process involves manual intervention on many or all hops along the path.) However, every network has constraints on what sort of edge-to-edge service can be requested— examples include limits on the number of simultaneous users, limits on bandwidth for specific users, and limits on the time of day during which services are available. The signaling mechanism must ensure that relevant constraints are observed. Policy is the abstract expression of the constraints that apply to any particular user's signaled request for edge-to-edge QoS.

Signaling approves or denies access to requested services in accordance with the network's capability to support a request, and the prevailing network policy as it applies to the user making the request. Whether the signaling mechanism is a dynamic and automated procedure or a slow provisioning process, a critical step is to authenticate the users making signaling requests. Authentication involves verifying (to some level of certainty acceptable to the network operator) the identity of a user making a request for service and confirming that the user is entitled to whatever network services the prevailing policy allows. Authentication may range from real signatures on a faxed order for service provisioning to digital signatures on signaling request packets.

In the IP world, signaling is still an evolving art form—in no small part because IP QoS itself has only just begun to reach a level of maturity in which signaling is even required. Nevertheless, the Internet Engineering Task Force (IETF) has worked for a number of years on a signaling protocol expected to have widespread applicability—the Resource Reservation Protocol (RSVP). Defined in RFC 2205, RSVP was developed to support the signaling of end-to-end IP QoS for individual unicast and multicast application flows under the Integrated Services model [RFC2205]. However, additional uses are being developed for RSVP—for example, establishing Multiprotocol Label Switching (MPLS) label-switched paths (LSPs) with specific paths and QoS [MRSVP], or configuring Differentiated Services parameters in end hosts [DCLASS].

After publishing RFC 2205, the IETF's Resource Allocation Protocol (RAP) working group was established to develop a scalable policy control model for RSVP. First, the working group is specifying RSVP protocol extensions allowing RSVP-capable network nodes to exchange policy data [RSVPPC]. Second, the working group is developing the Common Open Policy Service (COPS) that allows RSVP-capable network nodes to interact with external policy servers [COPS].

This chapter provides an overview of RSVP, discusses the policy and authentication extensions, and provides an overview of COPS.

5.1   Resource Reservation Protocol

For practical intents and purposes, RSVP is nothing more than a signaling protocol. However, confusion sometimes occurs in this area because the RSVP Applicability Statement (RFC 2208, published in 1997 [RFC2208]) uses the acronym to encompass the specific use of RSVP signaling in an Integrated Services environment. However, a number of more recent efforts (for example, the use of RSVP to establish MPLS paths) have made it clear that RSVP can be utilized without IntServ. RSVP is also independent of the IP protocol version—IP applies equally well to IPv4 and IPv6. This section focuses more closely on the key design goals and characteristics of RSVP.

5.1.1   Fundamental Architecture

RSVP was designed to meet a number of high-level goals. First, it had to support both unicast and multicast traffic flows (referred to as RSVP sessions, once resources have been assigned). Second, it had to allow parties of a multicast session to request different levels of QoS (that is, it had to allow heterogeneity). Third, RSVP had to be deployable as an addition to the existing IP routing infrastructure, rather than as a replacement.

Meeting these goals resulted in the following specific characteristics:

- RSVP operates in parallel with, and does not modify, existing IP routing protocols. A RSVP session's packets follow whatever path is currently valid toward the packet's destination. RSVP simply ensures that routers along the current path know which QoS-related handling is required for each session's packets. RSVP's signaling messages also follow the same routed path used by a session's traffic.

- RSVP uses receiver-oriented control. In a process known as *one pass with advertisement (OPWA)*, a source advertises its traffic's characteristics to the receivers, and the receivers then tell the network which specific traffic handling is desired.

- RSVP uses soft-state signaling. Routers along the traffic's path must regularly be updated (refreshed) with information about active RSVP sessions; otherwise, the router removes all state associated with the session.

- RSVP messages are extensible and can carry additional objects relevant to the traffic and policy control entities at every router along the path(s) between source and receivers.

RSVP assumes that QoS-capable routers implement one or more of the capabilities described in Chapter 3, "Per-hop Packet Processing." When a reservation message arrives with a request that can be supported, each router appropriately configures its packet classifier, queuing stage, scheduling parameters—the "resources" required to support the new session. Where the underlying link layers provide a range of QoS characteristics, each hop chooses appropriate parameters to support the desired IP-level service. However, the definition of *appropriate* is outside the scope of RSVP itself and depends on the type of QoS being supported—for example, IntServ's controlled load (CL) or Guaranteed Service (GS) classes. Flows for which specific traffic handling resources haven't been reserved get Best Effort service—whatever forwarding resources (link capacity, scheduler time, and queue space) are left over.

Finally, RSVP sessions are simplex—that is, they apply only in a single direction from source to destination. Reserving resources for bi-directional traffic flow requires two independent RSVP sessions—one in each direction.

5.1.2 Routing Independence

The RSVP working group made an explicit decision to decouple signaling of QoS requirements from the establishment of forwarding paths. Existing IP routing protocols continue to work as designed, establishing shortest-path forwarding trees according to prevailing static metrics. Routing does not take into account the number of flows that may have requested specific QoS support using RSVP or the level of resources that RSVP dedicates to these flows. Similarly, RSVP does not attempt to inform the routing protocols of new sessions appearing or of old sessions being removed. When a receiver requests the allocation of resources for a new flow, RSVP attempts to support the request using whatever resources are still available along the flow's shortest-path tree. The request fails if no resources are available (possibly because of earlier reservations still in force)—even if completely empty alternative paths exist through the network.

Decoupling signaling from routing was a very pragmatic decision. It allowed the RSVP working group to focus on a relatively tractable problem space, even though it meant network resources might not be used with complete efficiency. The alternative approach would have posed two difficult problems for the working group. First, as mentioned in Chapter 2, algorithms for QoS-based routing in connectionless IP networks are vastly less well understood than the existing single-metric, shortest-path algorithms in use today. Second, conventional destination-based IP forwarding simply cannot support arbitrary non-shortest paths. Specific paths for individual RSVP sessions would have required all routers to implement per-flow forwarding table entries and lookups. Not surprisingly, the working group shied away from developing such a recommendation.

5.1.3 *One Pass with Advertising*

RSVP's signaling messages are carried directly within IP packets (IP protocol number 46), following the same paths between source and destination(s) as the associated application's data packets. The two primary messages are PATH (path establishment) and RESV (reservation). Sources that want to allow RSVP reservations for their sessions emit periodic PATH messages toward the session's destination IP address (or group address in the case of a multicast session). PATH messages are tracked by routers along the path and by the receiver(s) of the session. Routers modify the PATH messages as they pass through to reflect local QoS capabilities. Receivers use the information carried by PATH messages to decide what the network is capable of delivering. Receivers respond to PATH messages with RESV messages identifying the session (and sources) for which the reservation is desired. Routers along the path correlate RESV messages (going upstream) with previously seen PATH messages (going downstream), deciding on a hop-by-hop basis whether resources can be successfully assigned to the session identified by each RESV message.

It is important for RESV messages to backtrack on the exact route taken by the corresponding PATH messages. Because IP routing doesn't guarantee symmetric forward and reverse paths, RSVP requires routers to keep track of the previous hop of every PATH message they process. When a RESV message is passed back upstream, it is sent to the previous hop of the associated PATH message; this occurs regardless of what conventional IP routing indicates is the next hop back toward the source.

Reservations are achieved by using a single pass of the RESV message upstream, using information "advertised" to the receiver by the PATH messages coming downstream. For this reason RSVP is said to use *one pass with advertising (OPWA)*.

Figure 5.1 shows an example of a single unicast session from host A (the source) to host B (the destination). PATH messages from host A follow the shortest-path IP route toward host B, installing path state as they go. RESV messages from host B retrace the steps of the matching PATH messages, establishing resource reservations (session state) in each router along the path. Ultimately, if the RESV messages reach host A, resources will be installed along the entire path for the specified session.

Figure 5.1   PATH and RESV flow in a unicast session.

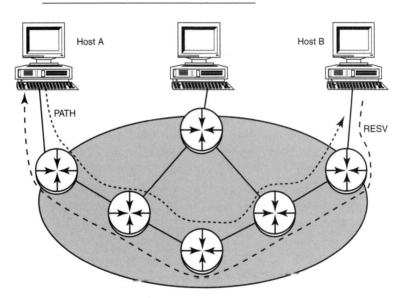

Figure 5.2 shows a single multicast session from host C (the source) to hosts D and E (the members of the destination multicast group). Router R is a branch point in the multicast-forwarding tree for this session. Host C's PATH messages branch at R—independent copies

of each PATH message are forwarded down the separate branches toward D and E, respectively. Each receiver creates independent RESV messages back toward C—RESV 1 from host D, RESV 2 from host E. These RESV messages are merged at R into a single reservation request (RESV 3), reflecting a superset of each receiver's request. This merged RESV is then propagated back toward C.

Figure 5.2   PATH and RESV flow in a multicast session.

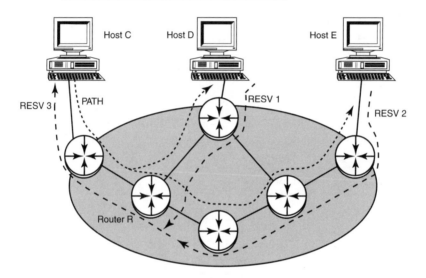

RSVP supports heterogeneity among reservation requests—receivers in a multicast sessions may choose to request different levels of QoS. For example, in Figure 5.2 host D might specify tighter jitter tolerance than that specified by host E. The network may well install different levels of resources between router R and host D than it does between router R and host E. Each branch of the forwarding path downstream from router R is maintained independently of the other. However, upstream from router R (toward host C) RESV 3 reflects the superset of each downstream host's QoS requirements (RESV 1 and RESV 2)—in this example, resources would be installed sufficient to meet the tighter jitter tolerance requested by host D. (An interesting consequence of heterogeneous merging is the so-called "killer reservation." It is possible for one downstream member of a multicast group to deny service to other downstream members by issuing reservation requests that cause the merged reservation to fail admission control further upstream. The IETF is still considering a range of solutions [RSVPKR].)

Sources do not have to wait for RESV messages back from receivers before beginning to transmit data, although they may choose to do so. Receivers that do not generate RESVs (perhaps because they are not RSVP capable) or whose RESVs are failing to reach the source for some reason (for example, failing admission control at some intermediate point in the network) receive Best Effort service. (In addition, a flow may find itself receiving Best Effort service for a brief period following a change in routing topology. Immediately after a route change, the flow will pass through some routers that have no reservation state installed until the next PATH and RESV message exchange occurs over the new route.)

5.1.4 Soft-State State Signaling

Unicast routes can change at any time (due to varying network conditions), and multicast routes change as group members come and go around the network. RSVP must track such changes to ensure that a session's resources are promptly reserved along a new route and released along an old route. However, decoupling RSVP from IP routing means that an indirect tracking mechanism must be used.

RSVP's solution is for resource reservations at each router (the "state" associated with a RSVP session) to have only a limited lifetime. Each session's PATH and RESV messages must be regularly retransmitted while the session is active. These retransmissions serve to refresh each session's state information held by routers along the path(s). If the state information isn't refreshed within a certain period of time, it is discarded and the associated local resources are released—such state is referred to as being soft, and RSVP is said to use *soft-state signaling*.

Soft-state signaling ensures that reserved resources along any given path will be automatically released if routes change during the lifetime of the session (routers on the session's original route[s] will no longer see matching PATH and RESV messages). Resources will be reserved along the new route(s) as soon as the next retransmission of PATH (and corresponding RESV) messages occurs. RSVP is, therefore, able to follow routing changes while remaining independent of the choice of a network's routing protocol. For example, Figure 5.3 shows what would happen to the unicast session from Figure 5.1 if the underlying IP routing changed between host A and host B.

A router is not required to keep its RSVP and routing protocols entirely independent. Where the routing protocol provides local (internal) indications of route changes, this information can be used to expedite retransmission of PATH and RESV messages along the new route for currently active sessions. This process is referred to as *local repair*.

Figure 5.3   Per-hop state times out if not refreshed.

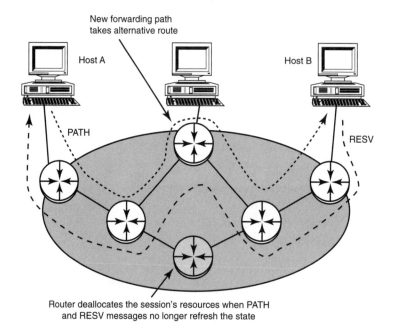

It is possible for resources to be explicitly released, through the use of PathTear messages (by a sender) or ResvTear messages (by a receiver). In each case these messages explicitly negate the reservations that may have been put in place in response to a previous corresponding PATH or RESV message. However, PathTear and ResvTear augment, rather than replace, soft-state signaling.

The soft-state model also allows RSVP to be relatively robust against network failures. Anything that causes the cessation of PATH or RESV messages through a segment of the network results in reserved resources being released back into the pool available for Best Effort traffic. Explicit signaling is not required for the network to revert to a "safe" state.

5.1.5   *Making Reservations*

An RSVP session is described by a specific triple of <*Destination IP Address, IP Protocol Type [, Destination Port]*>. IP packets belong to a specific RSVP session if their destination (either a unicast or multicast address) matches that of the session description, their protocol type field matches the IP protocol type in the session description, and if the payload is Transmission Control Protocol (TCP) or User Datagram Protocol (UDP), the session description's optional destination port matches the packet's TCP or UDP port number. A session description does not include any source criteria. Packets from many sources may simultaneously qualify as belonging to a specific session.

The basic `RESV` message contains two components—a *flowspec* and *filterspec*, which together represent a *flow descriptor*. The flowspec defines the QoS being requested and is used to configure each router's queuing and scheduling capabilities. The filterspec and session description are used to configure each router's packet classification engine—thus defining the set of packets that will receive the QoS described by the flowspec. A session may have multiple filterspecs associated with it, each having its own flowspecs. In this way, different QoS levels may be provided to session traffic originating from different sources. Packets matching the session description receive Best Effort service if they do not match any current filterspecs.

RSVP currently supports three *reservation styles* (defined in RFC 2205) that allow different sources to receive different types of resource reservations for the same session. Each reservation style one represents a different way of associating a set of sources (in a filterspec) with a particular flowspec. The styles are known as

- Fixed Filter (FF)
- Shared Explicit (SE)
- Wildcard Filter (WF)

FF style reservations allow a specific source to be explicitly associated with a particular flowspec and session. This style establishes the most precise association between an individual flow and a resource reservation. Routers along the path do not share the assigned resources with packets coming from any other source. The filterspec contains information on a single source.

SE style reservations allow multiple sources to be explicitly associated with a particular flowspec and session. In contrast to the FF style, routers may share the flowspec's resources between packets coming from all the specified sources. The filterspec contains information on multiple sources.

WF style reservations share a flowspec's resources among flows coming from any source. The router is allowed to apply a wildcard match to each packet's source information—in other words, the router's packet classifier looks only at the information sufficient to differentiate between sessions. No filterspec is required with a WF reservation. Unicast applications are most likely to use FF reservations, whereas SE and WF are intended for multicast applications (such as conference calls, where it may be expected that only one source will be transmitting—and, therefore, using the reserved resources—at any given time). RSVP's support for heterogeneity does not extend to reservation styles—FF, SE, and WF styles may not be mixed within a single session.

It might be argued that WF is equivalent to a SE reservation that specifies every participant in a multiparty session. However, in practice there's an important difference—a SE reservation forces a router's classification engine to have an entry for each member of the session, which could easily result in hundreds of entries. Unless such tight source control is required, a WF reservation is preferred because it allows the router to meet the reservation's goals with a single packet classifier entry (one matching only the session-specific destination fields).

If receivers request confirmation of a reservation (through a flag in the RESV message), *ResvConf* messages are returned when a router installs a resource reservation. However, there's no guarantee that any given ResvConf will make it back to the receiver because the message is sent unreliably just like any other packet. If an error is discovered in a RESV message or the reservation is rejected for certain reasons, a *ResvErr* message is sent back toward the receiver. If an error is discovered while processing a PATH message, a *PathErr* message is sent back toward the sender.

It is worth noting that many applications actually utilize a number of distinct flows to achieve their goals (for example, FTP uses separate control and data connections, a Web browser may open many distinct TCP connections while retrieving a single Web page, and so on). It is up to the applications themselves to decide how to best use RSVP reservations to meet their overall performance objectives. For example, a Web browser might use Best Effort when downloading text components of a Web page and use RSVP to reserve resources only when downloading multi-media page elements, such as streaming audio or video. (In principle, RSVP can tell routers to classify packets based on application-level information contained within them. However, the current filterspec definitions are restricted to UDP or TCP flows.)

5.1.6 Admission and Policy Control

Neither admission control, nor policy control is specifically defined in the RSVP specification, yet both functions mediate a router's acceptance of any given RESV request. First, the resources must be available to support the QoS requirements indicated by the receiver sending the RESV messages—RFC 2205 refers to this practice as *admission control*. Second, the RESV must be making a request that is in conformance with any local policies governing request fulfillment (for example, certain types of users may be excluded at certain times of day or from certain classes of request at all times)—RFC 2205 refers to this practice as *policy control.*

The choice of service model (for example, Integrated Service) influences how an individual router evaluates the traffic characteristics given in PATH messages and the reservation request in RESV messages. RSVP itself carries a number of opaque objects within PATH and RESV messages that characterize a source's traffic and a receiver's request. The RESV flowspec is one such opaque object, interpreted according to the rules of the chosen service model. In addition to a Sender Template (a filterspec indicating the fields a router can use to identify the packets from this source that are to be associated with a particular session), PATH messages contain two opaque objects—SENDER_TSPEC and ADSPEC. SENDER_TSPEC defines the source's traffic characteristics, and ADSPEC represents the "advertising" part of OPWA—the ADSPEC carries information that is modified at each router hop to reflect network characteristics (such as available link and router capacities) between source and receiver.

The interpretation of these opaque objects within an Integrated Services environment is defined in RFC 2210 [RFC2210] and was discussed in Chapter 4, "Edge-to-Edge Network Models." These objects may be used to support other service models, although no new definitions have been issued as RFCs.

RSVP messages carry policy information in an opaque POLICY_DATA object. This information is used at every hop to ascertain whether the message conforms to local administrative policies. One of the key uses for this object is to carry end user identification, allowing a network to reliably associate reservation requests with specific users. The RAP working group has developed specific rules for using POLICY_DATA objects, which are discussed later in this chapter.

5.1.7 Signaling Security

The RSVP working group is close to completing a specification for protection against fraudulent injection of path state or resource reservations [RSVPMD5]. Cryptographic authentication is provided by the INTEGRITY object carried by RSVP messages, which is verified at every hop. This process allows a RSVP-enabled network to protect against denial-of-service attacks and theft-of-service attacks (someone reserving resources without having the legitimate right to do so, either to deny resources to legitimate users or to use the resources him- or herself).

Correct use of the INTEGRITY object allows a recipient of a PATH or RESV message to verify that the message hasn't been tampered with in transit and that it has been generated by someone in possession of a shared secret key. The INTEGRITY object carries an authenticating digest (a keyed-hash of the RSVP message's contents, generated using the shared secret) and a monotonically increasing sequence number (to protect against replay attacks). As a RSVP message is forwarded (either upstream or downstream), each RSVP hop recalculates the authenticating digest, using the locally significant secret it shares with the next RSVP node along the RSVP message's path. Upon receiving a RSVP message containing an INTEGRITY object, RSVP nodes verify the authenticating digest, using the secret it shares with the RSVP node from which the message apparently came.

The default hash algorithm is HMAC-MD5 [RFC2104], although other algorithms may be utilized between consenting RSVP peers. Use of the INTEGRITY object assumes that an external key management method is in use—networks are free to use any measures they deem appropriate to distribute the shared, secret keys. Use of the INTEGRITY object does not obscure the actual RSVP signaling traffic. RSVP message contents are not encrypted in any way.

5.1.8 Encrypted Traffic

RSVP's basic session description and filterspec definitions assume the availability of TCP or UDP port numbers in the data stream to provide per-flow resource reservations. However, TCP or UDP port numbers are not necessarily available when the source's data stream consists of packets encoded in accordance with the IP Authenticating Header (AH) [RFC2402] or IP Encapsulating Security Payload (ESP) specifications [RFC2406]. AH and ESP modes add a new header between the IP and TCP/UDP headers, moving the TCP/UDP port numbers from where a conventional MF classifier expects to find them. In addition, ESP transport mode's payload encryption results in the TCP/UDP port fields being completely hidden. Therefore, only the destination IP address and IP protocol fields are available to differentiate between RSVP sessions, and only the source IP address is available to match a filterspec.

RFC 2207 augments the basic RSVP specification to allow more precise identification of specific traffic flows when AH or ESP encoding is being used [RFC2207]. The filterspec's source TCP/UDP port number is replaced by a generalized port identifier (GPI)—a 4-byte quantity corresponding to the Security Parameter Index (SPI) carried by AH- and ESP-encoded IP packets (immediately following the IP header where the TCP/UDP port fields would be in a regular packet). A filterspec specifying <Source IP address, GPI> will create a packet classifier entry matching the packet's source IP address and the SPI field in the AH or ESP headers. The destination TCP/UDP port in a session description is replaced by a virtual destination port (vDstPort)—a parameter that is signaled between RSVP endpoints but doesn't actually exist in the session's IP packets. A session descriptor now contains <Destination IP address, IP protocol number, vDstPort>, although the packet classifier will only be made aware of the destination IP address and protocol number.

The GPI (SPI) itself uniquely identifies specific security associations between a source and destination. Therefore, a packet classifier using <destination IP address, IP protocol, source IP address, GPI> provides finer control of resource allocation than does a classifier using only <destination IP address, IP protocol, source IP address>.

5.1.9 Configuring Specific Link Layers

RSVP signaling typically triggers related link-layer signaling or (re)configuration as each router attempts to meet the QoS requirements specified in the reservation request. However, RSVP does not specify how specific link layers are utilized—such decisions depend on the QoS service model represented by the objects carried in the RSVP messages. In the case of the Integrated Services model, the IETF's Integrated Services over Specific Link Layers (ISSLL) working group is developing rules for the use of a number of link layers—for example, Asynchronous Transfer Mode (ATM) networks, low-speed Point-to-Point Protocol (PPP) links, and Ethernets. ISSLL specifies particular combinations of link-layer parameters (and if applicable, connection establishment sequences) required to meet GS and CL QoS goals that RSVP signaling may express.

The Integrated Services model was introduced in Chapter 4, and various link layers are discussed in Chapter 6, "Link Layers Beneath IP," Chapter 7, "Low-Speed Link Technology," and Chapter 8, "High-Speed Link Technology." One general assumption is made for all link layers—some form of default forwarding path must exist prior to any RSVP reservations to carry conventional Best Effort traffic and RSVP's own signaling messages.

5.1.10 Scaling

During RSVP's development a number of criticisms were leveled—the most prominent being that RSVP will not scale. Such criticism makes a good sound bite but isn't immediately educational. However, it has an important level of truth—RSVP, specifically when used to support an Integrated Services service model, imposed a number of requirements that were onerous for routers in the mid-1990s.

The load imposed by RSVP can be broken into two parts:

- Soft-state signaling

- Per-packet processing

Signaling consumes memory and processing capacity to establish and continuously maintain path and session state. Per-packet processing involves all the stages described in Chapter 3—multifield (MF) classification, queuing, and scheduling (along with the embedded metering, policing, and shaping functions). How these demands affect any given vendor's router depends entirely on the router's internal architecture.

In the mid-1990s many popular routers were based on a generalized processor platform, and so finite processing capacity was shared between packet forwarding activities and router state maintenance (routing protocols, and now RSVP soft-state signaling). MF classification is more time-consuming than no classification, and maintaining queues and schedulers consumes more processing cycles than simple first-in, first-out (FIFO) output queuing. Routers located in densely trafficked areas of the network could find their processors unable to cope with the signaling and packet-processing load of hundreds or thousands of simultaneous RSVP sessions. For this reason, the RSVP working group recommended that early deployments be small, relatively controlled intranet environments where the numbers of simultaneous RSVP sessions would be low.

Backbone operators in particular were not convinced that distinct, per-flow sessions could be supported at the speeds required to handle OC-12c, OC-48c, and higher line rates. However, high-performance routers are now being designed with distributed architectures that decouple packet processing from router state management. Much of the focus in next-generation backbone routers is on hardware-assisted packet processing—enabling classification, queuing, and scheduling at tens of millions of packets per second.

Soft-state signaling also contributes to the load on RSVP-enabled routers. Using the default values given in RFC 2205, each hop chooses a random PATH and RESV refresh interval between 15 and 45 seconds for each session. Thus, for example, a router carrying 2,000 sessions will be parsing 2,000 PATH messages (including verification of authentication and policy objects) on average every 30 seconds (or approximately 67 PATH messages per second if you assume these refreshes are evenly distributed). If there's any correlation between PATH refresh arrival times, the transient load may well peak higher at certain points in the 30-second window. A similar load exists for RESV messages coming in the opposite direction (and it may be even higher for multicast sessions—routers at branch points in the traffic flow will have multiple RESVs converging on them for the same session). Finally, short-lived sessions generate frequent modifications to state information in a router's classification engines. This is a relatively slow process, especially on newer routers with distributed architectures.

Both the RSVP and ISSLL working groups are developing techniques for reducing the soft-state signaling load. One approach is to relax the refresh intervals [RREDUC], especially when the session's characteristics are essentially constant. This approach reduces the average processing load as the number of sessions rises but also increases the time for session reservations to be reestablished after routing changes occur. Another approach is to allow the aggregation of multiple RSVP sessions sharing common sections of the network, thereby reducing the soft-state signaling and packet processing requirements [RAGGR]. In principle multiple PATH and RESV messages are aggregated into a single PATH and RESV message representing the aggregate of sessions. In that region of the network carrying the aggregate, routers see a single "session," which represents the aggregated sessions. The packet classifier uses a piece of aggregate information (for example, the DiffServ Codepoint, or DSCP) to identify packets belonging to the aggregate session [ISDS99].

Concerns over the scaling characteristics of RSVP-signaled IntServ in backbone networks helped motivate the creation of the Differentiated Services model, described in Chapter 3. However, developments in router architectures and session aggregation techniques suggest that RSVP is likely to become prevalent and useful in both enterprise and backbone IP networks.

5.1.11   Configuring DiffServ Hosts

The general idea of using DiffServ networks as components of an end-to-end IntServ path was mentioned in Chapter 4 [ISDS99]. At a certain point in the end-to-end path, many sessions are aggregated onto a smaller set of DiffServ service classes. Then MF classification is used to assign a DSCP to packets. This DSCP is chosen to provide a service level that meets or exceeds the requirements of all the sessions being aggregated together. Correct assignment of DSCP values requires some means for the upstream IntServ router (the one performing the MF classification) to receive configuration information from a downstream router bordering the DiffServ network.

ISSLL is defining a DCLASS object for this very purpose [DCLASS]. At least one router within the DiffServ network is assumed to be RSVP-aware and participates in RSVP signaling (non-RSVP-aware DiffServ routers simply forward RSVP signaling messages without interpretation). When an individual session is established, the RSVP-enabled DiffServ router mediates access control through the DiffServ region. This same router is responsible for deciding to which DiffServ service class (and, hence, DSCP) this session's packets ought to be assigned. After the DSCP is allocated, a DCLASS object (carrying the DSCP) is added to the session's RESV messages heading upstream. The upstream aggregation point removes the DCLASS object and begins marking the session's packets appropriately.

This architecture allows the actual marking point to be anywhere upstream, decoupled from the router making the admission control decision within the DiffServ network. Taken to an extreme, DSCP assignment can be pushed all the way back to the source host (assuming the network operator trusts the source to use DSCPs only as indicated in received DCLASS objects).

5.2   Implementing Policies

Policies represent administrative boundaries, criteria, and limitations that must be imposed on edge-to-edge resource reservation requests. It is not generally practical for network administrators to individually configure policy rules into every router that they maintain. The IETF's RAP working group is developing a client/server architecture to support the efficient distribution and maintenance of policy rules among a set of network elements. Three key outputs are expected from this working group—a framework, a protocol for distributing policy rules, and guidelines for implementing policy in RSVP-based environments.

5.2.1   Common Open Policy Service

The RAP architecture consists of three basic components [RAPWRK]:

- **Policy Enforcement Points (PEPs)**—Network elements that admit or reject resource reservation requests based on network policy.

- **Policy Decision Points (PDPs)**—Network elements that maintain knowledge of current network policy rules and validate signaling requests against these rules (sometimes also referred to as *policy servers*).

- **Common Open Policy Service (COPS) Protocol**—A communication protocol between PEPs and PDPs.

A PDP is queried by PEPs whenever they have a specific policy decision to make. Although a PDP may be collocated with a PEP, a scalable deployment will utilize a single PDP to support multiple PEPs (clients). Taking RSVP as an example [RAPRSVP], every router that performs policy control decisions on PATH and RESV messages is considered a PEP.

The PDP function may also be partially distributed, insofar as a PEP may have a collocated Local PDP (LPDP). The LPDP (if present) is used by the PEP for preliminary verification that a signaling request complies with current policies. The PDP then makes its decision based on both the resource request and the results from the LPDP. The PDP's decision is always authoritative. (The LPDP is only used as the sole source for policy decisions if a PDP is unavailable for some reason.)

COPS is being developed as the protocol for PEPs and PDPs to use for the exchange of policy information and decisions [COPS], as shown in Figure 5.4. Each PEP establishes a TCP connection to its PDP, enabling reliable message exchange between client and server. PEPs issue *request (REQ)* messages containing their policy decision requests, and they receive *decision (DEC)* messages carrying the PDP's responses. How the PDP obtains policy rules is outside the scope of COPS. (It might be the Lightweight Directory Access Protocol (LDAP), or some other scheme.) How the PEP communicates with the LPDP (if any) is also outside the scope of COPS.

Figure 5.4   The Common Open Policy Service provides the link between Policy Enforcement Points and Policy Decision Points.

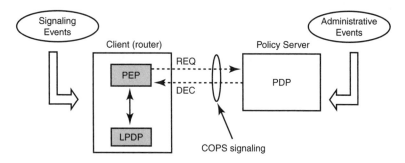

Initial focus of the RAP working group was on the *outsourcing* model of PEP-PDP interactions—a PEP requires a decision that it is unqualified to make and outsources this decision to a PDP. However, COPS also supports a *provisioning* model—where the provisioning of certain network elements (for example, bulk updates of a router's queuing and scheduling rules or specific updates to a packet classifier or metering stage) may be subject to network policies. COPS allows PEPs to request configuration data from their PDP through *REQ* messages and to receive configuration data in *DEC* messages [RAPPR]. PDPs may download new or updated configuration information in response to administrative events occurring asynchronously with events at the PEP. PEP requests contain client-specific information so that the PDP can customize the configuration information it supplies.

The outsourcing model is most likely to be used in RSVP-like environments, whereas the provisioning model is expected to be applicable to the configuration of Differentiated Services parameters. In either case, this work is still under development within the IETF.

5.2.2 RSVP Policy Control

A complete implementation of RSVP involves two orthogonal policy control mechanisms—interpretation of POLICY_DATA objects carried within PATH and RESV messages [RSVPPC][RSVPID] and the use of COPS between RSVP-enabled routers and a network's centralized policy server [RAPRSVP].

Not every RSVP-enabled router contains a PEP. A typical RSVP-enabled network is expected to install PEPs at the border routers (those routers directly attached to users or other networks). Interior routers (attaching only to other interior routers or border routers maintained by the same network administration) that rely on the border routers to enforce policies on sessions flowing through the network do not need to function as PEPs. Such routers are known as policy ignorant nodes (PINs) [RSVPPC].

Figure 5.5 shows a simplified example where the routers directly connected to hosts A and B must act as PEPs, enforcing policy on the PATH messages transmitted from host A and the RESV messages transmitted from host B. The two interior routers are entirely ignorant of policy considerations (although they still apply resource-based admission control on the session signaling). Logically, there are two PDPs; although in practice, they would be implemented on a common, centrally administered network node.

Figure 5.5   Border routers enforce policy.

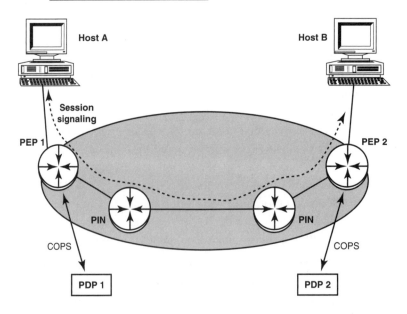

PINs are treated as transparent, untrusted elements in the PATH and RESV transport path between PEPs. POLICY_DATA objects are passed through untouched by PINs, although these objects can be created, modified, and removed by PEPs. (More precisely, when a PATH message must be replicated by a PIN along a multicast path, the POLICY_DATA object is replicated without further interpretation. When RESV messages are merged at a PIN on a multicast reverse path, the POLICY_OBJECTs from each RESV are simply concatenated together to form the merged RESV. Subsequent PEPs are responsible for knowing how to interpret multiple or single POLICY_DATA objects.)

In the same way that whole RSVP messages are protected by the INTEGRITY object, POLICY_DATA objects can have their own INTEGRITY object buried inside. A keyed-hash of the POLICY_DATA object is carried, using secret keys shared by peer PEPs (separated by zero, one, or more PINs). PEPs use the keyed-hash to verify that an intervening PIN hasn't tampered with the POLICY_DATA object(s).

Of significant importance is the transport of user identification within POLICY_DATA objects. The RAP working group is currently developing a generalized authentication data (AUTH_DATA) element that can be carried within POLICY_DATA objects [RSVPID]. The AUTH_DATA element is expected to support clear text, Kerberos session tickets, and public key digital signatures as methods of authenticating both users and applications.

The specific details of how a RSVP-based PEP utilizes COPS are still being worked out by the RAP working group [RAPRSVP]. Policy control is performed for every traffic flow for which a distinct reservation is being made. For example, a RSVP session defined using the FF style and having multiple sources will be considered to consist of multiple flows. Policy control will be applied independently to each source being listed as a member of the session.

PDPs themselves are expected to be RSVP-aware and to know how to interpret both POLICY_DATA objects and other RSVP objects carried by PATH or RESV messages. The PDPs are also responsible for tracking the state of a session (for example, to initiate or terminate billing processes). In addition to being queried for policy control decisions on a session reservation request, the PDP is informed as to whether the request has been honored or has failed resource-based admission control at the PEP. The PDP is also informed if the session is terminated.

Because RSVP uses soft-state signaling, it would be a scaling nightmare for a PEP to query the PDP each time a RESV or PATH was received. Instead, a distinction is made between the initial PATH and RESV message exchange (that establishes session state) and subsequent exchanges (that simply refresh session state). The PEP queries its PDP only when a PATH or RESV message arrives that is initializing new state or modifying existing state. The PEP caches the PDP's decision (response) in this case and can use that same decision to handle refresh PATH and RESV messages at the local level. If the PEP detects a change in the reservation parameters being requested for an existing session, the PEP must requery the PDP. However, while waiting for the PDP's new response, the PEP continues to handle the affected session in accordance with the previously cached PDP decision.

5.2.3 Billing

Billing is somewhat outside the scope of this book, although it will ultimately be a critical part of balancing a user's QoS requests against his or her willingness to pay. Establishing an adequate basis for billing requires the network not only to authenticate a user's request but also to track the actual consumption of the requested resources. Correct use of POLICY_DATA objects can allow a RSVP network to authenticate users and thereby allow a PDP to track their resource reservations. However, these mechanisms are insufficient if the service provider wants to offer billing based on actual network usage. If usage-based billing is required, the network must accurately track each user's traffic patterns and be able to prove that the traffic is associated with a specific user's resource reservation request. Unfortunately, at this stage the IETF offers little in the way of accepted solutions.

5.3 References

[COPS]   Durham, D. (ed.), J. Boyle, R. Cohen, S. Herzog, R. Rajan, and A. Sastry. "The COPS (Common Open Policy Service) Protocol." Internet Draft (work in progress) draft-ietf-rap-cops-08.txt. (November 1999).

[DCLASS]   Bernet, Y. "Usage and Format of the DCLASS Object with RSVP Signaling." Internet Draft (work in progress) draft-issll-dclass-01.txt. (October 1999).

[ISDS99]   Bernet, Y., R. Yavatkar, P. Ford, F. Baker, L. Zhang, M. Speer, R. Braden, B. Davie, J. Wroclawski, and E. Felstaine. "Integrated Services Operation over DiffServ Networks." Internet Draft (work in progress) draft-ietf-issll-diffserv-rsvp-03.txt. (September 1999).

[MRSVP]   Awduche, D., L. Berger, D. Gan, T. Li, G. Swallow, and V. Srinivasan. "Extensions to RSVP for LSP Tunnels." Internet Draft (work in progress) draft-ietf-mpls-rsvp-lsp-tunnel-03.txt. (September 1999).

[RAGGR]   Baker, F., C. Iturralde, F. Le Faucheur, and B. Davie. "Aggregation of RSVP for IPv4 and IPv6 Reservations." Internet Draft (work in progress) draft-ietf-issll-rsvp-aggr-01.txt. (December 1999).

[RAPPR]   Reichmeyer, F., Shai Herzog, Kwok Ho Chan, John Seligson, David Durham, Raj Yavatkar, Silvano Gai, Keith McCloghrie, and Andrew Smith. "COPS Usage for Policy Provisioning." Internet Draft (work in progress) draft-ietf-rap-pr-01.txt. (October 1999).

[RAPRSVP]   Boyle, J., R. Cohen, D. Durham, S. Herzog, R. Rajan, and A. Sastry. "COPS Usage for RSVP." Internet Draft (work in progress) draft-ietf-rap-cops-rsvp-05.txt. (June 1999).

[RAPWRK]   Yavatkar, R., D. Pendarakis, and R. Guerin. "A Framework for Policy-Based Admission Control." Internet Draft (work in progress) draft-ietf-rap-framework-03.txt. (April 1999).

[RFC1819]   Delgrossi, L., and L. Berger (eds.). "Internet Stream Protocol Version 2 (ST2) Protocol Specification—Version ST2+." RFC 1819. (August 1995).

[RFC2104]   Krawczyk, H., M. Bellare, and R. Canetti. "HMAC: Keyed-Hashing for Message Authentication." RFC 2104. (March 1996).

[RFC2205]   Braden, R. (ed.), S. Berson, S. Herzog, and S. Jamin. "Resource ReSerVation Protocol (RSVP)—Version 1 Functional Specification." RFC 2205. (September 1997).

[RFC2207]   Berger, L., and T. O'Malley. "RSVP Extensions for IPSEC Data Flows." RFC 2207. (September 1997).

[RFC2208]   Mankin, A. (ed.), F. Baker, B. Braden, S. Bradner, M. O'Dell, A. Romanow, A. Weinrib, and L. Zhang. "Resource ReSerVation Protocol (RSVP) Version 1 Applicability Statement: Some Guidelines on Deployment." RFC 2208. (September 1997).

[RFC2210]   Wroclawski, J. "The Use of RSVP with IETF Integrated Services." RFC 2210. (September 1997).

[RFC2402]   Kent, S., and R. Atkinson. "IP Authentication Header." RFC 2402. (November 1998).

[RFC2406]   Kent, S., and R. Atkinson. "IP Encapsulating Security Payload (ESP)." RFC 2406. (November 1998).

[RREDUC]   Berger, L., D. Gan, G. Swallow, and P. Pan. "RSVP Refresh Reduction Extensions." Internet Draft (work in progress) draft-ietf-rsvp-refresh-reduct-01.txt. (October 1999).

[RSVPID]   Yadav, S., R.Yavatkar, R. Pabbati, P. Ford, T. Moore, and S. Herzog. "Identity Representation for RSVP." Internet Draft (work in progress) draft-ietf-rap-rsvp-identity-05.txt. (September 1999).

[RSVPKR]   Talwar, M. "RSVP Killer Reservations." Internet Draft (work in progress) draft-talwar-rsvp-kr-01.txt. (January 1999).

[RSVPMD5]   Baker, F., and B. Lindell. "RSVP Cryptographic Authentication." Internet Draft (work in progress) draft-ietf-rsvp-md5-08.txt. (February 1999).

[RSVPPC]   Herzog, S. "RSVP Extensions for Policy Control." Internet Draft (work in progress) draft-ietf-rap-rsvp-ext-06.txt. (April 1999).

6

Link Layers Beneath IP

The preceding chapters have focused on the techniques required to build QoS capable routers and their role in QoS-enabled IP networks. But equally important are the inter-router links, each with their own unique QoS characteristics. Each link provides a packet transport between routers, and the link's QoS characteristics are the building blocks upon which IP-level QoS is created.

Links come in many varieties—configured or signaled, point-to-point or multipoint, always-on shared media or on-demand connectivity, local area or wide area, Best Effort or QoS enabled, low or high bandwidth, wireless or wired, symmetric or asymmetric... The list is quite long. Links may even be constructed from services supplied by other networks.

Each link has its niche where particular physical, technological or business considerations make it an appropriate choice. Every type of link has its own method for shipping bits from one place to another, as well as adaptation or convergence functions that delineate sequences of bits and bytes into structured packets. Some link technologies attempt localized error correction and data compression that can help or hinder the operation of end-to-end protocols such as Transmission Control Protocol (TCP) or adaptive codecs. Links may also be created through *tunnels*, where a packet transport is provided by a service at the same or higher layer than the packet being transported. A network designer needs to be aware of the potential interactions and how they will affect a customer's perception of network performance.

Two protocols stand out for being used across a number of bit and byte transport technologies—the Point-to-Point Protocol (PPP) and Asynchronous Transfer Mode (ATM). PPP finds itself used across a wide range of link technologies including low speed remote access links, and high-speed router-to-router links. ATM is the currently dominant solution for high-speed, wide area, QoS-capable data transport.

Network architects have even shown their ingenuity by developing solutions that layer PPP over ATM. This chapter reviews PPP and ATM and then discusses the nature and applications of tunnels. Subsequent chapters delve into specific link layer technologies such as Asymmetric Digital Subscriber Line (ADSL) (see Chapter 7, "Low-Speed Link Technologies"), Ethernet, and Synchronous Optical Network/Synchronous Digital Hierarchy (SONET/SDH) (both described in Chapter 8, "High-Speed Link Technologies").

6.1 Low-Speed Link Considerations

Every hop in an IP path effects the key QoS parameters—latency, jitter, and packet-loss probability. In Chapter 2, "The Components of Network QoS," a router's Classify, Queue, and Schedule-based (CQS-based) output interface was simplified by viewing the next-hop link as a single entity. In fact, multiple paths to the IP next-hop may be treated as a single link for routing purposes but treated separately when it comes to actually scheduling packet transmissions. An output interface may bundle parallel links to emulate a single (virtual) link of greater aggregate capacity. The offered packet load (in the queue) is spread across the available links, ensuring that packets are removed from the queue faster than if only a single link were in use.

A more sophisticated interface may partition the differentiated queuing and scheduling activities among subsets of the links making up a virtual link bundle, as shown in Figure 6.1. Certain links may be assigned to sub-bundles that serve only specific subsets of the possible queues, allowing traffic classes to be supported by links most optimally suited to them. For example, if Link A and Link B in Figure 6.1 were 1.5Mbit per second each, Port M would appear to have an aggregate capacity of 3Mbit per second. However, if Link A was known to have longer latency than Link B, the CQS parameters would direct traffic requiring low latency to the queues feeding into Link B rather than Link A.

However, for low-speed links—for example, dial-up or ADSL—in the tens and low hundreds of kilobits per second things are not quite as simple. Given the typical range of IP packet sizes, jitter control is difficult if low-speed link scheduling is performed solely on a per packet basis.

Figure 6.1   Scheduling per link within a virtual link.

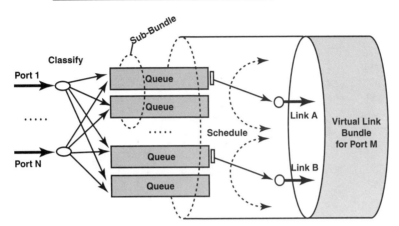

6.1.1 Low-Speed Scheduling Jitter

Variable scheduling granularity and shared queues both contribute to jitter. If a particular queue is being shared by many bursty flows, the queuing latency for any given packet passing through that queue is distributed randomly. When the scheduler pulls a packet from a queue, the link is held for the time it takes to transmit that packet, which represents the minimum granularity with which the scheduler can interleave traffic from different queues. Random variations in packet lengths results in random transmission latencies and, thus, jitter.

For high-speed networks, it may be reasonable to ignore the additional jitter (for example, at 155Mbit per second a 1,500-byte packet takes less than 100 microseconds to transmit). However, on low-speed links interleave-induced jitter becomes significant because the packet's lengths (in milliseconds) become quite large. Picking a limit of 20 milliseconds (a common sample time on cellular radio networks), it is clear that interleaving 1,500-byte packets is inappropriate on links slower than 600Kbit per second. At 128Kbit per second a 1,500-byte packet holds the link for approximately 94 milliseconds (and takes more than 400 milliseconds with a 28.8Kbit per second link). By contrast, a 64-byte packet holds a 128Kbit per second link for 4 milliseconds and holds a 14.4Kbit per second link for 36 milliseconds. Figure 6.2 shows how long links of various speeds are blocked by packets ranging up to 1,500 bytes long.

Figure 6.2   Packet length in milliseconds versus speed and packet size.

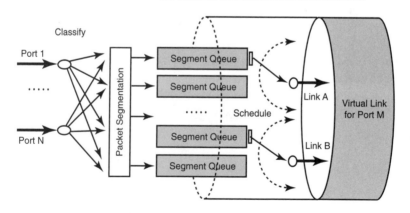

Schedule Link-Level Fragments

To ensure no packet holds a link for too long, it is important that access to low-speed links is scheduled on relatively short, atomic units. This requirement implies that some form of link-level fragmentation or segmentation process is applied before link scheduling occurs. Figure 6.3 shows the most general CQS-based expression of all these principles—segment the upper-layer packets into atomic units that, individually, do not consume too much time on any one link and then schedule across the links (or subsets of the links) at the segment level.

Figure 6.3   Constrained scheduling of segments rather than packets.

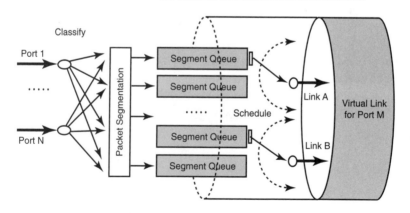

Such an interface imposes some requirements on the link-level segmentation scheme. It must be possible to interleave segments from different packets on a given link (and/or distribute them across multiple links in a virtual link bundle). Each segment requires link-level multiplexing or interleaving identifiers to enable the proper re-assembly of segments into packets at the receiving end of the (virtual) link. Scheduling, and ultimately the temporal ordering of segments on any given link, is solely the responsibility of the transmitting end of the link.

The receiver accepts segments over whatever links make up the bundle and in whatever order results from the sender's transmission sequence and the latencies of the links themselves. A link-level multiplexing identifier's primary role at the receiver is to unambiguously associate segments belonging to a given higher-level packet.

Don't Use IP Fragmentation

IP fragmentation is not an appropriate solution to this problem. Although the maximum transmission unit (MTU) for a link can be set to a low value (for example, 64 bytes), thereby forcing large IP packets to be fragmented by the IP interface transmitting directly onto the link, this approach has two major problems:

- If remote hosts are using PathMTU Discovery [RFC1191, RFC1981], there is a system-wide impact—such hosts send packets carrying barely any TCP payload after the IP and transport header overhead is removed from the low MTU.

- If PathMTU Discovery is not being used, IP fragmentation still utilizes the low-speed link inefficiently by forcing the replication of the IP packet's 20-byte header in each fragment.

Whichever scheme provides finely grained per-hop interleaving must be invisible to the IP layer.

Most link layer technologies support some form of payload segmentation to constrain interleave-induced jitter. The trade-off is additional overhead, which itself can be a problem on low-speed links where bandwidth efficiency is often critical.

6.2   Point-to-Point Protocol

PPP is a full Internet standard [RFC1661] developed to provide an auto configuring, multiprotocol mechanism for exchanging variable-length packets over bit-serial or byte-serial, full-duplex point-to-point links. PPP is, conceptually, a simple protocol architecture and has spawned an entire family of extensions. Its basic task is to isolate higher-level packet layers from the framing and multiplexing issues associated with the use of simple point-to-point links. Today PPP is very common and is used over many different types of media, ranging from low-speed (kilobit per second) dial-up lines to high-speed (gigabit per second) optical circuits. Arguably it has met its original design goals.

As shown in Figure 6.4, PPP can be described in three stages—framing and encapsulation, a Link Control Protocol (LCP) that auto negotiates parameters such as the type of encapsulation to be used, and one or more Network Control Protocol(s) (NCPs) that auto negotiate network layer parameters to be associated with the link (for example, the client's IP address [RFC1332] and/or the client's domain name server [RFC1877]).

Figure 6.4   Point-to-Point Protocol: Packet Framing, Link Control Protocol, and Network Control Protocol.

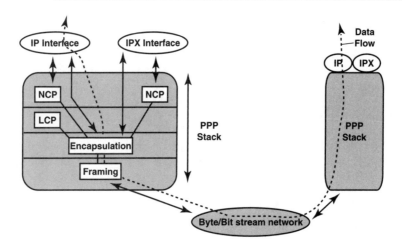

6.2.1 *Framing and Encapsulation*

Framing and encapsulation are two distinct functions—*framing* delineates packet boundaries within a continuous bit or byte (octet) stream, whereas *encapsulation* provides the means to multiplex/demultiplex packets belonging to different higher (network) layer protocols onto the same delineated stream. PPP encapsulation enables a single delineated packet stream to be shared between network layer packets, LCP control messages, and NCP control messages. It consists of an 8- or 16-bit header (Protocol field), preceding the network layer packet (Information field), and optional trailing padding. The Protocol field identifies the protocol to which the Information field's contents belong. Framing is often provided by a mechanism based on high-level data link control (HDLC) [RFC1662]. Figure 6.5 shows the complete HDLC/PPP encapsulation typically applied to a network layer packet.

Figure 6.5   Point-to-Point Protocol encapsulation within HDLC-like link framing.

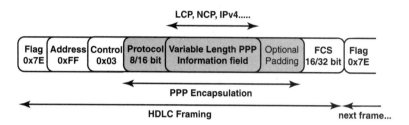

HDLC-link framing uses in-band indications for delineation—in this case, the octet value 0x7E (hexadecimal) in the byte stream is the Flag Sequence (FS) that indicates a frame boundary (or a zero, six ones, and a zero on bit-serial links, which is equivalent to 0x7E).

The HDLC Address and Control field is usually set to 0xFF03 (All Stations address and Unnumbered Information command). This field is immediately followed by the PPP encapsulation and the network layer packet. The end of the frame is indicated by the appearance of another FS (0x7E) octet. When this octet is received, the preceding 16- or 32-bit value is presumed to be the Frame Check Sequence (FCS) across the preceding frame. The FCS detects errors introduced by the link itself.

Clearly the value 0x7E may legitimately appear within the PPP frame, yet it must not appear "on the wire" lest the receiving HDLC-like framer mistakenly conclude that the frame boundary has been reached. Other values may also need to be hidden, for example, ASCII control characters that have special meaning to the link itself. (The characters to escape are defined by a negotiated Async-Control-Character-Map, or ACCM. On some links, control characters are already carried transparently, and the ACCM can be null.)

On byte-serial links, the desired transparency is achieved as follows: Take the octet X that needs to be escaped, exclusive-OR it with the value 0x20, precede it with the octet 0x7D (the Control Escape octet), and insert the resulting two-octet value back into the transmitted stream. For example, any occurrence of the 0x7E octet becomes a two-octet sequence 0x7D 0x5E. The Control Escape octet can also be escaped, 0x7D becoming 0x7D 0x5D in the transmitted octet stream.

On bit-serial links, transparency is achieved by inserting a zero bit after any consecutive sequence of five ones occurring between the legitimate 0x7E delimiting flags. This practice ensures that the only time the receiving end sees a consecutive sequence of six ones, that sequence is the frame delimiting flag. Control character transparency is not an issue on bit-serial links.

Bit or byte stuffing can affect link-capacity scheduling. (The link effectively has a fluctuating bandwidth because the transmission of some packets takes longer than expected.) A malicious user might create packets containing repeated 0x7E, 0x7D, and other escape codes to force such transparent expansion, reducing the available bandwidth on the link. The worst-case expansion when byte stuffing is being used can approach 100 percent of the frame's original length. (For example, a UDP packet carrying 200 0x7E bytes would initially result in a 238-byte PPP/IP/UDP frame. The PPP frame would be 438 bytes long on the wire after expansion of every 0x7E in the payload.)

If bit stuffing is used, the frame expands to at most six fifths of its original length. Byte and bit stuffing are never used at the same time on a given link. Some transport paths between PPP peers provide their own frame delimiting, allowing HDLC-like framing to be discarded completely. (When another link layer carries the PPP packet, there is no real need to carry the HDLC Address and Control header. However, IETF protocol development is not always consistent—some PPP transport solutions keep the HDLC header, while others discard it.)

Overhead is minimized wherever possible on low-speed links. Compression of the HDLC Address and Control fields may be negotiated on a per-link basis, and the two octets are simply not transmitted for network layer packets. LCP messages always start with the 0xFF03 Address/Control sequence so that there is never any ambiguity. Protocol field values for network layer packets are assigned. Therefore, they can never be mistaken for the regular Address/Control field preceding an LCP message.

6.2.2 Link and Network Control Protocols

A PPP link needs to be managed independently of the actual network-level protocol it supports. The LCP's role is to provide the negotiation and auto configuration of parameters that would be common to all network protocols sharing the link. These parameters include link state (up or down), encapsulation format options, packet-size limits in either direction, authentication of each end, link-quality monitoring, and detection of link misconfigurations. LCP control messages are carried as PPP frames with a Protocol field of 0xC021.

Typically when a link is established, LCP activity must first occur to determine that the link can safely be declared "up." Then NCP activity occurs to declare the linkup for each NCP-associated network layer protocol. If the LCP declares the link "down," every associated NCP immediately considers the link to be down.

Although the LCP always goes through a configuration phase for a link, the use of an authentication phase is optional. If authentication is used, it occurs after the link is configured. The NCPs are not informed that the link is up until configuration and authentication (if required) have occurred successfully.

A distinct NCP is defined for each network layer protocol to be supported across a given PPP link—for example, IP, internetwork packet exchange (IPX), or AppleTalk. Each NCP shares the services of the LCP and the underlying link to communicate with its peer on the other end of the link. An NCP for IP interfaces would support such things as the auto configuration of interface IP addresses and subnet masks (for example, when a remote user dials in to a central site, the remote user's IP address and mask is configured by the central site via the NCP over the newly established PPP link).

After LCP declares a link to be up, each NCP begins negotiating with its peer at the other end of the link to determine whether the link is suitably available for the purposes of that NCP's network layer protocol. In some cases, a link might be up as far as LCP is concerned but down as far as an NCP is concerned. Because each NCP operates independently, different up and down states can exist simultaneously.

NCP control messages are carried as PPP frames, and each network layer protocol has two Protocol field values—one in the range 0x0001 to 0x3FFF to identify the network layer's own packets and a matching value in the range 0x8001 to 0xBFFF to identify the associated NCP. A few currently defined Protocol field values and their meanings follow:

- 0x0021 and 0x8021 (IPv4 packets and IPv4 NCP) [RFC1332]

- 0x0057 and 0x8057 (IPv6 packets and IPv6 NCP) [RFC2472]

- 0x002B and 0x802B (IPX packets and IPX NCP) [RFC1552]

- 0x0281, 0x0283, and 0x8281 (MPLS unicast packets, MPLS multicast packets, and MPLS NCP) [MSENC]

After one or more NCPs consider a link to be established, the actual traffic on the link may consist of a mixture of LCP control messages, NCP control messages, and network layer packets.

6.2.3 Multilink PPP

Basic PPP assumes that the bandwidth of the effective link is limited by the capacity of the underlying path between two PPP peers. However, in many access scenarios, multiple parallel paths can be opened between two PPP peers (for example, a home with two or more phone lines, or an ISDN service with two distinct B channels).

Multilink PPP (MP) [RFC1990] allows parallel paths to be aggregated into a single virtual link (bundle), expanding the effective link capacity between any two PPP peers. It also supports the fragmentation of PPP packets so that a bundle can be built from links having small native data transfer units. MP appears as another network layer protocol from the perspective of each underlying LCP/link that makes up the bundle but appears as a link to real NCPs (see Figure 6.6).

Figure 6.6   Multilink PPP provides a virtual link layer.

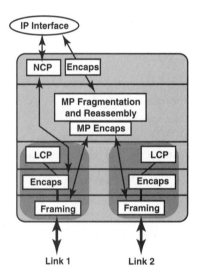

As shown in Figure 6.7, network layer packets are prepended with their normal PPP encapsulation, optionally fragmented and then transmitted on each link within an MP packet. (Although referred to as *fragments* in RFC 1990, they are not IP fragments—there is no replication of the IP header, and the effective MTU of the link is not reduced.) A MP packet is a regular PPP packet with the Protocol field set to 0x003D (rather than the value normally associated with that specific network layer protocol) and an additional MP header between the Protocol field and the fragment it is carrying. When a PPP packet is received with Protocol field 0x003D, the packet is passed to the local MP entity, which considers it a fragment of the original PPP packet. When all the fragments are received, the initial PPP packet can be considered to be reassembled and is processed according to its own Protocol field as though received across a regular link.

Figure 6.7   Multilink PPP fragments initial Point-to-Point Protocol packets.

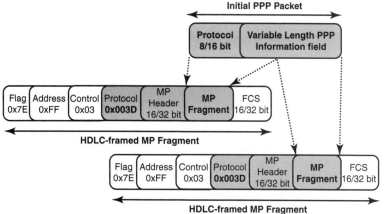

The 16-bit "short" MP header contains flags indicating the beginning and end of a fragmented PPP packet and a 12-bit sequence number. (A 32-bit "long" header can also be used if a 24-bit sequence number space is desired.) A single sequence number space is used across all links in the bundle to detect lost fragments and correctly reassemble them even if fragments arrive out of order. (Fragments may appear to be reordered at the receiver if spread over links with differing latencies—reordering *within* any one link breaks the lost-packet detection scheme and cannot be tolerated.) Using a single sequence number space means it is not possible to interleave the fragments of different initial PPP packets on any given link in the bundle.

A bundle may be as simple as a single link and may have new links added or dropped at any time. The MP entity is responsible for scheduling the transmission of MP packets between each of the actual links making up a bundle. However, the MP specification does not state or constrain how an MP-based interface should temporally distribute fragments across the links in a bundle.

Proposals in the mid-1990s used MP to create a two-level differentiated priority scheme over PPP. Although only one instance of MP can be active on any given link, MP can share the link with other PPP encapsulated network layer packets. The link would be shared by IP over MP running in parallel with conventional IP over PPP. High-priority IP packets would be forwarded across the IP-over-PPP path, and all other packets would be forwarded across the IP-over-MP-over-PPP path (see Figure 6.8).

Figure 6.8 High-priority packets get regular Point-to-Point Protocol; low-priority packets get Multilink PPP fragmentation.

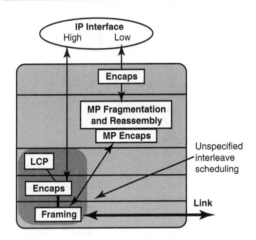

The MP fragmentation of low-priority packets allows the link driver to interleave a high-priority PPP packet between MP fragments belonging to a lower priority packet (see Figure 6.9). However, the high-priority packets are not themselves fragmented, and so they can easily steal significant amounts of bandwidth and time from the low-priority traffic.

Figure 6.9 Multilink PPP fragments can be suspended while sending high-priority packets.

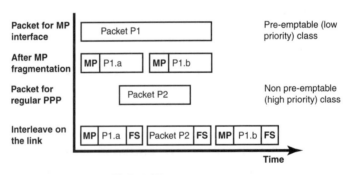

Two recent extensions to PPP—MultiClass MultiLink (MCML) PPP [PPPMCML] and Real Time Framing (RTF) [PPPRTF]—focus on providing more sophisticated control of jitter on low-speed links.

6.2.4 MultiClass MultiLink PPP

MCML extends MP fragmentation by using some previously reserved bits in the MP header to carry a per fragment multiplexing (interleaving) identifier, referred to as a "class"[PPPMCML]. The sequence number space is now interpreted per class, and as a consequence fragments from different packet-level queues may be concurrently interleaved on any given link in a bundle (see Figure 6.10). Depending on whether the MCML header is short (16 bits) or long (32 bits), there can be up to 4 or 16 classes.

Figure 6.10 MultiClass MultiLink supports interleaving of packets from up to 16 queues.

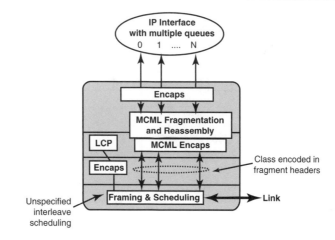

MCML fragmentation is shown in Figure 6.11. PPP packets are fragmented, the fragments encapsulated with an MCML header (containing a class identifier, sequence number, and begin/continue/end fragment flag), and then the fragments are transmitted as regular PPP packets in their own right (reusing MP's protocol value 0x003D).

Figure 6.11 MultiClass MultiLink fragments initial Point-to-Point Protocol packets.

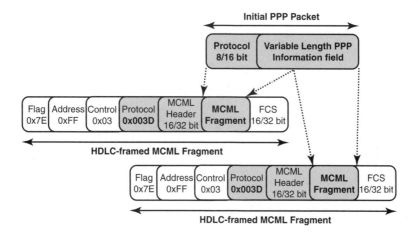

Initial PPP packets are assigned to different MCML classes if the packets belong to IP flows that require interleaving. At the PPP receiver, fragments are assigned to separate reassembly buffers based on the class identifier. As the sequence number spaces are now per class, lost and reordered fragments on one class do not affect the flow of fragmented packets on other classes (although fragments belonging to any given class must still be delivered in sequence on each link). With appropriate choice of fragment size, MCML can offer finely grained interleave intervals to the higher layer (for example, IP), as shown in Figure 6.12.

Figure 6.12   MultiClass MultiLink reduces interleave jitter.

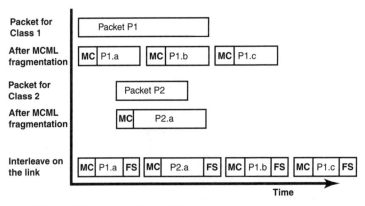

MC: Multiclass MP Header   FS: End of Frame

The MCML specification does not state or constrain how an MCML-based interface should temporally distribute fragments across the links in a bundle or how large a fragment ought to be. In its most general form an MCML implementation would look like Figure 6.3. MCML over a single link and MCML distributing packets evenly across the available links are subsets of Figure 6.3. In general the PPP receiver simply reassembles PPP packets and passes the payloads up to their appropriate network layers as quickly as they arrive.

MCML has one key limitation—IP packets are MP fragmented whether or not higher-priority traffic is waiting to be interleaved. For example, in Figure 6.12 packet P1 is split into three fragments simply because it is large, even though packet P2 is interleaved only between the first and second fragments of P1. Such behavior imposes fragmentation over-head (and, hence, wastes bandwidth) even when the other classes are otherwise idle. When HDLC framing is used, MCML also exhibits the unpredictable expansion characteristic due to byte or bit stuffing.

6.2.5 Real-Time Framing

MCML's constant fragmentation overhead led to a parallel IETF effort: PPP in a real-time oriented HDLC-like framing (referred to as real-time framing, or RTF) [PPPRTF]. RTF imposes lower average overhead than MCML does while still enabling interleaving of fragments from different packets. It utilizes dynamic manipulation of the sender's HDLC framer and, therefore, is typically tightly integrated with link scheduling and access. RTF allows a lower-priority packet's transmission to be suspended, a higher-priority packet to be interleaved, and then the original packet's transmission to be resumed.

RTF provides the lowest possible interleave latency for high-priority packets because RTF allows the transmission of a lower-priority packet to be interrupted on a byte boundary. The notion of priority is variable—a sender may choose to hold a short packet with low jitter tolerance if the packet currently using the link is almost completed but may choose to interleave if the current packet still has some time to go before transmission is complete. When no higher-priority packets require interleaving, packets are transmitted atomically, minimizing the overhead.

Somewhat akin to MCML, all initial PPP packets are encapsulated in an RTF header before transmission. This header is either 8 bits (compact) or 16 bits (extended compact) and contains a class number, a per class sequence number, and a fragment begin/resume flag. When no interleaving occurs, each initial PPP packet is contained within a single, HDLC-framed RTF packet (a PPP packet with protocol type 0x003D).

In general a RTF receiver is always reassembling only one packet at a time, the *current packet*. However, a number of classes may have packets in various stages of suspended reassembly. The current packet is the one whose class was specified in the most recent RTF header. An interleave is indicated by the presence of a new suspend/resume flag, the Fragment Suspend Escape (FSE, byte value 0xDE). When a receiver picks up a new HDLC frame in its entirety (sees the 0x7E and verifies the FCS against the preceding two or four octets), it begins parsing from the front of the frame—reassembling the current packet. FSE flags suspend the current packet (initiate a fragmentation and imply that a new current packet is about to be specified by the following RTF header), and FS flags terminate the current packet. Reassembly of a previously suspended packet continues when an RTF header is received, indicating a resume of a class for which fragments have already been received.

Figure 6.13 shows a simplified view of what occurs when interleave is required. Assume packet P1 is long and is of a lower priority than packet P2.

Figure 6.13   Real-Time Framing allows on-demand interleave with no unnecessary fragments.

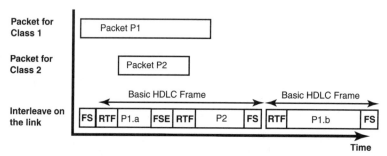

RTF: RTF MP Header (8 or 16 bit)   FSE: Fragment Suspend Escape   FS: End of Frame

1. P1 is encapsulated as an RTF packet, and a conventional bit-wise or byte-wise HDLC-like transmission begins.

2. The sender determines that P2 requires immediate transmission.

3. Without terminating the HDLC frame itself, P1 is suspended by the introduction of the FSE flag—the octets of P1 transmitted up to this point now constitute its leading fragment.

4. A new RTF header is inserted, identifying the class to which the preempting packet (P2) belongs. The entire contents of P2 follow.

5. P2 transmits to completion, and the HDLC frame is terminated by the usual FS flag.

The receiver can now fully process P2 and pass it up to the appropriate network layer entity. The next HDLC frame begins with a RTF header, indicating that it is resuming the transmission of P1. When this HDLC frame terminates normally, the receiver knows it has reassembled all of P1.

The suspend action can be recursive—if you have three packets P1, P2, and P3 of increasing priority, P2 could preempt P1, and P3 could preempt P2 within the same frame (holding both P1 and P2 in suspension while P3 transmits to completion). Interestingly, the resume action allows for P1 to be resumed before P2 because the RTF header explicitly tells the receiver which packet is being resumed. However, typically the resumption occurs in reverse order of suspension (to complete transmissions in order of initial priority).

RTF has two types of classes—suspendable (class 0 to 6) and nonsuspendable (class 7 to 14 for compact headers or 7 to 1030 for extended compact headers). Nonsuspendable classes are for packets that will not be interrupted by an FSE flag after they've begun transmission (the HDLC frame runs to completion).

RTF has lower fragmentation overhead than MCML has but retains the unpredictable payload expansion characteristic of the underlying HDLC framing. FSE transparency is also added, using a slightly convoluted algorithm based on expanding 0xDE bytes in the packet's payload with various 2-byte combinations.

6.2.6 Integrated Services Mappings for MultiClass MultiLink and Real-Time Framing

The MCML and RTF specifications do not mandate particular semantics for their class fields except that they enable correct demultiplexing of interleaved fragments at the receiver. Additional thoughts on the use of these classes have been developed under the auspices of the IETF's Integrated Services over Specific Link Layers (ISSLL) working group [ISLWSVC]. While focusing on the specific use of classes to support the IntServ Controlled Load and Guaranteed services, the observations are also generally valid for DiffServ and other schemes using MCML/RTF classes to interleave packets with different transmission priorities.

One may be tempted to ask the question of which classes represent higher priority and try to assign fixed interpretations (as DiffServ assigns certain behaviors to values of the DS byte). The PPP driver can use IP packet classification to assign the packet's MCML/RTF class. However, only a few MCML/RTF class values are available. If each class had a fixed mapping to a queue (and an implied scheduler priority or weighting), this factor would limit the granularity of traffic differentiation (because you could have only as many queues as MCML/RTF classes).

As it happens, MCML/RTF class values don't need fixed relationships to the IP-level class hierarchy within the traffic flowing across the link. Notice that the class value serves merely to identify fragments of different (interleaved) PPP packets. After a packet has traversed the link, the packet's MCML/RTF class value might be reused for another packet belonging to a different IP-level flow. To distinctly handle many IP-level flows, the following needs to hold:

- The queuing and scheduling characteristics applied to any given MCML/RTF class depend on the type of PPP packets currently utilizing that class value (derived from additional information within the PPP packets themselves).

- Packets being interleaved at any given instant are assigned different MCML/RTF classes if they belong to IP flows having different priorities.

When an IP packet is due to be transmitted, it is assigned to a MCML/RTF class having queuing and scheduling discipline appropriate to the packet's IP-level flow requirements. If no appropriate MCML/RTF class exists, an unused (or idle) MCML/RTF class must be reassigned with appropriate queuing and scheduling discipline. The process involves only the transmitting end because that's where the temporal ordering of packets is imposed. Class values serve only as reassembly indexes at the receiving end.

Although tens or hundreds of distinct IP flows may be active across a low-speed PPP link, it is statistically likely that no more than a handful of these flows will have a fragmented packet in transit across the link at the same time. Therefore, a small number of reusable MCML/RTF class values is sufficient.

6.2.7 QoS Characteristics

In general, the QoS characteristics of a PPP link are determined by the underlying bit, byte, or frame transport technology itself (for example, HDLC framing's variable payload expansion through bit or byte stuffing). MP, MCML, and RTF add their own perturbations due to the interactions between an initial packet's size and the choice of fragment size. Figure 6.14 shows performance (available bit rate at the IP level as a percentage of line rate) versus IP packet size for regular PPP using HDLC-like framing and for MCML with HDLC-like framing using fragment sizes of 64 and 192 bytes (approximately 4- and 12-msec interleave latency, respectively, at 128Kbit per second). In each case, assume a 16-bit PPP Protocol field, a 32-bit HDLC FCS, and no bit/byte-stuffed payload expansion. The PPP/HDLC plot shows an expected curve of increasing link utilization as the useful payload becomes significantly larger than the PPP encapsulation overhead. The two MCML curves reflect the higher MCML overhead and show discontinuities as the IP packet gets too large to be held in a single fragment. Network architects need to consider this loss of capacity against the improved control of interleave-induced jitter.

When no interleaving is required, RTF performance is close to that of regular PPP. Evaluating the performance of a RTF link when interleaving *does* occur is a nontrivial task. The analysis depends on the number of suspensions occurring within a particular time period and the distribution of packet lengths among the high- and low-priority classes. However, to an arm-waving approximation, the performance will never be worse than MCML using fragments around the size of the smallest high-priority packet. Payload expansion is not always going to be an issue—when PPP packets are transported over links that provide their own frame delimiting, bit/byte stuffing is not required.

Figure 6.14 Performance of basic Point-to-Point Protocol and MultiClass MultiLink with 64- and 192-byte fragments.

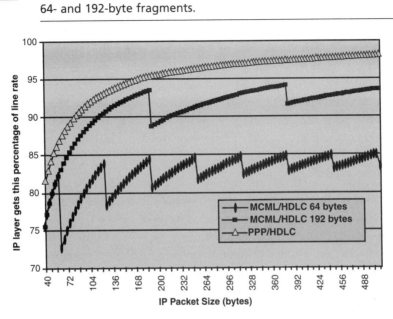

6.3 Asynchronous Transfer Mode

Much could be written about how Asynchronous Transfer Mode (ATM) came into being and its role in the networking world. The International Telecommunication Union's (ITU's) original vision of broadband ISDN (B-ISDN) encompassed the entire end-to-end networking architecture, complete with multiple grades of speed and service designed to integrate voice, video, and data transport functions. ATM was developed as the specific networking protocol to support that B-ISDN vision. However, along the way IP networking became a reality before ATM could begin to fully assert itself. As a consequence end-user applications based solely on ATM are rare. Today ATM technology is typically utilized for the high-speed transport of IP packets (both router to router and router to host) and to emulate fixed-bit-rate, circuit-oriented services. Specifications from the ITU Telecommunications Standardization Sector (ITU-T) and industry agreements from the ATM Forum combine to define what most of us experience as ATM networking today.

6.3.1 Network Model

The vision for ATM networking is far-reaching, akin in scope to that of the Internet. A clear distinction exists between an end station using the ATM network's resources (attached at a User Network Interface, or UNI) and the ATM network itself. Fundamentally the ATM network provides a *cell transport service* between UNIs—shipping data in the form of 53-octet long *ATM cells.* These cells are made up of 5 octets of header and 48 octets of user payload. The header contains information used by the ATM network to carry the cell's payload transparently from one UNI to another. The use of short, fixed-length cells is a unique feature of ATM intended to aid its capability to provide controllable QoS at high speeds. The end stations use the ATM cell transport service to send their data 48 octets at a time.

In the same manner that IP endpoints have globally significant IP addresses, ATM end stations have globally significant ATM addresses. However, unlike IP, an ATM network is connection oriented. Paths between end stations must be established explicitly prior to use—the ATM addresses of the end stations are used during path establishment (for example, by dynamic signaling), but are not carried along with the ATM cells after transmission begins across the path (see Figure 6.15). (However, it is possible to manually provision ATM connections, and under such circumstances the endpoints may not actually have specific ATM addresses.)

Figure 6.15   ATM provides cell transport between globally addressable end stations.

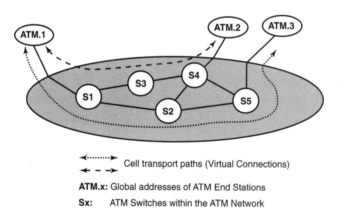

◄┈┈┈┈► Cell transport paths (Virtual Connections)
◄ - -►
ATM.x: Global addresses of ATM End Stations
Sx: ATM Switches within the ATM Network

In section 2 of ITU-T recommendation I.150, ATM is described as, "A connection-oriented technique. Connection identifiers are assigned to each link of a connection when required, and released when no longer needed" [I150]. Each cell carries a connection identifier subdivided into two fields—a virtual path identifier (VPI) and a virtual channel identifier (VCI). In section 3.1.1 of I.150, an ATM connection is described as consisting, "of the concatenation of ATM layer links in order to provide an end-to-end transfer capability to endpoints" [I150]. An ATM link consists of any cell path between points where the VPI or VCI are switched or terminated.

Figure 6.16 shows the hierarchical relationship, established by the ITU-T, between the VPI, VCI, and the cell transport media (for example, a SONET/SDH circuit) [I311]. Virtual channels are considered to exist within virtual paths, which are themselves unique only within a given cell transport media. The combination of cell transport media, VPI, and VCI defines a given ATM link.

Figure 6.16 A link carries virtual channels within virtual paths over cell transport media.

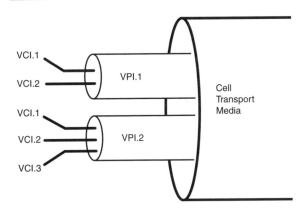

A virtual channel connection (VCC) provides an end-to-end cell path between users of the ATM transport service. (In this book, the term *VCC* is used interchangeably with the terms *virtual connection*, or VC, and *virtual channel*.) A VCC is made up of the concatenation of virtual path connections (VPCs). A VPC provides a cell path between points where the VCI field is switched. Each VPC is made up of the concatenation of links between points where switching occurs solely on the basis of the VPI. The cell transport media are responsible for providing internode links—carrying ATM cells between switching or terminating nodes. A node may provide VPI- or VPI/VCI-based cell switching (an ATM switch) or may terminate the virtual connection (an end station).

VPCs may be as short as a single link in cases when both the VPI and VCI may be switched at the next switching node. At the other extreme, a VPC may span an entire network of switching nodes and be terminated only at a customer's endpoint equipment. Cell sequence is preserved within VPCs and, hence, VCCs. However, cell integrity is not guaranteed.

The VPI and VCI values representing a virtual connection may change on every hop (they are not globally significant) and are assigned either by a dynamic signaling protocol or operator provisioning. Figure 6.17 represents a virtual connection spanning three switching nodes and four links. From End Station 1 cells are injected to node 1 with VPI = x/VCI = y. At node 1 the VCI is switched, at node 2 both the VPI and VCI are switched, and at node 3 the VPI and VCI are unchanged even though the cells are switched to another link. VCCs are bi-directional, so traffic can also flow from right to left on the VC in Figure 6.17. Cells injected by End Station 2 with VPI = p/VCI = m traverse the reverse path with the sequence of VPI/VCI mappings reversed at each switch.

Figure 6.17   A virtual connection is the concatenation of switched hops.

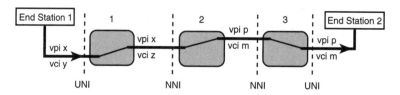

ATM switches have CQS architectures to deal with the case where multiple VCCs are routed from separate input ports to the same output port. The VPI/VCI information is used to differentiate cells for the purpose of queuing and scheduling, allowing the switch to interleave cells from different VCCs in whichever manner achieves the desired QoS goals for each VCC.

The Network Node Interface (NNI) exists between ATM switches making up a single ATM network and sometimes at the boundary between peer ATM networks. When an end-user (end station) desires specific service, it makes the request over the UNI using UNI-specific signaling [UNI31, UNI40]. Typically the request identifies the destination end station, using its globally significant ATM address. A distributed routing protocol runs within the ATM network to decide the best-switched route for the end station's VC. Routing and signaling messages are exchanged between switches over the NNI.

VCs established on-demand through user signaling across the UNI are known as switched virtual connections (SVCs), and those established through administrative configuration are permanent virtual connections (PVCs). An intermediate form, called the Soft PVC (SPVC), appears as a PVC to the end station at the UNI but is dynamically established and maintained within the ATM network (for example, if an internal link fails, the ATM network reroutes the SPVC without disrupting the VPI/VCIs allocated across the UNIs at either end).

6.3.2 ATM Cells

Figure 6.18 shows the structure of an ATM cell (the unit of transport within an ATM network). Within the ATM network only the header has importance, the payload is carried uninterpreted between the ends of a VC.

Figure 6.18   ATM cell structure.

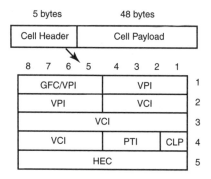

The VCI field is 16 bits wide, allowing each virtual path to carry 65,535 virtual channels. At the NNI the VPI is 12 bits, and at the UNI the VPI is 8 (with the initial 4 bits reserved for generic flow control, or GFC, across the UNI but generally not used) [I361]. The payload type indication (PTI) distinguishes between cells carrying data and network management cells and may also carry indications about the network congestion observed by the cell. The most important user service is the ATM user-to-user (AUU) indication—a form of out-of-band signal between ATM layer users at either end of a VC. ATM adaptation layer (AAL) type 5 (described in Section 6.3.3, "Adaptation Layers") uses the AUU to signal the last cell of a user packet.

The cell loss priority (CLP) bit may be used to divide the cell stream on a given VC into two tiers—normal cells (CLP=0) and low-priority cells (CLP=1). At the onset of local congestion, switch nodes preferentially discard cells with CLP = 1. The CLP is typically initialized to zero and set to one if the cell passes through a policing function (for example, at an ingress ATM switch) that determines the cell to be violating whatever profile is allowed for the cell's VC.

The header error check (HEC) is an 8-bit cyclic redundancy check (CRC) code calculated over the entire header [I432]. The HEC has two distinct roles—cell delineation and cell header protection. When acting to protect a cell's header, the HEC is capable of single-bit error correction or multibit error detection. However, before header's can be checked for correctness, the receiver must be synchronized with the incoming cell stream and know where to find the header. If the cell transport media is bit serial or byte serial (for example, SONET/SDH), the delineation mechanism uses the known relationship of the HEC to the preceding four octets [I432]. Sequences of five octets are sought out where the fifth represents a correct HEC for the previous four. The receiver considers itself synchronized when matches occur regularly (the exact thresholds depend on the encoding technique).

The HEC generator polynomial is applied to a group of 4 bytes and matched to the fifth. This process occurs on a bit-by-bit basis (if bit serial) or byte-by-byte basis (if byte serial) until a match is found. The preceding 4 bytes are then considered to "probably" represent a cell header. The header of the probable next cell, 53 bytes along in the media stream, is then checked for a match. If this check results in a match for the next N cells, synchronization is assumed to have been achieved. Subsequent 53 octet sequences are processed as valid ATM cells. If the HEC fails for M cells in a row, synchronization is assumed to have been lost, and the bit-by-bit checking is resumed. Values for N and M depend on the underlying cell transport but are likely to be in the range 6 to 8.

6.3.3 Adaptation Layers

Because the ATM network provides only cell transport, the ITU-T defined a collection of AALs whose role is to map an end station's natural data stream onto the network's underlying cell transport service. ATM Switches along a path are unaware of the end-to-end AAL services being utilized over any given VC.

Figure 6.19 shows a VC endpoint (end station), consisting of a cell transport media interface, an ATM layer, and an AAL. The ATM layer demultiplexes received cells based on their VPI and VCI before passing the cells upward to the AAL. The ATM layer filters out and drops cells that do not belong to any VC currently open to the AAL.

Figure 6.19   An end station with ATM layer and AAL.

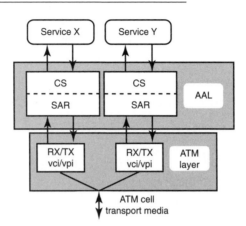

The AAL consists of two internal sublayers: a convergence sublayer (CS) and a segmentation and reassembly sublayer (SAR). The CS provides any necessary encapsulation of user data before the SAR segments the result into 48-byte cell payload fields. In general the SAR function provides transmission and error-detection facilities on a cell-by-cell basis. The CS function provides transmission and error-detection facilities over the natural unit of data utilized by the user service (bytes, bit streams, or variable-length packets). In some applications the SAR or CS functions may be empty.

The primary source of information on AALs is ITU-T specification I.363 [I363]. The four AALs are

- **AAL 1**—Designed for circuit emulation services where bit streams must be transported with strict delay, jitter, and timing constraints.

- **AAL 2**—Designed for delay sensitive, bit- or byte-stream services having variable bit rates.

- **AAL 3/4**—Designed for frame oriented service where no specific timing relationships exist between frames and where multiple frames may be simultaneously multiplexed across a VC.

- **AAL 5**—Designed for frame oriented service where no specific timing relationships exist between frames and where a single frame at a time may be transmitted across a VC.

The IP industry has firmly backed the use of AAL 5 as the protocol for carrying variable-length IP packets across ATM virtual connections. It provides nothing more than the ability to recognize packet boundaries within a serial stream of cells and to verify that cells were not lost, corrupted, or accidentally introduced between packet boundaries. The QoS achieved from one end to another depends on the underlying VC rather than AAL 5 itself.

Figure 6.20 shows the AAL 5 hierarchy. An AAL service data unit (AAL_SDU, the atomic unit of transmission of the layer above the AAL) is turned into a common part convergence sublayer protocol data unit (CPCS_PDU) by padding it out and appending a CPCS_PDU trailer.

The SAR layer then breaks the CPCS_PDU into 48-octet segments, filling the payloads of consecutive ATM cells. The padding ensures that the CPCS_PDU trailer falls in the last eight octets of the last ATM cell making up the transmission of this AAL_SDU.

Figure 6.20   AAL 5 processing.

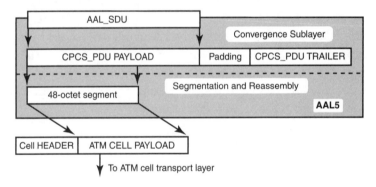

Delineation of CPCS_PDU boundaries is performed by the ATM layer AUU parameter in the PTI field of the ATM cell header. Operating essentially as an end-of-frame marker, the AUU is set to one to mark the last cell of a CPCS_PDU (or only cell if the CPCS_PDU is 48 octets or smaller). Cells arriving with AUU set to 0 are presumed to represent the beginning and middle of a CPCS_PDU spanning more than one cell.

Figure 6.21 shows the details of a CPCS_PDU. For ease of location, the CPCS_PDU trailer is always placed in the last eight octets of the final cell (the one with AUU = 1). This practice implies that between 0 and 47 octets of padding (PAD) exist between the last octet of the AAL_SDU and the CPCS_PDU trailer. Primary error detection is provided by the 4-byte CRC field, which covers the entire CPCS_PDU (up to but excluding the CRC itself). The Length field specifies the actual payload (AAL_SDU) size in bytes. For the purposes of IP over ATM, the CPCS user-to-user (CPCS-UU) and CPI fields are ignored.

Figure 6.21   AAL 5 common part convergence sublayer protocol data unit format.

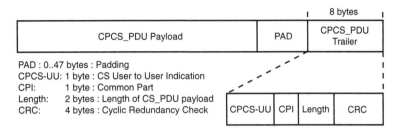

Because AAL 5 does not support the interleaving of CPCS_PDUs on a single virtual connection, all cells carry segments for either the current or next CPCS_PDU. The first cell to arrive after a cell with AUU set to one is assumed to be the beginning of the next CPCS_PDU. A CPCS_PDU shorter than 41 bytes may be represented by a single cell with AUU set to one (40 bytes of CS_PDU and 8 bytes of trailer fit within a single cell payload).

6.3.4   *Signaling and Routing*

As in an IP network, end-users do not concern themselves with routing within the ATM network. An end-user *signals* to the network (across the UNI) that it desires a VC to a certain destination, conforming to certain QoS parameters. The network itself then uses internal signaling among the participating ATM switches to discover an optimal route (path) for the VC to follow, one that will enable the VC to meet whatever QoS constraints have been specified while still reaching the specified destination end station (at another UNI). This step constitutes a VC *routing* phase and is typically performed only once each time an end-user requests a new VC. Once the VC is up, the path is fixed and cell traffic is switched along it. (This behavior contrasts to the Best Effort IP model where routing protocols regularly reevaluate their shortest-path trees and can change them while IP traffic is flowing.) Two forms of ATM addressing exist:

- A native E.164 format (for public ATM networks, it looks like a phone number)

- A 20-octet ATM End System Address (AESA) (for private and public networks, encoding a number of different addressing hierarchies in Network Service Access Point, or NSAP, format)

Although hierarchy exists within ATM address spaces, this hierarchy is not as tightly linked to the network's topology as IP address hierarchy is. The ATM address hierarchy allows for an efficient routing of signaling (call establishment) requests, but it imposes no constraints on the path that the VC eventually follows.

The ATM Forum's user signaling protocol has gone through three revisions—UNI 3.0, UNI 3.1, and now UNI 4.0 [UNI31, UNI40]. The ATM Forum also developed a routing protocol for use within commonly administered ATM networks called Private NNI (PNNI). Interestingly, many IP over ATM backbones have stuck with manual or operator provisioning of VCs (permanent virtual connections, or PVCs) across their ATM networks. The usual response when queried about this decision was that operators were having enough trouble understanding the behavior of their IP routing layers and did not relish the idea of another dynamic layer underneath!

6.3.5 QoS Characteristics

One clear difference between ATM and IP is that end-to-end service quality was a design consideration from the beginning of ATM. Cell transport links between ATM switches are required to provide predictable latency and jitter, and ATM switches themselves are built around a CQS architecture for the very purpose of ensuring controllable isolation between VCs that desire it. The ATM world began by treating QoS and high-capacity networking as its primary focus, whereas the IP world was initially obsessed with far-reaching connectivity at whatever speed was available.

It remains as a matter of historical record that the Internet gained mind-share first, arguably because of its focus on connectivity. However, this book exists because the IP world is now expanding beyond connectivity alone. The Internet needs to support signaled and provisioned QoS, too (even if not in quite the same form envisaged by ATM's original designers).

Classes of Service

VCs can be established with strict or loose QoS constraints on parameters such as bandwidth, latency, and jitter bounds. The essential attribute from an end-user's perspective is that the VC's characteristics are pretty much guaranteed after the network has signaled back successful VC establishment. These guarantees are enabled by the coordinated use of:

- Call admission control (CAC) to decide if a new connection request can be honored given the user's specified QoS requirements

- Usage parameter control (UPC) similar to policing—to ensure no individual user's traffic exceeds its previously negotiated QoS parameters

• Per-hop differentiated queuing and scheduling of cell traffic on a per-VC or per-VP basis

Several traffic classes of service have been defined, building on the preceding capabilities. These classes are currently defined in the ATM Forum's Traffic Management specification version 4.1 [ATMTM41]:

• **Constant Bit Rate (CBR)**—This is used by connections that require a specific bandwidth to be available at all times during the life of the connection (characterized by a peak cell rate, or PCR). If the user transmits faster than the negotiated PCR, the network may aggressively discard excess cells. The network is expected to keep jitter (cell delay variation) tightly controlled.

• **Real Time Variable Bit Rate (rt-VBR)**—This is used by connections whose delay and jitter tolerances are tight, but whose bandwidth usage isn't constant enough to warrant CBR service. Typically the user characterizes their bandwidth use with a PCR, a sustained cell rate (SCR), and maximum burst size (MBS). rt-VBR is intended for bursty real time applications.

• **Non-Real Time Variable Bit Rate (nrt-VBR)**—This is used by connections supporting bursty traffic sources that do not have tight delay or jitter requirements, but do have an expectation of low cell loss ratio (CLR) while the cell rate is within negotiated PCR, SCR, and MBS parameters.

• **Unspecified Bit Rate (UBR)**—This is used by connections that have no specific delay, jitter, loss rate, or bandwidth requirements (the ATM equivalent of "Best Effort" service). This service was introduced specifically to support the efficient transport of traditional data (for example, IP) over ATM.

• **Available Bit Rate (ABR)**—This is used by connections that can flexibly adapt to available network capacity within an upper bound (PCR) and lower bound (minimum cell rate, or MCR). After the call is established, the network may signal the endpoints to slow down or speed up within the negotiated rate range in order to most efficiently utilize the capacity available at any given time. The user expects that cooperating with the network will result in very low cell loss rates. No specific delay or jitter bounds are supported by ABR service.

• **Guaranteed Frame Rate (GFR)**—This is used by connections that require a minimum rate guarantee, know they are carrying AAL 5 frames, and want the network to either deliver frames whole or not at all. The network commits to delivering frames transmitted at the MCR and may deliver frames at the PCR if sufficient capacity exists at any instant. The network attempts to ensure congestive loss results in the loss of entire AAL 5 frames, rather than just single cells within frames.

Together with the fact that ATM networks are able to flexibly span far larger geographical areas than any other high-speed technology, these QoS capabilities makes ATM an understandable choice for predictable point-to-point IP packet transport.

Payload Expansion

Of course, nothing is completely perfect or predictable. Although the ATM network can provide bandwidth guarantees when requested, the guarantees are expressed in terms of cell rates (bit rates at the cell transport level) rather than AAL user-level bit rates. The relationship between cell rates and user-level bit rates depends largely on the AAL service employed. In the case of IP over ATM, the use of AAL 5 results in a form of payload expansion that oscillates as a sawtooth function with increasing AAL_SDU size (from mapping the AAL_SDU into an integral number of ATM cell payloads).

Consider an AAL 5 virtual connection limited to 10,000 cells per second. When carrying 2,000-byte AAL_SDUs, the apparent user bit rate is

2000-byte AAL_SDU → 2008-byte CPCS_PDU

→ 42 cells per AAL_SDU

→ (10,000/42) AAL_SDUs per second

→ 3.81 Mbit per second at the AAL_SDU level

However, if the AAL_SDUs were 98 bytes long, the allowed maximum rate drops to

98-byte AAL_SDU → 106-byte CPCS_PDU

→ 3 cells per AAL_SDU

→ (10,000/3) AAL_SDUs per second

→ 2.61 Mbit per second at the AAL_SDU level

For the smaller AAL_SDU sizes, substantial interactions occur between the achievable peak bit rate at the AAL_SDU level and the cell rate signaled for the VC. Figure 6.22 shows how the maximum achievable throughput on a 10,000 cell per second AAL 5 connection varies with the size of the IP packet being carried (*throughput* being the number of bits of IP packet transmitted per second). Achievable throughput converges to the expected value as packet size increases (just over 3.81 Mbit per second). The graph shows quite dramatic swings for packets below around 500 bytes.

Figure 6.22 Effective IP bit rate over a 10,000 cell per second AAL 5 VC.

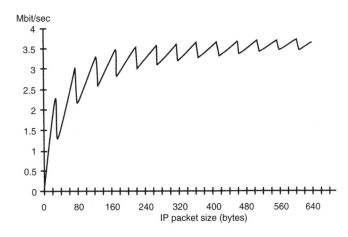

This variability becomes less important as the average packet size increases. However, our working assumption is that there's an increasing amount of real-time IP traffic carrying small voice samples. Small changes in a codec's voice sample size may generate quite unexpected disparity between the IP packet stream's nominal bit rate and the required cell rate on the VC.

Cell Transports

ATM cell transports have been defined across an extremely wide range of link types and speeds. By the mid 1990s, cell transport ranged from 1.5Mbit per second (T1) leased lines to high-speed 622Mbit per second (OC-12/STM-4) optical circuits [ATMT1, ATMOC12]. More recently, cell transport over 2.4Gbit per second (OC-48/STM-16) optical circuits has been defined [ATMOC48].

However, speed is not the defining factor for an acceptable ATM link. The link technology must have temporal characteristics that are easily described and quantified. Knowing the characteristics of every link in the network allows each VC to be appropriately routed—for example, VCs with strict QoS requirements would be routed around links that have only soft jitter guarantees. (The existence of a completely QoS-free UBR class even led a Cells In Frames consortium to make a serious effort to carry ATM cells over Ethernet between hosts and switches. Although technically not unreasonable, this idea left some ATM purists bemused!)

6.4 Virtual Links and Tunnels

Links are an entirely abstract notion, representing a service providing per-hop transport for IP packets. Often our poor brains cope by asserting that links are built from technologies at layers below IP or that links have a one-to-one relationship to the physical path between two points. But in the real world, this is rarely the case. Conventional link-level paths frequently do not exist between two points that desire to exchange packets even though a packet transport service may exist at the IP, UDP, or TCP level. If you can accept the inevitable layering violations, you can enter the world of the virtual link—where packets theoretically belonging to one layer are transported using services of an equivalent or higher layer. These virtual links are often referred to as *tunnels*, and the act of transporting a packet over a higher-layer service is *tunneling*.

Tunnels are a compromise—they trade raw bandwidth efficiency for topological flexibility and are a popular tool for network designers. Tunnels come in a number of flavors (for example, IP-in-IP, PPP over UDP, PPP over ATM, and so on) and have been used to develop a number of prototype and/or deployed services (for example, the Multicast Backbone, or MBone, and the development of distributed PPP services that tunnel PPP from regional modem banks back to centralized network access servers). Tunnels may represent links within the topology of the network they run over or links quite independent of the network over which the tunnel runs.

The CQS model for an output interface still applies—by design a tunnel looks like a packet-based link as far as the endpoints are concerned. As with more conventional links, tunnels have particular QoS characteristics, but in this case the characteristics are usually inherited from the network over which they run.

6.4.1 IP-in-IP

As its name suggests, an IP-in-IP tunnel transports IP packets within IP packets. At a tunnel's source, the IP packet to be tunneled is placed within the payload of another IP packet (the *tunneling* or *encapsulating* packet, as shown in Figure 6.23). The identity of the tunnel's endpoint (another router or host with an IP interface on the tunneling packet's network) defines the tunneling packet's destination IP address field.

The tunneling packet is then transmitted, using regular IP forwarding, toward the desired tunnel endpoint. When the tunneling packet reaches its destination, the tunnel endpoint extracts the original IP packet and processes it as though it had arrived over a regular interface. Tunneling packets use a unique IP Protocol Type to distinguish themselves from packets carrying other payloads such as TCP, UDP, or Internet Control Message Protocol

(ICMP)—for example, protocol type 4 indicates the payload is an IPv4 packet [RFC2003]. Because a tunnel represents a single hop from the perspective of the tunneled packet, its time to live (TTL) field is decremented by one (rather than the number of hops between the tunnel endpoints).

Figure 6.23   Packet encapsulation for IP-IP tunneling.

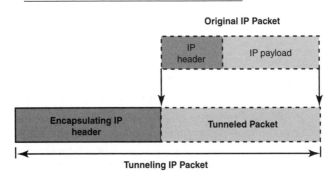

Such tunnels are frequently used when an IP packet must be transported without the intervening IP routers seeing or acting on the packet's header. Only the tunnel's end-points perform any special processing—routers along the tunneling packet's path between source and destination consider the tunnel to be just another stream of IP packets. A non-obvious aspect of tunnels is that the tunneled and tunneling IP packets may belong to the same IP routing domain, or they may belong to entirely *different* IP routing domains. Tunnel endpoints are specified using IP addresses belonging to the network over which packets are being tunneled. These addresses may be entirely unrelated to the IP address space of the network for which this tunnel is represents a (virtual) link.

One trade-off is the additional overhead of the encapsulating IP header. RFC 2003 speci-fies the basic IPv4 in IPv4 tunnel [RFC2003], which results in the effective MTU of the virtual link being at least 20 bytes smaller than the smallest MTU along the tunneling packet's path. (RFC 2004 suggests a more efficient encapsulation mechanism incurring only 8 or 12 bytes of overhead but with some loss of generality—for example, fragmented IPv4 packets cannot be tunneled [RFC2004]. The protocol type in the encapsulating header is 55.) When tunneling over IPv6 networks, the MTU drops by at least 40 bytes (the size of the encapsulating IPv6 header)[RFC2473]. Overhead also consumes link bandwidth.

The jitter, latency, and packet-loss characteristics of a tunnel depend entirely on the IP path between the tunnel endpoints. If the IP network offers only Best Effort service, the tunnel represents a packet-oriented link with random QoS characteristics. If the IP network implements some of the techniques described in this book, the tunneling packet might well be provided with specific per-hop queuing and scheduling services, thereby providing the virtual link with some predictable QoS characteristics. Although the IP network does not know that any given packet stream is a tunnel, the network can be told to classify the packets (for example, based on the ToS/DS byte or the full header classification) and provide them with specific QoS treatment.

Any router or host IP interface is likely to have its own CQS architecture feeding into a tunnel—providing for differentiated scheduling of tunneled IP packet streams onto the virtual link (that is, into tunneling packets). The packet classification scheme used to schedule tunneled packets onto the tunnel may be quite unrelated to the classification used on the tunneling packets by the IP network between the tunnel endpoints. For example, the ToS/DS byte interpretations applied to the tunneled packets may be different to the rules used along the tunnel to interpret ToS/DS byte in the tunneling packet's header. An interesting design choice exists with respect to ToS/DS bytes—whether congestion indications picked up along the tunnel itself (and reflected in modifications to the tunneling packet's ToS/DS byte) ought to be reflected in the ToS/DS bytes of the tunneled packets when they are de-capsulated. A strict definition of "tunnel as transparent link" suggests not, but the alternative can be useful in expediting the trigger of end-to-end congestion avoidance mechanisms.

MBone

In the early days of multicast experimentation, few IP backbone routers were capable of natively supporting IP multicasting forwarding or the associated routing protocols. Indeed, many backbone operators were wary of allowing IP multicast traffic to run natively across their networks because the typical applications were badly behaved bandwidth hogs (that is, the applications did not run on top of TCP, and the backbone operator's own routers were not equipped to perform traffic shaping and policing at the time).

To work around this problem, the MBone was established as a tunneled network on top of the existing IPv4 unicast network. Workstations were turned into multicast-capable IP routers and interconnected by links built from IP-in-IP tunnels. When a multicast packet was received by these workstation-based multicast routers and the multicast forwarding tables indicated it ought to be forwarded to other sites around the MBone, the packet would be replicated across all the appropriate unicast tunnels out from that multicast router. These modified workstations also supplied the rate limiting and policing required by the operators of the IPv4 unicast backbones over which the MBone was being tunneled.

6Bone

As this book is being written, interest is growing in the next generation of IP, known as IPv6. It represents both an evolution and revolution in IP networking—on the one hand it represents how IP would have been built if its designers knew then what they know now (evolution); on the other hand today's IPv4 networks need wide-ranging upgrades before they can start carrying IPv6 packets (revolution).

To create a test bed for wide area (indeed, global) IPv6 experimentation and proof-of-concept trials, the IPv6 community turned to IP-in-IP tunneling. An IPv6 backbone—the 6Bone—was created as an overlay on top of the existing IPv4 unicast Internet. IPv6-capable routers are interconnected by tunnels that carry IPv6 packets within IPv4 packets—basically an extension of the RFC 2003 model but with an IPv4 protocol type of 41 to indicate that the payload is an IPv6 packet. RFC 1933 specifies the rules for explicitly established IPv6 in IPv4 tunnels where only unicast IPv4 is available [RFC1933], and RFC 2529 assumes that the IPv4 network offers native multicast service that can be leveraged to enable automatic discovery and assignment of tunnel endpoints [RFC2529].

6.4.2 Tunneling PPP

Service providers have found the session abstraction provided by PPP to be quite valuable. However, a bit- or byte-serial, point-to-point link between PPP peers—typically a customer and the service provider's centralized network access server (NAS)—is often not possible or particularly efficient. A number of solutions have been developed to leverage alternative connectivity options (for example, an ATM service, Ethernet, or a hybrid of dial-up and IP transport), each revolving around a fully or partially tunneled path between PPP peers.

Layer 2 Tunneling Protocol

Layer 2 Tunneling Protocol (L2TP) was developed to provide PPP packet transport across a range of packet-oriented, potentially unreliable transport services (for example, UDP/IP and AAL 5 ATM) [RFC2661]. It has evolved from two similar solutions—Layer 2 Forwarding (L2F) and Point-to-Point Tunneling Protocol (PPTP) [RFC2341, PPTP]. Neither L2F nor PPTP are IETF standards-track work items, but both have been implemented by a number of vendors.

A primary application of L2TP involves dial-in or leased-line PPP service to an ISP. In the regular PPP model, a customer's link-level connection terminates at the same point as its PPP session, directly on a service provider's NAS. However, in L2TP the dial-in link's termination point can be decoupled from the PPP session termination point, thus allowing the implementation of a distributed NAS function.

As shown in Figure 6.24, L2TP tunnels connect the customer link's termination point (the L2TP access concentrator, or LAC) and the PPP session's termination point (the L2TP network server, or LNS). In general L2TP can be used anywhere a hybrid link is required between the two PPP peers making up a PPP session. Where the customer's device has connectivity to the same network as the LNS, LAC functionality may be co-resident with the customer's own PPP entity, thereby avoiding having to go through a real LAC.

Figure 6.24   L2TP distributes the network access server between a L2TP access concentrator and L2TP network server.

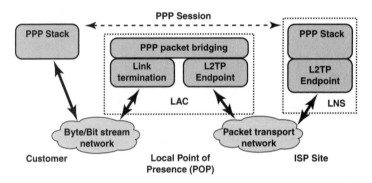

L2TP is a moderately complex protocol in its own right. It builds a reliable control channel and unreliable data path over any unreliable, packet-oriented transport service and can cope with an underlying transport that reorders packets. A rich set of control and error indications is available so that a LNS has a good idea what is happening to the associated customer link connection at the LAC.

A L2TP frame consists of a 3- to 12-octet L2TP header and the link-level frame being tunneled. Because of its origins in the dial-in and ISDN access worlds, the link-level frame is often assumed to be the HDLC-like frame stripped of its delimiter (0x7E) octets, trailing FCS octets, and bit/byte stuffing, leaving only the Address and Control fields (0xFF03, although this can be removed on a per session basis if the PPP session's LCP negotiates Address and Control field compression). The resulting L2TP frame is shown in Figure 6.25. Each L2TP header contains a 16-bit tunnel ID and 16-bit session ID that allow a single LAC-LNS transport connection to be subdivided into tunnels and the tunnels further subdivided into sessions.

Figure 6.25   L2TP supports sessions within tunnels within a packet transport connection.

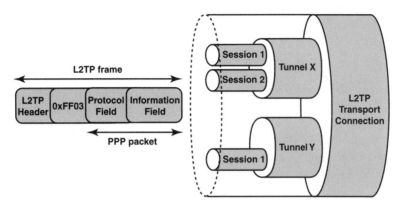

The QoS characteristics of a L2TP tunnel depend on both the nature of the transport connection between LAC and LNS and the mechanisms LAC and LNS use to multiplex packets from different tunnels onto the transport link. As it currently stands, the L2TP specification provides a very simple "priority" bit indicating that a packet "…should receive preferential treatment in its local queuing and transmission" [RFC2661]. No rules currently cover scheduling between sessions or tunnels vying for access to the underlying transport connection.

A number of transport connections are being defined. Initially the most important one is L2TP over UDP/IP. In this scenario, an IP network between the LAC and LNS is assumed, and a transport connection is established between specific UDP ports on the LAC and LNS. L2TP frames are carried as the payloads of regular UDP packets, and therefore the entire transport connection receives whatever IP-level QoS the intervening IP network provides. L2TP is also being defined over other packet-oriented transport services—for example, AAL 5 ATM [L2ATM] and Frame Relay (FR) [L2FR].

PPP and L2TP over ATM

ATM virtual circuits can provide a very useful source of wide area, QoS-controlled connectivity for other link-level protocols. ATM is used two different ways in the PPP world. An ATM VC can directly transport a PPP session between PPP peers [RFC2364] or provide the L2TP transport connection between a LAC and LNS [L2ATM].

In both cases, the AAL 5 service is used for frame delineation, error detection, and mapping packets onto the underlying cell stream. When used for native PPP transport, this service replaces HDLC-like framing and removes the need for bit or byte stuffing. The PPP packets or L2TP frames may be carried in two ways:

- Directly in an AAL 5 AAL_SDU (VC multiplexing)

- Encapsulated with an LLC/SNAP header with the resulting LLC frame transmitted directly in an AAL 5 AAL_SDU (LLC multiplexing)

VC multiplexing (shown in Figure 6.26) is the most efficient—each AAL_SDU carries a PPP packet or L2TP frame directly. The type of packets carried in each AAL_SDU is fixed during VC establishment—a VC between PPP peers must carry only PPP packets; likewise, a VC between LAC and LNS must carry only L2TP frames. (LLC/SNAP headers are added if a VC is to be concurrently shared between different protocols or when the VC is mapped through an ATM/FR interworking unit at some point along its path.)

Figure 6.26   VC multiplexed Point-to-Point Protocol or L2TP packets are AAL 5 AAL service data units.

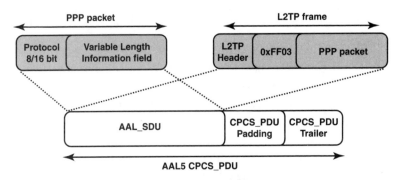

ATM does provide good per VC QoS control. However, packet interleaving becomes an issue on low-speed VCs (in the low hundreds of kilobit per second) because AAL 5 doesn't provide any tools for subdividing the capacity of any single VC. Two possibilities exist for PPP over AAL 5—if VCs are scarce, MCML can be run across a single VC; and if VCs are plentiful, parallel AAL 5 VCs can be established between the PPP peers (possibly avoiding the need to use MCML if there's one VC for each IP traffic class). When ATM is used as an L2TP transport, an additional relationship exists between each L2TP tunnel within the transport connection and sessions within the tunnels. The LAC/LNS may choose to use one VC for all tunnels, distinct VCs for each tunnel, or even VCs specific to sessions within the tunnels.

Figure 6.27 shows the performance curves for PPP over AAL 5, using distinct VCs and using MCML fragmenting initial PPP packets on 64- and 192-byte boundaries, respectively. Clearly running PPP over AAL 5 is a choice made for flexibility rather than performance. MCML with small fragment sizes is a major performance hit, with MCML fragmentation and ATM segmentation interacting to provide a very uneven performance curve. A network designer needs to carefully balance the cost of establishing parallel VCs with the performance hit of running MCML over a single VC.

Performance for L2TP over ATM is even lower because of the additional overhead per AAL_SDU. When both ends of the PPP session are on the same ATM network, running PPP directly over an AAL 5 VC generally makes more sense than co-locating a LAC in each customer's device just to run L2TP over ATM.

Figure 6.27   Performance of regular Point-to-Point Protocol and MultiClass MultiLink over AAL 5 VCs.

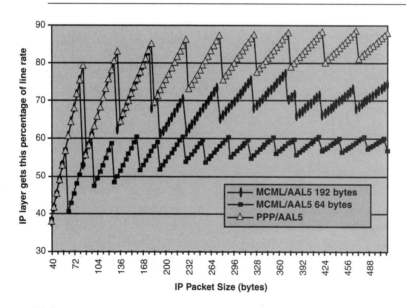

PPP over Ethernet

For something a little different, here is a brief look at PPP over Ethernet (PPPoE). PPPoE was developed for situations where the path between one or more PPP-based customers and their local ISP is (or emulates) a shared Ethernet. (Ethernet itself is covered in Chapter 8, "High-Speed Link Technologies.") Described in RFC 2516, the scheme supports the unicast exchange of PPP packets carried within Ethernet frames between one or more customer interfaces and the ISP's access server (concentrator) [RFC2516]. Because the access server must handle multiple PPP customers over a single Ethernet interface, PPPoE utilizes a 16-bit session ID to multiplex concurrent PPP sessions—essentially splitting the shared Ethernet into multiple virtual links, one for each PPP session. Unicast Ethernet transmissions provide a packet-oriented transport link between PPP peers.

As shown in Figure 6.28, PPPoE frames are created by prepending the PPP packet (no HDLC header) with a 48-bit PPPoE header (containing the session ID and other flags). The PPPoE frame is then placed into an Ethernet frame, and its specific payload identified with EtherType code 0x8864. Ethernet provides the delineation and FCS. PPPoE also defines an automatic discovery/configuration protocol to locate access servers and establish session IDs. (These packets have EtherType 0x8863.) The access server or concentrator may actually terminate the ISP's end of the PPP session or may be a LAC tunneling the PPP sessions back to the ISP's central facilities.

Figure 6.28   PPP over Ethernet encapsulates Point-to-Point Protocol packets in Ethernet frames.

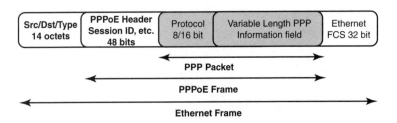

Because a real Ethernet layer runs between 10 and 1000Mbit per second, individual PPP sessions probably won't need to utilize MCML. Emulated Ethernet services may have lower rates between the customer and access server/concentrator (for example, when the Ethernet is being bridged over a lower-speed access link such as ADSL), and MCML might be required because PPPoE provides no packet interleave functionality of its own. In either case, other traffic on the Ethernet may significantly effect the QoS perceived by any given PPP session.

6.5 References

[ATMT1]   ATM Forum. "DS1 Physical Layer Specification." af-phy-016.000. (September 1994).

[ATMTM41]   ATM Forum. "Traffic Management Specification version 4.1." af-tm-0121.000. (March 1999).

[ATMOC12]   ATM Forum. "622.08 Mbps Physical Layer Specification." af-phy-0046.000. (January 1996).

[ATMOC48]   ATM Forum. "2.4 Gbps Physical Layer Specification." af-phy-0133.000. (October 1999).

[I150]   CCITT SGXVIII—Report R109, Draft recommendation I.150. "B-ISDN Asynchronous Transfer Mode Functional Characteristics." (July 1992).

[I311]   ITU-T Recommendation I.311. "B-ISDN General Network Aspects." (August 1996).

[I361]   Helsinki. ITU-T Recommendation I.361. "B-ISDN ATM Layer Specification." (March 1993).

[I363]   ITU-T Recommendation I.363. "B-ISDN ATM Adaptation Layer (AAL) Specification." (March 1993).

[I432]   ITU-T Recommendation I.432.1. "B-ISDN User-Network Interface—Physical Layer Specification: General Characteristics." (February 1999).

[ISLWSVC]   Jackowski, S., D. Putzolu, E. Crawley, and B. Davie. "Integrated Services Mappings for Low Speed Networks." Internet Draft (work in progress) draft-ietf-issll-isslow-svcmap-08.txt. (17 May 1999).

[L2ATM]   Davison, M., A. Lin, A. Singh, J. Stephens, R. Turner, and J. Senthilnathan [online]. "L2TP over AAL5 and FUNI." Internet Draft (work in progress) draft-ietf-pppext-l2tp-atm-02.txt. (April 1999).

[L2FR]   Rawat, V., R. Tio, and R. Verma. "Layer Two Tunneling Protocol (L2TP) over Frame Relay." Internet Draft (work in progress) draft-ietf-pppext-l2tp-fr-02.txt. (June 1999).

[MSENC]   Farinacci, D., Y. Rekhter, E. Rosen, G. Fedorkow, D. Tappan, T. Li, and A. Conta. "MPLS Label Stack Encoding." Internet Draft (work in progress) draft-ietf-mpls-label-encaps-04.txt. (April 1999).

[PNNI]   ATM Forum. "Private Network-Network Interface Specification, Version 1.0." af-pnni-0055.000.

[PPPMCML]   Bormann, C. "The Multi-Class Extension to Multi-Link PPP." Internet Draft (work in progress) draft-ietf-issll-isslow-mcml-06.txt. (June 1999).

[PPPRTF]   Bormann, C. "PPP in a Real-Time Oriented HDLC-like Framing." Internet Draft (work in progress) draft-ietf-issll-isslow-rtf-04.txt. (April 1999).

[PPTP] Hamzeh, K., G. S. Pall, W. Verthein, J. Taarud, W. A. Little, and G. Zorn. "Point-to-Point Tunneling Protocol (PPTP)." Internet Draft (work in progress) draft-ietf-pppext-pptp-10.txt. (April 1999).

[RFC1191] Mogul, J., and S. Deering. "Path MTU Discovery." RFC 1191. (November 1990).

[RFC1332] McGregor, G. "The PPP Internet Protocol Control Protocol (IPCP)." RFC 1332. (May 1992).

[RFC1552] Simpson, W. "The PPP Internetwork Packet Exchange Control Protocol (IPXCP)." RFC 1552. (December 1993).

[RFC1661] Simpson, W. (ed). "The Point-to-Point Protocol (PPP)." STD 51. RFC 1661. (July 1994).

[RFC1662] Simpson, W. (ed). "PPP in HDLC-like Framing." STD 51. RFC 1662. (July 1994).

[RFC1877] Cobb, S. "PPP Internet Protocol Control Protocol Extensions for Name Server Addresses." RFC 1877. (December 1995).

[RFC1981] McCann, J., S. Deering, and J. Mogul. "Path MTU Discovery for IP version 6." RFC 1981. (August 1996).

[RFC1933] Gilligan, R., and E. Nordmark. "Transition Mechanisms for IPv6 Hosts and Routers." RFC 1933. (April 1996).

[RFC1990] Sklower, K., B. Lloyd, G. McGregor, D. Carr, and T. Coradetti. "The PPP Multilink Protocol (MP)." RFC 1990. (August 1996).

[RFC2003] Perkins, C. "IP Encapsulation within IP." RFC 2003. (October 1996).

[RFC2004] Perkins, C. "Minimal Encapsulation within IP." RFC 2004. (October 1996).

[RFC2341] Valencia, A., M. Littlewood, and T. Kolar. "Cisco Layer Two Forwarding (Protocol) L2F." RFC 2341. (May 1998).

[RFC2364] Gross, G., M. Kaycee, A. Lin, A. Malis, and J. Stephens. "PPP over AAL5." RFC 2364. (July 1998).

[RFC2472] Haskin, D., and E. Allen. "IP Version 6 over PPP." RFC 2472. (December 1998).

[RFC2473] Conta, A., and S. Deering. "Generic Packet Tunneling in IPv6 Specification." RFC 2473. (December 1998).

[RFC2516]   Mamakos, L., K. Lidl, J. Evarts, D. Carrel, D. Simone, and R. Wheeler. "A Method for Transmitting PPP over Ethernet (PPPoE)." RFC 2516. (February 1999).

[RFC2529]   Carpenter, B., and C. Jung. "Transmission of IPv6 over IPv4 Domains without Explicit Tunnels." RFC 2529. (March 1999).

[RFC2661]   Townsley, W. M., A. Valencia, A. Rubens, G. S. Pall, G. Zorn, and B. Palter. "Layer Two Tunneling Protocol (L2TP)." RFC 2661. (August 1999).

[UNI31]   ATM Forum. *ATM User Network Interface (UNI) Specification Version 3.1.* Englewood Cliffs, N. J.: Prentice Hall (June 1995).

[UNI40]   ATM Forum. "ATM User-Network Interface (UNI) Signalling Specification Version 4.0." af-sig-0061.000. (July 1996).

Low-Speed Link Technologies

In this chapter, the term *low-speed* covers the range from typical dial-up modem links (in the 14.4Kbit per second to 56Kbit per second range) to Asymmetric Digital Subscriber Line (ADSL) and cable modem (CM) techniques (from a few hundreds of Kbits per second to a few Mbits per second). Low speed links tend to either be Access or wide area network (WAN)—typically providing point-to-point connectivity over moderate to wide geographical areas (a few miles to hundreds or thousands of miles) with customers or clients either being provisioned with connectivity to a local common carrier's exchange (for example, a T1 or E1 circuit) or signaling connectivity on an as-needed basis (for example, dial-up modem connections).

This chapter provides a basic overview of dial-up modem, Integrated Services Digital Network (ISDN), ADSL, and CM technologies and explains how they're typically used to provide inter-router links for IP networks. Observations are given on the particular QoS characteristics of each link type.

7.1 PPP over Dial-Up Links

Today's low-speed dial-up is almost universally through some form of analog modem connected to the traditional public switched telephone network (PSTN) service, which is also referred to as *plain old telephone service (POTS)*. Byte stream connectivity is provided between two Point-to-Point Protocol (PPP) peers—one usually being in a client's PC or home terminal adapter and the other in a service provider's remote access server (RAS), which is a device developed specifically to terminate hundreds or thousands of simultaneous modem and PPP sessions. PPP is deployed with byte-oriented, HDLC-like framing across modem connections, and Multilink PPP is often available [RFC1990]. Most consumer dial-up configurations offer connection rates ranging from 14.4Kbits per second to 56Kbits per second.

> **Note**
>
> An even earlier protocol called Serial Line IP (SLIP) is still sometimes used over dial-up connections [RFC1055]. However, SLIP lacks PPP's authentication and parameter negotiation capabilities, and it is fading out.

Modem connections pose an interesting problem from a QoS perspective because they are not particularly predictable and not always symmetric.

7.1.1 Modems and the Public Switched Telephone Network

A brief description of the problem being solved by modems can help explain their QoS characteristics. The PSTN traditionally provides subscribers with an electrical *analog local loop* connection between homes and the nearest telephone exchange—often at a central office (CO). This local loop connection is not inherently compatible with the digital technologies used in serial lines or computer local area networks (LANs). At its most basic level, a modem (*mo*dulator *dem*odulator) converts arbitrary sequences of ones and zeros into distinct analog signals (modulation) and then reconverts analog signals into ones and zeros (demodulation).

A modem link consists of two modems between which an analog "voice call" has been established through the PSTN (see Figure 7.1). Today's PSTN uses its own digital, circuit-switched core network between telephone exchanges, which means another conversion between analog and digital signal formats is occurring at each exchange. However, this conversion is not the same as the modulation/demodulation occurring in the modems. The analog information coming in to an exchange undergoes analog-to-digital conversion (ADC) to generate a digital bit stream representing the analog signal. At the receiving exchange, a digital-to-analog conversion (DAC) reconstructs the analog signal and transmits it to the receiving modem. The analog signal is then demodulated to reconstruct the originally transmitted bit stream.

The PSTN's internal digital signal represents the analog signal sampled at 8,000 samples per second, with 8- or 7-bit samples—the traditional pulse coded modulation (PCM) scheme for encoding POTS calls—resulting in a bit rate of 64Kbits per second in Europe or 56Kbits per second in North America. However, the signal looks nothing like the original bit stream driving the transmitting modem's modulation process. The need to work through a conventional analog local loop results in a modem call consuming a 64Kbit per second or 56Kbit per second channel inside the PSTN to deliver a variably reliable sub-56Kbit per second channel to the end-user.

Figure 7.1   Modems allow digital communications across an analog public switched telephone network service.

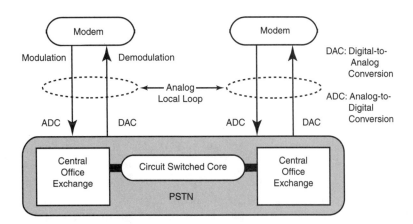

The two following related limitations affect the speed of modem connections:

• Density of bit encoding by the modulation scheme

• Noise introduced into the analog signal prior to ADC or demodulation

Voice calls are explicitly limited to an analog bandwidth of around 3.3KHz at the local exchange. This value sets the upper limit to the number of line transitions (symbols) that may be transmitted per second (the Nyquist rate). The achieved bit rate depends on how many bits per symbol can be encoded by the modulation scheme (for example, through relative phase shifts between successive line transitions). For example, a modulation scheme sending 2,400 symbols per second (*baud*) with an encoding of 4 bits per symbol renders an effective bit rate of 9600 bits per second. However, the demodulation process is sensitive to analog line noise misleading it into incorrectly recognizing symbols. As the bit density per symbol rises, the tolerance to line noise drops. Line noise can be introduced on the loop leading to the receiving modem, but a bigger problem comes at the ADC of the transmitting modem's exchange—analog noise from the hundreds and thousands of other lines in the exchange (known as *crosstalk*) is faithfully digitized, carried across the PSTN, and rendered at the receiving end's modem. Much of the work in developing higher speed modem standards has focused on defining denser symbol encoding schemes that are reliable in the face of line noise.

7.1.2 Variable Line Rates

Two transmission protocols cover most analog dial-up connections in common use today:

- **V.34**—A specification covering bit rates of 28.8Kbits per second and 33.6Kbits per second.

- **V.90**—A specification allowing downstream rates—from Internet service provider (ISP) to client—to theoretically reach 56Kbits per second and the upstream rate—from client to ISP—to reach 33.6Kbits per second [V34, V90].

When a modem connection is established, the modems will negotiate an initial modulation scheme that appears to cope with the existing line quality. This determines the bit rate that can then be announced to the local PPP drivers at each end. However, this rate may change during the call itself. Both V.34 and V.90 protocols continuously monitor the quality of the analog circuit between the two modems to ensure that they are using the most robust encoding scheme at any given time. Because encoding robustness increases as the bit rate decreases, the modems lower their effective bit rate in response to deterioration of the line quality or raise the rate if the line quality improves. The process of dynamically establishing a new bit rate is called *retraining*. In addition to causing an unannounced change in the link's effective throughput, the retraining process itself often results in the modems suspending all data transfer across the link for periods of seconds (a fairly serious jitter!).

7.1.3 Compression and Error-Correction Latency

Another source of jitter and latency is the use of data compression and error correction (for example, V.42 error correction [V42] or V.42bis data compression [V42BIS]) in conjunction with the V.34 or V.90 link. Typically the connection between a computer and its modem allows the PPP driver to send bursts of bytes far more quickly than the established line rate (for example, up to 115Kbits per second or higher with many personal computers). When compression is turned on, modems buffer up the bytes from the PPP driver and attempt to compress each burst before transmitting. Although this buffering and compression process can increase the effective throughput of a link, it also introduces additional latency. An extra wrinkle occurs when error correction is turned on. The modems retransmit any burst that is not correctly received by their peer (most commonly because analog noise is interfering with the encoding/decoding process). Retransmissions consume bandwidth and add latency to that burst being retransmitted. (Continuously poor link quality triggers retraining, and under severe conditions the modems may drop the link entirely.) As with retraining, this activity occurs beneath the PPP interface and is hard to predict.

7.1.4 Asymmetric Throughput

Although the V.34 specification optionally allows for asymmetry (the bit rates can be negotiated independently in each direction and need not be the same), such connections typically have closely matched upstream and downstream speeds. However, the V.90 specification (a convergence of two earlier, proprietary protocols—K56flex and x2) is explicitly asymmetric. It allows up to 56Kbits per second in the downstream direction but limits the upstream to V.34 rates (peaking at 33.6Kbit per second). The trade-off is a consequence of the engineering trick that enables 56Kbits per second in the first place.

The achievable bit rate of a modem connection ultimately depends on the level of noise interfering with the analog signal as it passes through the PSTN. However, as noted earlier the PSTN core is mostly digital. Many companies with large demands for call capacity in and out of the PSTN utilize direct digital connections into the local exchange (carrying tens or hundreds of 64Kbit per second channels on a small number of physical connections, rather than running hundreds of individual analog local loop lines). The V.90 architecture recognizes that ISPs can do the same and thereby removes half of the analog/digital conversions occurring in a typical modem call (see Figure 7.2).

Figure 7.2   V.90 assumes ISP connects via digital loop.

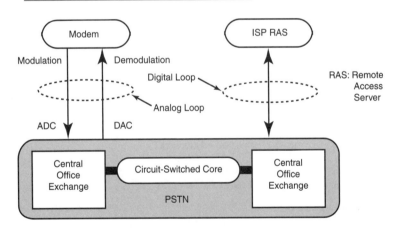

The V.90 specification makes the following assumptions:

- The ISP has a purely digital connection to its local exchange.

- The customer has an analog connection to his or her local exchange.

- Asymmetric bandwidth (higher in the downstream direction) is acceptable for most consumer Internet access applications.

The ISP's modems directly generate the 64Kbit per second or 56Kbit per second digital representation of the analog signal that would have been received at the exchange had the ISP utilized a conventional modem over an analog loop. The advantage is that there's no ADC process on the downstream traffic to pick up crosstalk noise at the ISP's exchange. At the other end, the DAC process generates a clean analog signal for demodulation by the customer's V.90 modem. This practice enables modulation schemes capable of achieving up to 56Kbits per second in the downstream direction (allowing for optimal analog conditions). Because of the uncertainty around the remaining ADC process in the upstream direction, the V.90 specification uses the earlier V.34 scheme toward the ISP (allowing up to 33.6Kbits per second).

The sensitivity to noise being introduced during ADC is such that V.90 cannot function properly on any path that contains more than one conversion process. (The only one allowed is DAC to the customer's local loop.) Interestingly, the downstream bit rate is limited in the United States to 53Kbits per second because of concerns over the signal level being injected into the local loop by the DAC at the customer's end. The V.90 modulation schemes would exceed the Federal Communications Commission (FCC) signal strength limit of –12dbm if they attempted to encode 56Kbits per second. V.90 may run slightly faster downstream in other countries that do not have the same limitation.

Asymmetry is not necessarily a problem—many forms of Internet access generate asymmetric bandwidth demands (for example, Web surfing is often carrying only page requests upstream, but actual page content downstream). However, users need to be careful if they're attempting to engage in interactive video or audio conferencing. Even if a V.90 modem announces a connection speed around 50Kbits per second, outbound transmissions will at best have around 33Kbits per second to play with. From a QoS perspective the biggest concern with modems is their tendency to unexpectedly retrain and shift link speeds without informing the upper-level drivers.

7.1.5 Summary of QoS Characteristics

The QoS characteristics of modem-based dial-up links depend greatly on the call-by-call (and intra-call) behavior of the analog PSTN circuits between each modem. They can be summarized as follows:

- Variable bit rate due to unpredictable retraining.

- Asymmetric bit rates, especially for V.90 connections. Each direction's bit rate can vary separately through retraining.

- Latency due to compression and error correction beneath the PPP driver.

- Jitter due to error correction and retraining events beneath the PPP driver.

- Unpredictable frame expansion due to byte "stuffing."

Although they are the most common method for the average consumer to receive their Internet connectivity, current dial-up links are poorly suited to the reliable support of real-time, interactive, and QoS-sensitive applications. The Integrated Services over Specific Link Layers (ISSLL) working group notes that modem-based dial-up PPP links are unsuitable for guaranteed service and are difficult to use reliably even for controlled-load service [ISLWSVC].

Despite these limitations, dial-up links are extremely common in comparison to some of the more advanced digital access technologies such as ISDN and ADSL. One major benefit is that POTS modems can be deployed without requiring additional equipment from the local telephone company—a perceived (and often real) saving in red tape and headaches! The following sections look at faster, more predictable digital access transports that require upgrades to the telephone company's own infrastructure.

7.2 *Integrated Services Digital Network*

Telephony companies designed Integrated Services Digital Network (ISDN) to provide a consumer digital network service that leveraged their existing investment in electrical analog loops to their customer sites. From the perspective of an IP network builder, ISDN provides on-demand, signaled point-to-point connectivity in the form of one or more 64Kbit per second bit-serial or byte-serial clear channel circuits. You can run PPP, Frame Relay (FR), or something else entirely over these circuits. Because of the costs associated with installing ISDN, the most common scenario has the ISDN link providing a router-to-router link between remote (or home) offices and a router (or RAS) on a corporate or ISP backbone.

As with POTS dial-up service, users may set up and tear down ISDN calls whenever the need arises. However, unlike modem-based dial-up connections, an ISDN connection offers quite predictable QoS characteristics.

7.2.1 Interfaces over the Analog Loop

One goal for ISDN was that it should reuse the existing analog loop infrastructure. ISDN utilizes a technology known as *Digital Subscriber Line (DSL)* in which bit streams are modulated into an analog waveform for transport over the local loop between customer and PSTN exchange. Although this process may seem similar to the use of voice-band modems in the dial-up scenario, DSL differs in two ways:

- A DSL link is terminated at the local exchange (not the remote exchange, as in a typical POTS modem call).

- ISDN's DSL "modems" are not limited to the 3.3KHz analog bandwidth of a voice modem, using a broader spectrum from 0 to 80KHz–120KHz to achieve higher symbol rates (and, hence, higher bit rates).

Terminating the analog section of an ISDN link at the local exchange allows the digital bit stream to be reconstituted (demodulated) and switched natively through the PSTN's digital core. Because DSL overlaps the frequency band used by POTS, an upgrade of a POTS line to ISDN displaces the original POTS service. (It must be replaced by an ISDN-based phone.) Two types of ISDN service are defined:

- Basic Rate Interface (BRI)

- Primary Rate Interface (PRI)

These interfaces consist of two or more B-channels (*bearer* channels, for carriage of user data) and a D-channel (for signaling of B-channel connections and an optional end-to-end packet-switched service). B-channels are 64Kbits per second (derived from the standard PCM sample rate for a single voice channel), whereas the D-channel may be 16Kbits per second (BRI) or 64Kbits per second (PRI).

A BRI is intended for low-capacity connections, consisting of one 16Kbit per second D-channel and two B-channels (often referred to as D+2B) for a total capacity of 144Kbits per second. A PRI is intended for sites with aggregate capacity needs in excess of a single BRI. In the United States and Japan, a PRI consists of one 64Kbit per second D-channel and 23 B-channels (D+23B) to fit within a standard 1.544Mbit per second T1 transport (the remaining 8Kbits per second are used for framing). In many other parts of the world (for example, Europe), the PRI consists of one 64Kbit per second D-channel and 30 B-channels (D+30B) to fit within a standard 2.048Mbit per second E1 transport (the remaining 64Kbits per second are used for framing).

Figure 7.3 shows a highly simplified view of the ISDN connection between a user and local exchange. The box labeled ISDN NT is the network termination equipment that provides ISDN modem functionality at either end of the traditional analog local loop. The digital link between network terminations (NTs) is always on. The D-channel terminates on an ISDN switching component at the local exchange. Users may initiate signaling on the D-channel at any time to set up and tear down B-channel connections. The remote PRI or BRI on which the B-channel must terminate is specified during the setup signaling. An open B-channel represents a synchronous, bidirectional 64Kbit per second circuit through the PSTN's switched core to the selected remote PRI or BRI.

Figure 7.3   ISDN interfaces are analog only to the local exchange.

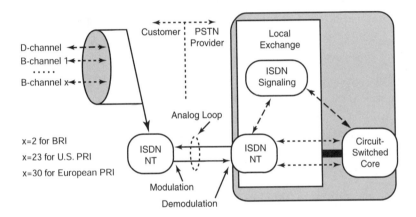

7.2.2 *PPP over the B-Channel(s)*

Depending on the nature of the terminating equipment, an ISDN customer's host or router may see a bit-serial or byte-serial connection over a B-channel to the remote peer. The default is to use bit-serial HDLC framing over a bit-serial circuit with byte-serial HDLC framing a configurable fall back [RFC1618]. In either case, the B-channel is a clear digital connection between the peer PPP entities. Conventional Link Control Protocol (LCP) and Network Control Protocol (NCP) negotiations are required before the link is finally declared up from the IP layer's perspective.

Multiple B-channels may be established between the same two ISDN interfaces, allowing an aggregate point-to-point bandwidth in excess of the basic 64Kbit per second rate. Although a scheme called *BONDING* has been proposed to spread traffic across B-channels at the bit level, the recommended approach of the Internet Engineering Task Force (IETF) is to spread traffic at the packet level using Multilink PPP [RFC1990].

When only a single B-channel is available (for example, across a BRI where the other channel is dedicated for some non-PPP application), Multiclass Extension to Multi-Link PPP (MCML) and/or real-time framing (RTF) may be employed to interleave QoS-sensitive traffic [PPPMCML, PPPRTF]. Of course, because the B-channels are independently signaled digital circuits, numerous combinations of Multilink PPP, MCML, and RTF may be employed between ISDN-attached PPP peers. The fixed 64Kbit per second capacity of each B-channel means that the perturbation of point-to-point QoS comes solely from HDLC payload expansion.

7.2.3   Uses for the D-Channel

Without going into the details of ISDN signaling, it is sufficient to note that an end-user can establish and tear down B-channel connections at any time by appropriate signaling across the D-channel. Signaling messages are carried between the end-user and the ISDN signaling entity in the local exchange.

Although not always supported by every PSTN provider, the ISDN signaling service can allow short frames to be sent from one end-user to another in a connectionless mode (no preestablishment of a circuit is required). In this mode the D-channel offers a frame-oriented service and may be used to support a low bit rate PPP link between two BRIs or PRIs.

7.2.4   Summary of QoS Characteristics

ISDN links do not adapt to varying line conditions by retraining or in any other way unexpectedly varying their transmission rate. The D- and B-channels are either functioning or not. For this reason, they provide a fairly predictable link technology upon which to build a QoS-enabled IP service. All that remains is the variable payload expansion characteristics of HDLC-like framing when running PPP over such links.

7.3   Asymmetric Digital Subscriber Line

An entire family of DSL technologies—generically referred to as *xDSL*—offers varying degrees of complexity, symmetry, bit rates, and robustness. ISDN utilizes the original DSL. The most interesting next-generation xDSL technology for high-speed Internet access to homes and businesses appears to be ADSL. Although other types exist—such as High-speed DSL (HDSL), Very high- speed DSL (VDSL), and so on—the focus, here, is on ADSL.

Three things differentiate ADSL service from DSL-based ISDN:

- ADSL offers significantly higher (albeit asymmetric) bit rates across the existing analog loop. Typically, installations support up to 9Mbits per second downstream (toward the customer site) and up to 640Kbits per second upstream.

- ADSL is not an end-to-end network service. It simply provides the last hop to a customer site for a wide area cell or packet transport service—for example, ATM or PPP—running in parallel to the existing PSTN. This technique allows high-speed cell or packet-switched services to be delivered to customer sites simply by piggybacking onto the existing analog loop. Wide area connectivity is achieved through separate cell or packet-switched backbone networks, running entirely independently of the telephone company's existing circuit-switched core.

- The frequencies used by ADSL do not overlap those used for POTS or ISDN service. So with appropriate splitters, ADSL installations do not displace preexisting POTS or ISDN use of a local loop.

7.3.1 Enhancing the Analog Loop

Figure 7.4 shows a grossly simplified view of the ADSL architecture. Each end of the analog loop has an ADSL modem—transmission unit (TU). Somewhat similar to the ISDN case, the digital bit stream is modulated onto frequencies above the voice band, both to share the loop with existing POTS services and to achieve far higher bit rates. Unlike ISDN, the ADSL link is typically assumed to be a single-hop transport for ATM cell or variable-length packet traffic between a customer site and an edge device on the parallel cell-switching or packet-switching core network. At the local PSTN exchange, the ADSL traffic is tapped off and passed directly to this edge device (multiplexer, or mux).

In each direction, ADSL supports two distinct paths with different latency and error-rate characteristics (defined in ITU specification G.992.1 [G9921] and ANSI T1.413 [T1413]). The *Fast* path provides minimal residual latency but does nothing special to reduce the bit error rate. The *Interleave* path utilizes additional encoding to increase the channel's robustness against bit errors at the expense of increased residual latency (configurable up to 60msec, typically 20msec). Fast and Interleave paths do not have to be in use simultaneously and may be configured differently in each direction. A splitterless version of ADSL, which supports only the Interleave path, is defined in ITU specification G.992.2 [G9922].

Figure 7.4   Asymmetric Digital Subscriber Line piggy-backs dedicated cell/packet access onto the local loop.

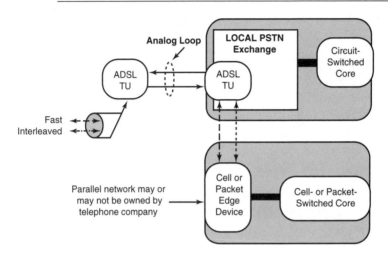

As noted earlier, modulation schemes typically trade off bit rates and error rates for given levels of electrical noise (crosstalk) on the analog loop. Because bit recovery is more robust at the customer's end than at the electrically noisy local exchange, ADSL is designed for higher bit rates toward the customer. ADSL modems typically provide a duplex (bidirectional) channel running between 16Kbits per second and 640Kbits per second and an additional simplex channel providing downstream rates from 1.5Mbits per second to 9Mbits per second. The actual speeds depend on the quality of the local loop over which the ADSL modems are to operate—longer or older loops lead to lower speeds.

When both Fast and Interleave paths are supported by the ADSL modems, each duplex or simplex channel's capacity is distributed between the two paths in a configurable manner. ANSI and ITU-T are looking at methods for dynamically reconfiguring the distribution of bandwidth between Fast and Interleave paths when both are in use (dynamic rate repartitioning, or DRR) and dynamic adjustment of a channel's total bandwidth (dynamic rate adaptation, or DRA). The expectation is that these schemes allow changes within 125msec without disrupting the ADSL connection although they may perturb the higher-layer protocols running over the ADSL link. G.992.2 links do not have dual paths, but they do have a Fast Retrain mode that can suspend the ADSL link for up to 3 seconds while renegotiating channel rates up or down.

7.3.2 *PPP over Asymmetric Digital Subscriber Line*

By itself, ADSL provides an unstructured point-to-point bit-serial link, which immediately suggests that ADSL can be used to connect two PPP peers. The ADSL Forum's recommendation covering native PPP over ADSL [TR003] is that bit-serial HDLC-like framing be used as per RFC 1662. The HDLC link terminates within the local exchange, either at a network access server, or NAS (if the PPP session is also being terminated at the exchange) or at a L2TP access concentrator, or LAC (if L2TP is being used to terminate the PPP session elsewhere on the parallel data network [TR011]). All the usual PPP extension protocols may be run across such a link.

The ISP terminating the PPP session can be different from the company providing the ADSL link or local loop. However, HDLC-framed PPP directly over ADSL allows only one PPP session, and therefore one ISP at any one time. Because of this limitation, most deployments are likely to have an additional multiplexing function between the ADSL and PPP layers.

7.3.3 *ATM over Asymmetric Digital Subscriber Line*

ADSL is also finding favor as a custom access technology for ATM service. The ADSL Forum recommendation for ATM over ADSL [TR017] specifies that the ATM transport layer utilize the ADSL link as a regular synchronous bit stream—that is, using Header Error Check (HEC)-delineation of cell headers to find cell boundaries. Using ATM across an ADSL link provides two key benefits:

- Different virtual path/virtual channel identifier (VPI/VCI) values enable the ADSL channels to be subdivided into distinct logical links (channels).

- ATM cells provide a finer granularity for interleaving real-time and non-real-time traffic.

From the ATM layer's perspective, little about ADSL requires unique consideration—it simply provides a cell transport between a customer site and an ATM switch—via a DSL Access Multiplexor (DSLAM) at the local exchange. Conventional User Network Interface (UNI) signaling and VPI/VCI assignment rules apply and are dictated by the ATM equipment at either end of the link. Switched virtual connections (SVCs) and permanent virtual connections (PVCs) can be configured between the customer site and endpoints anywhere on the ATM backbone network.

However, from a QoS perspective the ATM layer needs to account for asymmetry and variability in the ADSL bit stream's bandwidth. Either Fast or Interleave paths may be used (with consequential variation of the latency) although only the Interleave path is available when the link is G.992.2 compliant. Fast Retrains (G.992.2) or dynamic rate adaptation/repartitioning can result in temporary glitches in the cell transport. The relationship between ADSL rate changes and ATM QoS is still under study.

7.3.4 PPP over ATM over Asymmetric Digital Subscriber Line

As noted earlier, HDLC-framed PPP consumes the entire ADSL link for a single PPP session between customer site and ISP. If a customer site is to have simultaneous access to multiple ISPs, some method involving tunneling or virtual links has to be established, either above or below the PPP layer.

From the ADSL Forum's perspective, the obvious solution is to place a virtual link technique below the PPP layer. Given the prevailing assumptions about ATM being essential for "good QoS" (and the perceived requirement to support native ATM services to customer sites anyway), running ATM over the ADSL link seems natural. Distinct ATM virtual connections then support separate PPP sessions to each ISP (as noted in Chapter 6, "Link Layers Beneath IP," AAL 5 service provides frame delineation) [RFC2364]. This practice has the additional benefit of allowing the NAS function to be located outside the local exchange; indeed it can be located anywhere an ATM virtual connection can be terminated.
The familiar sawtooth efficiency curve for packet service over AAL 5 means that the achievable PPP/ATM/ADSL link rate depends on the distribution of PPP packet sizes.

7.3.5 Frame User Network Interface over Asymmetric Digital Subscriber Line

The ADSL Forum also describes how frames may be transported across an ADSL link using the ATM Forum's Frame User Network Interface (FUNI) format [FUNI, TR003]. The HDLC-framing is similar to that used for PPP with the major difference being that FUNI frames carry a virtual circuit identifier in a 2-byte FUNI header after the HDLC start flag (see Figure 7.5). This feature enables a number of virtual links to be established across the ADSL link. Although TR-011 [TR011] describes how parallel PPP sessions may be carried over FUNI, this solution does not have as much industry support as running PPP over ATM over ADSL [TR011]. FUNI is still a variable-length frame technique like basic PPP and lacks the capability to interleave real-time traffic at the cell level.

Figure 7.5   Basic Point-to-Point Protocol/Frame User Network Interface format over Asymmetric Digital Subscriber Line.

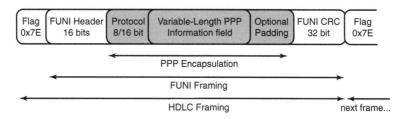

7.3.6   Summary of QoS Characteristics

ADSL links provide configurable downstream bandwidths between 1.5Mbits per second and 9Mbits per second and upstream bandwidths from 16Kbits per second to 640Kbits per second. If the Interleave path is chosen for robustness against impulsive noise-induced bit errors, a 20msec latency is typically added to the link's normal propagation delays. Depending on the desired robustness, the Interleave path's latency can be as high as 60msec. For ATM over ADSL installations, the Interleave path is the recommended default (and the only option when the ADSL link is compliant with G.992.2). Although likely to be infrequent, ADSL does allow for channel capacity to be altered while in use—redistribution between the Fast and Interleave paths may disrupt transmission for up to 125msec, and G.992.2 Fast Retrain can halt transmission for up to 3 seconds. The implications of these characteristics on QoS-enabled IP networking are still under consideration.

7.4   Data over Cable TV

Whereas DSL techniques are designed to leverage a telephone company's existing infrastructure in analog (copper) loop, the cable TV industry has been working on an alternative approach to digital connectivity. In many parts of the world, a substantial investment has been made in the cable TV infrastructure, and not surprisingly its owners are looking to utilize this infrastructure for residential and business Internet access.

7.4.1   An Asymmetric Tree

Initially designed as a private distribution network for regular TV signals (the common acronym, CATV, stands for *community area* TV), a cable TV network is typically deployed as an inverted tree of optical and/or coaxial cables serving a neighborhood, town, or city. At the root of the tree is the *head end*, where programming is injected by the cable system's owner. The head end feeds intermediate branches of the tree spanning across the operator's region. These intermediate branches then split again to feed individual streets and houses in the streets. Each house receives an analog, radio frequency (RF) signal compatible with its TV receiving equipment.

A TV channel is around 6MHz wide. Early networks based solely on coaxial cables operated between 50MHz and 450MHz in the downstream direction, supporting roughly 60 channels. More recent designs utilize fiber optics from the head end and reserve coaxial cable for the last hop into the customer premises (called hybrid fiber coax, or HFC). They are capable of operating to at least 750MHz for up to 110 channels. The bandwidth from 5MHz to 42MHz is reserved for upstream traffic.

Broadband RF modems are quite capable of encoding a multi-Mbit per second bit stream onto a 6MHz TV channel. However, using a cable network for digital access is not as easy as simply assigning one TV channel each for downstream and upstream traffic and handing everyone cable modems (CMs). First, many cable TV networks tend to be only weakly bidirectional or completely unidirectional (not entirely surprising, considering their original goal of carrying TV signals from the head end to customers). Second, cable networks experience analog noise interference and loss characteristics (especially in the upstream direction from customer to head end), making life difficult for CMs. Third, the cable network is a shared medium—capacity must be shared among all the downstream subscribers.

Asymmetry in the distribution network's analog performance means that the head end, or CM terminating system (CMTS), is the best place for data to be modulated *onto* a TV channel. Whereas the customer sites are the best places for data to be demodulated *off* a TV channel. In the downstream direction, a 6MHz channel can support 27Mbits per second—64 level quadrature amplitude modulation (64QAM) encoding—or 36Mbits per second (256QAM encoding). However, IP support requires bidirectional connectivity.

Figure 7.6 shows two existing solutions. When the cable network is old and/or essentially unidirectional, an external network (typically the PSTN) is used as the reverse channel. (Tight coupling is required at the packet level at each end so that the disjoint paths appear to be a single bidirectional link that just happens to have asymmetric bandwidth and latency characteristics.) On newer (for example, two-way HFC) networks, the CMs may transmit upstream toward the head end over the cable itself, using a channel in the 5MHz to 42MHz range. More robust encoding schemes—for example, 16QAM or quadrature phase shift keying (QPSK)—are used on the noisier upstream paths, leading to lower bit rates (between 320Kbits per second and 10Mbits per second, using a variable-width 200KHz to 3.2MHz RF channel).

Figure 7.6 Basic cable TV architectures.

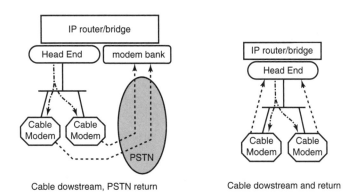

Cable downstream, PSTN return

Cable downstream and return

7.4.2 *Data over Cable Service Interface Specification and IEEE 802.14*

As tends to happen sometimes, an official standards development effort has been superseded by a grassroots industry effort. IEEE's 802.14 committee began developing an ATM-based solution for data over cable TV but has since been overtaken by a packet-oriented alternative referred to as Data over Cable Service Interface Specification (DOCSIS) [DOCSIS]. The development of DOCSIS was motivated by a group of cable operators intent on rapidly finding a solution to their desire to offer high-speed Internet access. Both approaches utilize almost equivalent digital encoding schemes at the physical layer (mentioned above).

DOCSIS focuses on supporting Ethernet-framed packet transport between CMTS and CMs on the assumption that the overall service is transparent bridging between the customer's LAN to an ISP-run router co-resident with the CMTS. (The CMTS may simply support LAN bridging with the ISP router located elsewhere at the head-end location.) In the downstream direction, the CMTS is the sole transmitter onto a shared medium—every CM sees every bit transmitted by the CMTS. Upstream transmissions are essentially point to point—CMs transmit directly to the CMTS, rather than to each other. The CMTS implements an internal media access control (MAC) forwarder function that reflects upstream frames back downstream—thereby emulating a shared LAN between all CMs and the CMTS. (Because the cable network is effectively open, link-level encryption provides some basic security against eavesdropping neighbors who are not part of the emulated LAN.)

Downstream transmissions from the CMTS are actually formatted as regular sequences of 188-octet MPEG-2 frames, carrying 4 octets of header and 184 octets of user payload [MPEG2] (intended to allow future flexibility for the CMTS to interleave data and digital video over the infrastructure). Flexible encoding rules allow DOCSIS MAC frames (which carry Ethernet frames or DOCSIS control messages) to span multiple MPEG-2 frames or to have multiple consecutive MAC frames carried by a single MPEG-2 frame. As a consequence, no direct equivalent exists to the AAL 5 segmentation and reassembly (SAR) overhead and jitter of mapping IP packets into ATM.

In the upstream direction, the channel is divided into "minislots," and a form of time-division multiple access (TDMA) between the CMs is directly and dynamically regulated by the CMTS. Every CM listens to regular bandwidth allocation map (MAP) messages coming from the CMTS that announce who is entitled to upcoming minislots. A CM spreads the transmission of its own MAC messages (carrying Ethernet frames or DOCSIS control messages) over minislots whenever it is entitled to transmit. By dynamically regulating minislot assignments, the CMTS controls bandwidth allocations and synchronizes CM transmissions on the upstream path.

7.4.3 Data over Cable Service Interface Specification QoS

It is expected that CMs may need to concurrently support multiple QoS classes. This mechanism can be modeled as a distributed scheduler with each CM representing one or more queues feeding onto the upstream link. A CM requiring only one type of scheduling from the CMTS can be considered as one queue. A CM supporting two or more traffic classes can be considered as multiple queues with the CMTS assigning different minislot distributions to the individual queues. Minislot assignment is achieved through the use of service IDs (SIDs). Every CM is assigned a unique SID for each distinct upstream scheduling service (also known as traffic class) it requires, and the CMTS distributes minislots on a per SID basis according to the temporal needs associated with that SID.

For jitter-sensitive traffic, a CM requests the CMTS to assign minislots with rigid regularity to one of its SIDs. The CMTS can be more relaxed in its assignment of minislots to SIDs for Best Effort or jitter-insensitive traffic. With such a finely grained unit of allocation (a minislot is $2^N \times 6.25$usec, where N = 0,1,...7), the CMTS can accurately slice the upstream channel between SIDs (whether associated with the same or different CMs). Ultimately MAC frames may be interleaved with fine granularity at the minislot level.

Clearly, the QoS characteristics of a DOCSIS system are highly configurable and dependent on the minislot allocation algorithm(s) implemented on the CMTS. No specific algorithms are mandated by the DOCSIS specification, and the industry itself is still fairly new, so analyzing a "typical" case is difficult. In the end, downstream and upstream channel capacity is shared among all the users of a particular CMTS (which may number in the hundreds or thousands). Sharing means that available capacity for any single user may be significantly lower than the peak channel capacity. In the absence of fixed minislot assignments, a user's achieved throughput may fluctuate quite widely from instant to instant due to the instantaneous demands from other users sharing the same CMTS.

7.5 References

[DOCSIS] CableLabs. "Data-over-Cable Service Interface Specifications Radio Frequency Interface Specification SP-RFIv1.1-I01-990311." (1999).

[FUNI] ATM Forum. "Frame Based User-to-Network Interface (FUNI) Specification v2." str-saa-funi-01.01. (December 1996).

[G9921] ITU-T Recommendation G.992.1. "Asymmetrical Digital Subscriber Line (ADSL) Transceivers." (June 1999).

[G9922] ITU-T Recommendation G.992.2. "Splitterless Asymmetric Digital Subscriber Line (ADSL) Transceivers." (June 1999).

[ISLWSVC] Jackowski, Steve, David Putzolu, Eric Crawley, and Bruce Davie. "Integrated Services Mappings for Low Speed Networks." Internet Draft (work in progress) draft-ietf-issll-isslow-svcmap-08.txt. (17 May 1999).

[MPEG2] ITU-T Recommendation H.222.0. "Information Technology—Generic Coding of Moving Pictures and Associated Audio Information Systems." (July 1995).

[PPPMCML] Bormann, C. "The Multi-Class Extension to Multi-Link PPP." Internet Draft (work in progress) draft-ietf-issll-isslow-mcml-06.txt. (June 1999).

[PPPRTF] Bormann, C. "PPP in a Real-Time Oriented HDLC-like Framing." Internet Draft (work in progress) draft-ietf-issll-isslow-rtf-04.txt. (April 1999).

[RFC1055] Romkey, J. "A Nonstandard for Transmission of IP Datagrams over Serial Lines: SLIP." Internet Request for Comment 1055. (June 1988).

[RFC1618] Simpson, W. "PPP over ISDN." RFC 1618. (May 1994).

[RFC1990] Sklower, K., B. Lloyd, G. McGregor, D. Carr, and T. Coradetti. "The PPP Multilink Protocol (MP)." RFC 1990. (August 1996).

[RFC2364] Gross, G., M. Kaycee, A. Lin, A. Malis, and J. Stephens. "PPP over AAL5." RFC 2364. (July 1998).

[T1413]   ANSI. "Network and Customer Installation Interfaces—Asymmetric Digital Subscriber Line (ADSL) Metallic Interface." T1.413. Issue 2, T1E1.4/98-007/R5. (1998).

[TR003]   ADSL Forum. "TR-003: Framing and Encapsulation Standards for ADSL: Packet Mode." (1997).

[TR011]   ADSL Forum. "TR-011: An End-to-End Packet Mode Architecture with Tunneling and Service Selection." (1998).

[TR017]   ADSL Forum. "TR-017: ATM over ADSL Recommendation." (1999).

[V34]   ITU-T Recommendation V.34. "A modem operating at data signalling rates of up to 33 600 bit/s for use on the general switched telephone network and on leased point-to-point 2-wire telephone-type circuits." (February 1998).

[V42]   ITU-T Recommendation V.42. "Error-correcting procedures for DCEs using asynchronous-to-synchronous conversion." (October 1996).

[V42BIS]   ITU-T Recommendation V.42 BIS. "Data compression procedures for data circuit terminating equipment (DCE) using error correction procedures." (January 1990).

[V90]   ITU-T Recommendation V.90. "A digital modem and analogue modem pair for use on the Public Switched Telephone Network (PSTN) at data signalling rates of up to 56 000 bit/s downstream and up to 33 600 bit/s upstream." (September 1998).

CHAPTER

8

High-Speed Link Technologies

In this chapter *high-speed* refers to link technologies that provide speeds upward of 100Mbits per second. In the LAN environments, both electrical (copper wired) and optical (fiber based) techniques are used at these speeds and are usually arranged as shared or switched media in arbitrary mesh topologies. In WAN environments, the solutions are usually based on optical fiber transport, which are topologically arranged as point-to-point links or rings built from a closed loop of point-to-point segments.

Although a number of conceivable permutations exist, this chapter focuses on a few key and interesting examples. The Synchronous Optical Network/Synchronous Digital Hierarchy (SONET/SDH) transmission hierarchy clearly dominates discussion of WAN techniques but new high-speed framing methods such as simplified data link (SDL) and link-multiplication techniques such as wave-division multiplexing are becoming equally important. In the LAN, the predominant technology is Ethernet, a shared-medium solution that is becoming commonly deployed in switched hub-and-star topologies.

8.1 IEEE 802.3/Ethernet

Generically known as Ethernet, the IEEE802.3 specification defines what is probably the most well known high-speed LAN technology today [8023]. Although a number of variations exist running over different physical media, Ethernet a provides a very familiar service model—variable-length packets may be transmitted in a connectionless mode to one or more destinations attached to the network. Ethernet interfaces are identified by one or more globally unique (at least within the scope of the local Ethernet network) 48-bit addresses, and packets carry the full 48-bit addresses to explicitly identify their source and destination(s). Ethernet addresses have no routing hierarchy and, therefore, have limited topological significance—an Ethernet network is generally considered "flat."

> **Note**
>
> Unicast addresses identify a single destination. Group addresses identify one or more Ethernet destinations that take a copy of (receive) the packet if they consider themselves members of the group at the time the packet is transmitted. Every interface receives a packet with a *broadcast* destination address of all ones.

Reliability is not built into the service—the source Ethernet interface can confirm that it transmitted the packet, but cannot confirm that any given packet was received by its destination(s). Likewise, classic Ethernet provides very limited control of transmission latency and jitter, although solutions do exist to extend Ethernet's QoS capabilities.

Various physical layer technologies have been used to support Ethernet. It became popular with a 10Mbit per second shared broadcast, bus technology and has evolved along a number of axes—alternative media configurations (stars, trees, and point-to-point) and speeds (100Mbits per second and 1Gbit per second with 10Gbits per second being developed). The physical layers have evolved from simple electrical shared base-band technology to optical point-to-point technology while always retaining the basic Ethernet frame format.

Ethernet's success is no doubt due to its simple and effective service model and relatively flexible physical layer designs. (Other LAN technologies, such as Fiber Distributed Data Interface, or FDDI, and token ring, are not described here.)

8.1.1 Frame Format

Figure 8.1 shows the basic Ethernet frame format. Every frame's transmission is preceded by 64 bits of preamble and start flag delimiter (SFD) during which all other receivers on the media synchronize with the sender. The destination address leads the frame and is read by other Ethernet interfaces in real time to determine whether they are the frame's intended recipient. The source address carries the identity of the frame's source Ethernet interface, and the 16-bit Type field (*EtherType*) identifies the upper-layer protocol whose bytes make up the payload. After the payload, the frame terminates with a 32-bit Frame Check Sequence (FCS).

Figure 8.1   Basic Ethernet frame format.

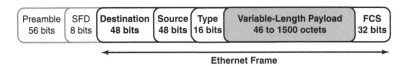

Some examples of EtherType values include

- 0x0800 (IPv4 packets)

- 0x86DD (IPv6 packets)

- 0x8847/0x8848 (MPLS frames)

For comparison, Figure 8.2 shows how the IEEE 802.3 committee originally defined its version of Ethernet. The EtherType becomes a Length field (whereas Ethernet determines the frame's length from the media-specific layer), and it is followed by a logical link control/sub network access point (LLC/SNAP) header precisely defining the contents of the variable-length payload. Most networks have no need to run the LLC link layer protocols between end stations, and so this form is not as popular as regular Ethernet. (Ethernet and original IEEE 802.3 frames may share the same media—the Length/EtherType field is less than 0x600 if it is a legal packet length, an 802.3 frame, or more than 0x600 if it's an EtherType for an Ethernet frame.)

Figure 8.2   Basic IEEE 802.3 frame format with logical link control/sub network access point encapsulation.

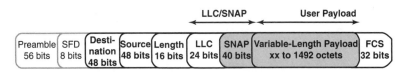

8.1.2   *Carrier Sense Multiple Access with Collision Detection*

Ethernet has frequently been characterized by the use of Carrier Sense Multiple Access with Collision Detection (CSMA/CD) to mediate link access in its earliest incarnations. The classic 10Mbit per second Ethernet utilizes a bit-serial, shared base-band network in which only one interface can transmit at any time. CSMA/CD provides a distributed method for time-division multiplexing of everyone's traffic onto the shared medium. However, the notable issue from a QoS perspective is that CSMA/CD is *probabilistic*—it can take variable and unpredictable amounts of time for an interface to obtain uncontested access to the shared medium each time it has a frame to transmit. In the extreme, the transmission is aborted when an interface decides too much time has elapsed without successfully obtaining access. The lack of guaranteed time slots ensures jitter and latency rises as the average offered load (and number of senders) rises.

CSMA/CD allows senders to attempt transmission whenever they have a frame to send and the shared medium has been quiet for a period of time (known as the interframe gap—9.6 microseconds on 10Mbit per second Ethernets) with the proviso that they wait a short random period if previous attempts have resulted in a *collision*. While transmitting, the sender also monitors the medium to detect possible collisions with other senders who started transmitting their frame's preamble at the same time. The frames are long enough to ensure that all parties on the shared medium detect the collision, at which point everyone "backs off" for a random short period before trying again. When a collision is detected, the sender continues to transmit a short jam signal before ceasing to ensure that everyone is aware of the collision. The retry algorithm uses *truncated exponential back off,* where the sender waits a random number of *slot times* between 1 and 2^N before making another transmission attempt (N is the number of collision/back-off events so far for this frame). For 10Mbit per second Ethernet, a slot time is 512 microseconds.

Frames must be of a minimum size to ensure that any two distant interfaces transmitting simultaneously will "see" the collision before completing their packet's transmission. (For 10Mbit per second Ethernet, the minimum frame must be 512 bits, 64 bytes, long.)

Statistically one sender is going to eventually begin its preamble early enough so that all the other senders see that the medium is busy and defer until the first sender's packet transmits to completion. Per-packet transmission jitter increases as the number of concurrent senders (and, hence, the probability of access collisions) increases. Back off does not occur indefinitely—after an interface cycles through 15 collision/back-off events (16 attempts to access the media), it aborts the packet's transmission entirely.

The probabilistic nature of CSMA/CD makes it difficult to predict the performance of an Internet Protocol (IP) path flowing over an Ethernet link. Many studies often end up vastly simplifying their model of the upper-layer traffic driving the network to make the problem tractable, but without helping the average engineer reach useful conclusions.

8.1.3 Bridging

A number of media- and frame-level devices are available to extend the scope of an Ethernet network. At the media-level, CSMA/CD's correct operation requires that all senders and receivers are able to see the consequences of each other's transmissions (to sense other transmissions and collisions). Ethernet *repeaters* may be used to tie two Ethernet networks together at the bit (media) level. However, CSMA/CD itself imposes a practical limit on the size of a repeater-joined network (because collision detection must be reliable between the two most distant nodes on the combined network).

Larger Ethernet networks require the use of CSMA/CD to be de-coupled from the scope over which Ethernet frames may be transmitted. This condition is achieved by connecting individual Ethernet networks through *bridges*. An Ethernet bridge receives and copies entire frames from one network to another by using independent CSMA/CD media access on each interface. If a sender on one network (LAN segment) begins transmitting at the same time as a sender on another segment, no collision occurs because the bridge is not acting as a repeater (although CSMA/CD still controls media access within each segment). When the two senders have completed, the bridge attempts to forward copies of their frames to the other segment in each case. As shown in Figure 8.3, a *bridged Ethernet* network can be larger than any single CSMA/CD-constrained LAN segment.

Figure 8.3   A bridged Ethernet is larger than any individual LAN segment.

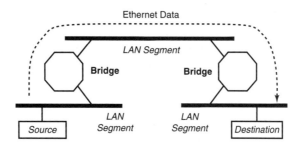

A simple bridge might flood copies of a frame out of every interface except the one on which the frame was received and is sufficient for simple topologies that contain no loops. (Most bridges today are actually "learning" bridges that track the addresses of Ethernet stations from which they see traffic. Using this learned information, the bridge is able to forward Ethernet frames directly toward the destination, rather than blindly flooding frames to all ports.)

However, a loop-free physical topology implies that no redundant paths exist between segments making up the Ethernet network. Introducing redundant bridges provides protection against any single bridge failure-isolating sections of the network. However, redundant paths also introduce loops. Using flooding bridges under these circumstances causes permanent looping of Ethernet frames around the network. To avoid loops while still supporting redundant paths, real Ethernet bridges are required to run a *spanning tree* protocol and only forward frames out interfaces indicated as being on the spanning tree. (A *spanning tree* is the set of branches that cover all nodes in the network once without crossing each other and, thus, is loop free.) In practice bridges must conform to the IEEE 802.1D's bridge and spanning tree protocol specification [8021D]. The protocol dynamically rebuilds the tree in response to events such as individual networks being disconnected or rearranged.

8.1.4 Virtual LANs

Virtual LAN (or VLAN) techniques enable a single physical Ethernet infrastructure (possibly bridged) to simultaneously emulate multiple parallel Ethernets. One application is to enable multiple subnets of an IP network to co-exist on the same Ethernet network without requiring any convoluted IP-level routing magic—each VLAN represents a distinct link-level shared network. The IEEE 802.1Q specification applies to the introduction of VLANs into bridged and nonbridged Ethernet networks [8021Q].

Figure 8.4 shows how VLAN information is carried per-frame as a form of encapsulation. (The IEEE 802.3 committee increased the maximum legal Ethernet frame length by four octets, and so unlike normal encapsulation, the additional four octets do not shrink the maximum size of the user payload.) The EtherType of 0x8100 indicates to all attached receivers that the payload is a VLAN frame. IEEE802.1Q refers to this EtherType as the Tag Protocol ID (TPID). The frame's next two octets are a Tag Control Information (TCI) field containing a 12-bit VLAN ID, a one-bit canonical format indicator (CFI), and a 3-bit User Priority field (discussed in the next section). Following the TCI field is the EtherType for the actual user payload that follows. The receiver(s) identified by the frame's destination address are assumed to support one or more virtual Ethernet interfaces—the VLAN ID specifies which of these interfaces will receive the frame. Further processing occurs based on the payload's EtherType as though received over a regular (non-VLAN) interface.

Figure 8.4   Ethernet frame with 802.1Q VLAN header.

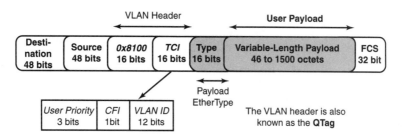

Because VLANs are a *topological* abstraction above the media access layer, they do not, per se, bring any more or less QoS control to an Ethernet environment. However, the 3-bit User Priority field in the TCI is useful in a broader context described next.

8.1.5 Managing QoS

The Internet Engineering Task Force (IETF) working group on Integrated Services over Specific Link Layers (ISSLL) has been working on the issue of providing predictable latency and jitter characteristics over Ethernet-based IP hops [IS802]. In Ethernet networks, such control boils down to constraining the unpredictable behavior of CSMA/CD media access—the media bit rates are fixed, and octet transparency does not rely on high-level data link control (HDLC)-like stuffing. Ideally the solution ought to be deployable in existing LANs with minimal disruption and be able to share resources with conventional CSMA/CD-based interfaces running just fine today.

Efficiency

Unlike Asynchronous Transfer Mode (ATM), no segmentation into fixed-size cells occurs with CSMA/CD; and unlike HDLC-framed services, there is no random payload expansion due to bit or byte transparency. Figure 8.5 shows the maximum efficiency of a CSMA/CD Ethernet against user payload size. Overhead includes the 56 bits of preamble, 8 bits of SFD, 14 octets of Ethernet header, 32 bits of FCS, and 96 bit times of enforced interframe gap (9.6usec on 10Mbit per second Ethernet). For example, a 64-byte IP packet would be wrapped with a total of 38 bytes of overhead, leading to an efficiency of 62.7 percent (a 10Mbit per second Ethernet is a 6.27Mbit per second link for 64-byte IP packets). IP packets around 1,500 bytes are carried with 97.5 percent efficiency. Note that in practice, CSMA/CD back off creates additional idle time between successfully transmitted frames, reducing the average throughput. However, in all cases the most efficient use of Ethernet occurs when higher layer applications utilize maximum sized packets.

Figure 8.5   Efficiency of Ethernet—payload bits versus bits "on the wire."

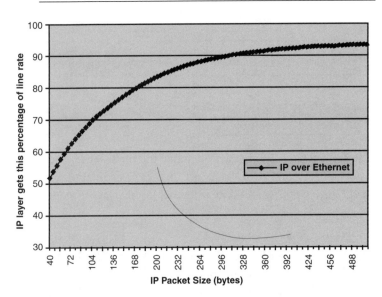

Modified Carrier Sense Multiple Access with Collision Detection

Modifications to the CSMA/CD algorithm itself may be nice if you start with a blank slate. However, QoS guarantees can be made only if the entire path (bridged or not) between source and destination is made up of rule-abiding modified CSMA/CD interfaces. Any LAN segment shared with regular CSMA/CD interfaces would be a source of jitter. An overlaid token-passing scheme would suffer a similar fate—the interfaces playing by the rules would be overwhelmed by the uncontrolled media access of even one regular CSMA/CD interface.

As it turns out, practical deployment considerations have handed us a solution. The 10Base-T Ethernet standard led to the popularization of a hub/star wiring arrangement in which Ethernet endpoints are wired directly into a nearby hub over a nonshared twisted-pair cable. The hubs themselves might well be wired directly back to a core router, or to another hub, over their own nonshared cables. Although originally favored because it gives network administrators great control (for rerouting services or troubleshooting), this wiring architecture is the basis for the QoS solution.

> **Note**
>
> It is worth noting that the phrase "hub" is also used to refer to a multi-port Ethernet repeater. The terminology comes from the fact that the first hub/star installations used multi-port repeaters at the focal points of the star. Later developments replaced hubs with multi-port Ethernet bridges interconnect the legs of the star at the Ethernet-frame level.

Switch Rich

Shown in Figure 8.6, the hub/star architecture is the most extreme form of bridged network with each point-to-point cable a LAN segment with only two interfaces on it. Most of the cost of installing an enterprise Ethernet network is the cabling of each desk, floor, wing, and building. After the basic hub/star architecture is in place, deploying (or upgrading to) frame-aware hubs (bridges) with per-interface frame-based CQS architectures—essentially smart bridges at every hub location—becomes relatively simple. Such advanced hubs are also referred to as *switches*, and the environment is said to be "switch rich."

Figure 8.6   Star topology of hubs and end stations is basis for Ethernet QoS.

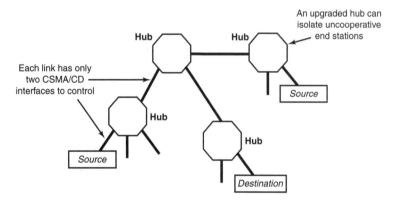

Controlling QoS between any two Ethernet end-stations now boils down to the concatenation of classic per-hop CQS. The source schedules frame transmission toward the first hop hub/switch, and each next-hop hub/switch forwards the frame out along the spanning tree's branches, using independent queuing and scheduling processes on each output port. Where a hub port is half-duplex, some CSMA/CD-related jitter still occurs. However, a QoS-capable network would be best built with hub ports that support full-duplex connectivity. Both ends can transmit whenever the frame-level scheduler dictates, completely avoiding CSMA/CD-induced jitter.

Naturally, frame buffers are finite resources within any switch, and if a frame is transmitted toward a port with no buffer space left, the frame is lost. Some half-duplex switches implement a form of back pressure by deliberately forcing collisions if the switches sense an incoming frame while their buffers are full. Full-duplex 802.3Z switches may implement back pressure using Pause Frame messages sent to their upstream neighbors.

Traffic Classification

No particular limits apply to just how sophisticated an Ethernet switch can choose to be when classifying frames for queuing and scheduling—possibly even looking into the user payload and utilizing IP-level information. However, at minimum a switch ought to provide two queues and classify based on the User Priority field in the 802.1Q VLAN header. (When a VLAN header is used simply to provide QoS differentiation, the 12-bit VLAN ID is set to zero.) The User Priority field allows up to eight queues to be meaningfully utilized, and 802.1D defines a range of mappings from user priority to distinct queuing and scheduling behaviors (referred to as traffic classes in 802.1D).

By default, Ethernet frames without any User Priority field are treated as having a user priority of zero. For switches having less than four queues, a user priority of zero is mapped to the lowest priority class/queue. However, for switches having between four and seven queues, user priority of zero is mapped to the second lowest priority class/queue. Switches supporting eight queues map user priority zero to the third lowest class/queue. This allows advanced switched-LANs to provide service levels both better and worse than "default."

The advantage of switch-rich topologies is that QoS-capable services can be rolled out piecemeal into an already-operational Best Effort Ethernet network. Only hubs along the path(s) between sources and destinations demanding QoS control need to be upgraded to QoS-capable switches. QoS-sensitive traffic can also be protected from the older sections of the network by these upgraded switches.

It should come as no surprise that the ISSLL working group is developing an architecture for QoS over Ethernet that looks like IntServ/DiffServ in small scale—the Subnetwork Bandwidth Manager [ISSBM]. Their issues are very similar—edge-to-edge signaling (to associate User Priority values with specific queuing and scheduling behaviors), policing/rate shaping (to smooth out traffic classes on ingress to the switched network), and admission control (to ensure the limited number of User Priority classes are not overloaded).

QoS control for IP across Ethernet depends on the Ethernet topology being switch rich, using full-duplex links, and with every switch and end station having configurable CQS architectures operating at the Ethernet frame level. Given those basic features, achieving edge-to-edge IP QoS is quite possible even when some or all of the traffic's path takes it across Ethernet links—for example, in enterprise networks or high-speed Ethernet interconnects between backbone routers at Internet service provider (ISP) peering points.

8.2 ATM over Synchronous Optical Network/Synchronous Digital Hierarchy

Most of today's WAN ATM services are built using SONET/SDH links for wide area cell transport between ATM switches. A SONET/SDH circuit provides a link between ATM switches that has very predictable QoS characteristics. As discussed in Chapter 6, "Link Layers Beneath IP," ATM has its own CQS architecture at every switch hop and is able to support QoS guarantees on a per virtual connection (VC) basis. However, the earliest IP over ATM architectures did not make much use of ATM's own QoS capabilities—mostly because the IP routers themselves were providing little more than Best Effort service anyway.

8.2.1 Mapping Cells into Synchronous Optical Network/Synchronous Digital Hierarchy Payloads

ATM cells are mapped into SONET/SDH frames octet by octet (see Figure 8.7). Cell payloads are scrambled to avoid any possibility of particular cell payload patterns confusing the SONET/SDH-level clock recovery circuitry with the scrambling reversed at the receiving end. No bit- or byte-transparency issues cause random payload expansion.

Figure 8.7   Cells map directly into a STS-3c frame.

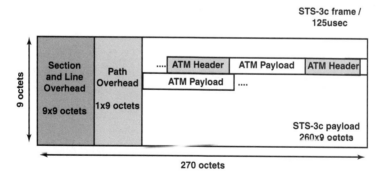

8.2.2 IP over ATM

Both the IETF and ATM Forum worked on architectures and protocols for deploying IP networks on top of ATM. Whereas the IETF started from the classical assumption of ATM as just another link layer for IP packet transport, the ATM Forum's first solution was to emulate an Ethernet—making it IP over Ethernet over ATM. Architecturally, the IETF's classical IP/ATM (CIP) approach had the greater long-term flexibility. (It directly exposed the IP layer to ATM's QoS-controllable VCs.) However, the ATM Forum's LAN emulation (LANE) approach gained popularity in the enterprise ATM market because it could easily leverage autoconfiguration tools already developed for IP over Ethernet environments. LANE became the foundation for the ATM Forum's subsequent Multiprotocol over ATM (MPOA) specification.

Classical IP/ATM

CIP's design goal is to support intrasubnet connectivity within an IP subnet of two or more IP interfaces [RFC1577, RFC2225]. The IETF recognized that a single ATM service might be capable of establishing VCs directly between members of many different subnets. However, modification of the classic IP routing model was an explicit non-goal (hence, "classical" IP/ATM)—in this case, intersubnet traffic must traverse a router. An ATM-based IP subnet is referred to as a logical IP subnet (LIS)—in contrast with a "regular" IP subnet, at the time associated with a single, isolated link-level network. More precisely, a LIS is made up of those IP/ATM interfaces on the same ATM network that are part of the same IP subnet at the IP level. Many unrelated, self-contained, and independently running LISs can simultaneously overlay an ATM network.

Every link driver has two concerns:

- **Address resolution**—Discovering the link-level next hop corresponding to a given IP next-hop address known to be on the link.

- **Packet transport**—Actually establishing link-level resources to transfer the packet to the indicated next hop.

ATM's lack of an all-nodes broadcast service means that CIP uses a client/server address resolution model. Each LIS member registers its own IP and ATM address mapping with a well-known Address Resolution Protocol (ARP) server, and queries the ARP server for the ATM address of other LIS members to determine a packet's ATM-level next hop. Each LIS is required to have its own ARP server.

Packet transport between any two LIS members requires establishing a VC, either on demand (a switched virtual connection, or SVC, set up only when a packet actually requires forwarding to that IP/ATM interface), or preprovisioned (a permanent virtual connection, or PVC). When the CIP architecture was being developed, IP QoS was nonexistent and the focus was efficient utilization of high-speed, but relatively scarce, VCs.

SVCs are established only when needed and released if idle for a period of time. (The default was 20 minutes.) When an IP packet needs to be sent to a next hop for which a SVC does not already exist, the ARP server is queried for the appropriate ATM destination address, and a new SVC is established.

Intra-LIS IP multicast requires an additional multicast address resolution server (MARS) to hold mappings of IP multicast group addresses to one or more ATM addresses [RFC2022]. To forward a multicast IP packet to its on-LIS destinations, IP/ATM interfaces establish a point-to-multipoint (pt-to-mpt) SVC to the ATM addresses returned by the MARS.

AAL 5 service provides framing for both unicast and multicast packet forwarding. As shown in Figure 8.8, LLC/SNAP multiplexing is the default for unicast, although VC multiplexing can be used with the IP packet carried directly as payload [RFC1483]. (In the RFC 2022 architecture, it is possible for sources to find their AAL 5 PDUs looping back to them. Additional encapsulation is defined under RFC 2022, enabling an interface to detect copies of its multicast packets coming back.)

By default, VCs are established with traffic parameters suited for Best Effort IP forwarding—typically the unspecified bit rate (UBR) service where available [RFC1755, RFC2331].

Figure 8.8   RFC 1483 encapsulation of IP in AAL 5.

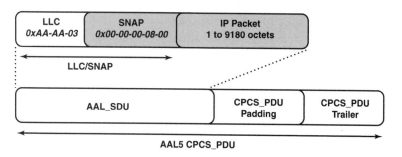

In the long run, most commercial CIP deployments have been large IP backbones, using PVCs to interconnect routers. (Not only were SVCs hard to obtain across commercial WAN ATM networks, but after a SVC was set up, the high volume of backbone traffic meant that it would never go idle long enough to be torn down.)

In the LAN arena, CIP never made much headway against the ATM Forum's LANE specification. While LANE provided rudimentary support for broadcast and multicast from its inception, CIP required the MARS extension, which was developed sometime after CIP and LANE were defined. However, MARS was over-kill for the market segment in which CIP and LANE competed. As a consequence, CIP+MARS never posed much competition to LANE for enterprise IP/ATM environments.

LAN Emulation

As its name suggests, LAN emulation, or LANE, was developed to allow ATM interface cards and their device drivers to provide an Ethernet-like (or token ring-like) service to end stations (hosts, routers, and bridges). An emulated LAN (ELAN) is made up of LANE/ATM interfaces that want to communicate directly via ATM VCs. Each LANE/ATM interface has its own Ethernet (IEEE MAC) address and uses a client/server address resolution protocol that supports the dynamic mapping of Ethernet addresses to ATM addresses. Address mappings are stored in a LANE emulation server (LES), one LES per ELAN (although the LES function may be distributed over multiple physical nodes). Forwarding a typical Ethernet frame involves querying the LES for the ATM address corresponding to the frame's destination Ethernet address and establishing a SVC to the returned ATM address.

Unlike CIP, a very rudimentary broadcast/multicast emulation mode was defined from the beginning—a key design decision in that it enabled existing IP/Ethernet autoconfiguration protocols to run "as is" over an ELAN. If a frame's destination was a group or broadcast address, the frame would be passed to the broadcast and unknown server (BUS), which then repeated the frame out to all members of the ELAN on a special point-to-multipoint VC.

Support for differentiated QoS does not exist in the first version of LANE—mostly because Ethernet at the time had no QoS service model to emulate. However, it did lead many users to question why they would deploy an ATM infrastructure only to get something just like Ethernet. Wide area ELANs are a possibility, but most cases can be solved using conventional Ethernet bridging over dedicated WAN links.

8.2.3   QoS Considerations

Both CIP and LANE inherit the familiar sawtooth efficiency curve typical of packet services running over ATM. Because of LANE's higher overhead (carrying the Ethernet header, too), its efficiency is slightly lower than CIP (see Figure 8.9, assuming that CIP is using LLC/SNAP encapsulation).

Figure 8.9 CIP efficiency with logical link control/sub network access point encapsulation versus IP packet size.

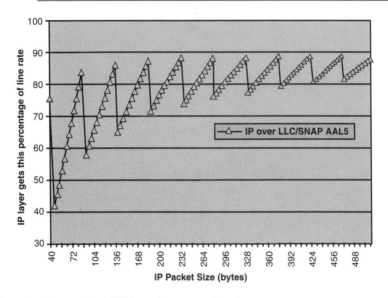

Controlling QoS in an IP/ATM environment involves two aspects:

• Upgrading the IP node with sufficient CQS architecture to provide differentiated scheduling of traffic toward any next hop

• Defining rules for establishing and using parallel ATM VCs toward a given next hop

The IETF's ISSLL working group outlined the design issues for IP/ATM QoS in RFC 2382 [RFC2382] and made specific recommendations in RFC 2380 [RFC2380], RFC 2381 [RFC2381] and RFC 2379 [RFC2379]. The group's focus was how to utilize Resource Reservation Protocol (RSVP) signaling at the IP layer (described in Chapter 5, "Establishing Edge-to-Edge IP QoS") to guide the establishment of parallel VCs toward a given intra-LIS (or intra-ELAN, for LANE) next hop. Figure 8.10 shows their general CQS architecture for a router or host IP/ATM interface. A lot of similarity exists in the VC management rules for supporting QoS in CIP and LANE, and so the ISSLL group's guidelines are pertinent to both services. These guidelines also have some relevance to "provisioned QoS" schemes such as DiffServ, keeping in mind that classification, queuing, and link selection are common issues.

Figure 8.10   Parallel virtual connections to carry different QoS classes.

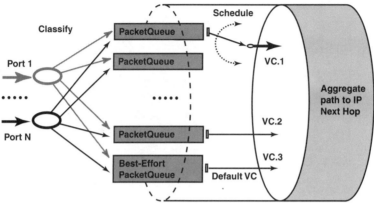

Focusing on the CIP case, a default Best Effort VC will always be established by regular CIP that can support the initial IP forwarding of RSVP path establishment (PATH) messages across the LIS (a point-to-multipoint VC if the IP destination is a multicast group). When the returning RSVP reservation (RESV) messages (arriving over the default VC for the reverse path back to the source) indicate to the on-LIS source that specific QoS handling is required for a certain IP traffic class, a new VC (with appropriate QoS characteristics) is established. Appropriate queuing and scheduling rules are established at the source IP/ATM interface to ensure the RSVP-signaled traffic class is forwarded on the newly established VC, rather than on the default VC. If the VC cannot be established because of ATM-level resource exhaustion, RSVP treats it as a reservation failure, and the traffic continues to be forwarded along its default Best Effort VC.

Packet-level scheduling of multiple classes (queues) onto a specific VC is possible, or an implementation may simplistically open new VCs for every RSVP-signaled traffic class. The former approach conserves VCs across the LIS, whereas the latter approach simplifies the source interface's internal packet-scheduling architecture by pushing the complexity down to the ATM level. Establishing a VC per queue also avoids the problem of interleave jitter being caused by packet-level scheduling between multiple queues onto a slow VC. Multiple queues should not feed into a single VC if that VC is likely to be "slow" (for example, 100Kbits per second). Packet level queuing and scheduling interacts closely with each VC's ATM service class to create the temporal forwarding behavior experienced by any given packet.

The choice of an appropriate service class for each VC is discussed in RFC 2381 [RFC2381]. This RFC provides a detailed examination of how existing Integrated Services classes—Guaranteed Service (GS) and Controlled Load (CL), described in Chapter 4, "Edge-to-Edge Network Models"—can be mapped to ATM service classes (described in Chapter 6, "Link Layers Beneath IP") and makes the following general recommendations:

- For GS use Constant Bit Rate (CBR) or real-time Variable Bit Rate (rt-VBR)

- For CL use non-real-time Variable Bit Rate (nrt-VBR) or Available Bit Rate (ABR) with a minimum cell rate

- For Best Effort use Unspecified Bit Rate (UBR) or ABR

RFC 2381 observes that mapping IP service classes to ATM service classes involves some approximations and assumptions about how the VCs are used. For example, the GS class requires tight delay bounds with the option of demoting packets that are out of profile. The preferred ATM match is the nrt-VBR service class. However, if nrt-VBR service is not available, a similar result can be achieved using a CBR VC to carry in-profile traffic, and a parallel UBR VC to carry out of profile traffic.

Regular CIP's "idle VC release" behavior is required only on the default VC. Any VC established through RSVP activity is presumed to be controlled by RSVP soft-state mechanisms and will be explicitly torn down when appropriate. RFC 1483 encapsulation rules are retained (because this step is orthogonal to correct packet scheduling), but it is noted that VC multiplexing (null encapsulation) is preferred where possible to reduce overhead.

Two key issues face an RSVP-based IP/ATM environment:

- Receiver heterogeneity within the LIS or ELAN

- RSVP renegotiation of traffic parameters

Receiver heterogeneity (where receivers can ask for different QoS levels—for example, peak bit rate or jitter bounds) is allowed by RSVP and is an issue for multicast groups. On-LIS destinations might request (via their returned RESV messages) different QoS requirements, suggesting that the ATM-level path toward these destinations be heterogeneous. However, an ATM point-to-multipoint VC supports only homogeneous QoS parameters across all its endpoints (leaf nodes). One solution is to simply establish a VC covering a superset of the required QoS and let the downstream nodes deal with it. Alternatively, an interface can establish parallel, nonoverlapping, point-to-multipoint VCs that, in the aggregate, cover all the on-LIS destinations, but with each VC having QoS parameters suitable for a subset of the on-LIS destinations. The former approach consumes QoS resources along all branches of the VC, whereas the latter approach consumes as many VCs as there are uniquely different downstream requirements. Various methods for aggregating traffic onto VCs and spreading traffic across VCs are under study.

RSVP also allows receivers to modify their QoS requirements during the lifetime of a traffic flow. This can lead to heterogeneity among the receivers if only some of the receivers decide to change their requirements. IP/ATM interfaces need to cope with VCs being established and torn-down to satisfy changing QoS requirements and heterogeneity.

Although the ISSLL work focused on RSVP-signaled IntServ traffic, similar CQS architectures are required to support DiffServ over ATM links. The main difference lies in the fact that a DiffServ-compliant IP/ATM interface has only a few queues to manage and, therefore, few VCs to establish. Traffic class/queue parameters (and, hence, matching VCs) are modified infrequently through provisioning rather than signaling. Typically, DiffServ-based IP/ATM interfaces are deployed in wide-area, high-capacity IP/ATM backbones or major network peering points.

8.3 PPP over Synchronous Optical Network/Synchronous Digital Hierarchy

Many current IP backbones were developed on top of an ATM service because it was the first high-speed WAN offering available from many long-distance carriers. However, if native SONET/SDH circuits are provisioned between backbone routers, a clear alternative exists—simply run PPP over the high-speed, octet-oriented duplex SONET/SDH circuit (for the purposes of defining PPP over SONET/SDH, SONET and SDH standards are essentially the same).

One major consideration driving interest in PPP over SONET/SDH (POS) is the possible efficiency gain—no ATM layer means no per-cell segmentation overhead. A second consideration is performance—a number of vendors can show POS interfaces running at OC-48/ATM-16 rates (2.4Gbit per second), whereas commercially viable ATM segmentation and reassembly engines are proving troublesome to develop at those speeds. However, disposing of ATM also loses the "virtual circuit" abstraction (useful for traffic engineering), leading many operators to assume they'll be running Multiprotocol Label Switching (MPLS) over POS to completely replace the functionality of ATM.

A POS-based network would rely on the IP routers to be the core switching points. SONET/SDH links typically run at OC-3/STM-1 (155Mbit per second) and higher, and so interleave jitter ought to be insignificant. Differentiated QoS relies solely on IP packet-level CQS within the routers to mediate POS link access.

8.3.1 HDLC-Like Framing

POS is defined in RFC 2615 [RFC2615] (an update to RFC 1619 [RFC1619]). Octet-based HDLC-like framing is used, treating the SONET/SDH circuit as nothing more than an extremely high-speed version of a dial-up or leased line circuits. Figure 8.11 shows how the HDLC-framed PPP appears within a simplified SONET/SDH payload. The frame may span the boundaries of consecutive payloads.

Figure 8.11   HDLC-like framing directly into STS-3c frame.

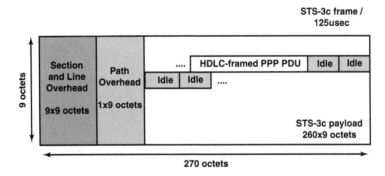

RFC 2615 covers circuits ranging between OC-3c to OC-192c rates. Transport for PPP at higher rates is currently open and being worked on by the IETF. One possible track will be the use of entirely different framing (such as SDL, discussed in Section 8.4).

8.3.2 Scrambling and Stuffing

The original POS specification allowed a PPP frame to be directly inserted into the SONET/SDH payload. At the end of 1997, the IETF became aware that IP packets carrying specially constructed sequences of octets could disrupt SONET/SDH-level clock synchronization with potentially annoying and disruptive operational consequences in public networks. RFC 2615 introduces a $x^{43} + 1$ *self-synchronous scrambler* to avoid this problem—octets from the HDLC-like framer are scrambled before insertion into the SONET/SDH payload. For backward compatibility with RFC 1619–based OC-3c circuits, the scrambler may be turned off.

Although a SONET/SDH circuit itself has very predictable QoS characteristics, the use of HDLC-like framing creates random payload expansions due to byte stuffing of the 0x7E frame delimiter. This process creates an interesting (and currently unsolved) issue for operators desiring close control of their link QoS: User packets can be deliberately filled with 0x7E bytes to trigger fluctuations of the apparent aggregate bandwidth of a POS link.

Interestingly, a possible solution exists by modifying the RFC 2615 scrambler process. If a PPP packet's octet stream is scrambled before HDLC-like framing, rather than after, the scrambled octet stream would have a low (and random) occurrence of 0x7Es. It would be virtually impossible for a user to force the HDLC-like framer into uncontrolled payload expansion.

8.4   PPP over Simplified Data Link

Simplified data link (SDL) is a recent alternative to HDLC-like framing, primarily focusing on the high-speed (OC-48 and up) packet-switching market [SDL]. Its development has been driven in part by a desire to avoid HDLC's byte-stuffing expansion and concerns over the perceived complexity of implementing HDLC-like framing at OC-192c rates and above.

SDL uses an ATM-like delineation scheme that allows frame boundaries to be discovered without any special in-band "flags." As shown in Figure 8.12, the SDL header is a fixed four-octet field carrying a 16-bit Length field (indicating the size of the SDL frame's contents, up to 64K long) and a 16-bit cyclic redundancy check (CRC) over the preceding Length field. The CRC calculation establishes a known signature, or relationship, between the four octets of a valid SDL header. Frame synchronization is achieved by searching for groups of four octets with such a relationship.

When the receiver believes it has synchronized with the incoming signal, the Length field determines the size of the user payload and locates the trailing 32-bit CRC (calculated over all octets from the SDL header to the end of the user payload). The size of the Optional Padding field (typically zero) is administratively configured at each end of the link. SDL's delineation scheme can be used over electrical or optical bit-stream circuits.

Both the user payload and trailing 32-bit CRC are scrambled before transmission to avoid bit-density problems in the underlying media. Scrambler state is reestablished by each end of the SDL link on a regular basis, using special in-band control messages. Special SDL messages are indicated by the Length field being 0, 1, 2, or 3.

Figure 8.12   Basic simplified data link frame format.

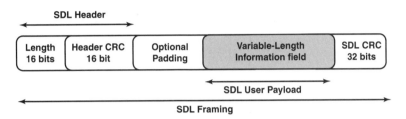

When the packet length is four or more, the distance in octets between the current SDL header and the next is the sum of the Packet Length field, length of the optional padding, and the SDL CRC field size. The user payload carries valid information.

Two proposals have been presented for PPP over SDL—one in which SDL replaces HDLC for PPP over SONET/SDH [SDLPOS] and the other in which SDL replaces both HDLC and SONET/SDH over the underlying media [SDLOPT]. In both cases, SDL framing adds eight octets of fixed overhead to the PPP packet (shown in Figure 8.13). (The 0xFF03 HDLC header and four-octet trailing FCS are no longer required.) The equivalent overhead for PPP/HDLC is nine octets, and so SDL's performance curve is virtually identical to PPP/HDLC (assuming no payload expansion).

However, SDL's lack of bit or byte stuffing prevents malicious users from unexpectedly consuming link capacity—a feature that might well justify it replacing HDLC-like framing on links carrying QoS-sensitive traffic.

Figure 8.13   Point-to-Point Protocol with simplified data link framing.

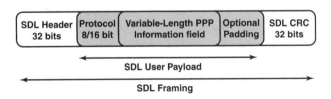

SDL itself does not provide VC functionality. As with HDLC-framed SONET/SDH links, VCs in an SDL-based IP network requires running MPLS over PPP over SDL.

8.5 *Wave Division Multiplexing*

Traditional telecommunications theory has two fundamental methods for creating multiple logical channels from a single physical channel—time-division multiplexing (TDM) and frequency-division multiplexing (FDM) . There are any number of permutations and some combinations (for example, spread spectrum radio techniques can be considered a form of both time division and frequency division in so far as they frequency hop based on regularly timed sequences). At their core, they allow a medium to be subdivided into manageable, independent chunks that can be shared by a number of sources.

Earlier in this century, engineers discovered how to selectively "tune" radio transmitters and receivers so that multiple channels could use the radio spectrum simultaneously. Cable TV systems utilize concurrent channels in the ultra high frequency (UHF) bands to multiplex many tens of channels over a single cable. Wave-division multiplexing (WDM) is a generic name for FDM in the optical domain. It was born when engineers developed methods to selectively tune optical transmitters and receivers and enable multiple light beams (on different frequencies, or *wavelengths*) to concurrently share a single optical fiber *without* mutual interference.

Adding wavelengths is a nontrivial effort. Optical fibers do not have uniformly linear characteristics—some wavelengths are attenuated or distorted differently from others, limiting the practical distances between transmitters and receivers. Tuning of both transmitters and receivers must be accurate to minimize interference—greater accuracy and control allows more wavelengths to be activated. Marketing terms such as coarse WDM (CWDM), dense WDM (DWDM), and ultra WDM (UWDM) have been coined to indicate increasing numbers of wavelengths supportable by specific vendor's equipment.

WDM is best understood as a *fiber-multiplication* technology. Where previously a single physical fiber strand supported a single high-speed optical circuit, now it can support multiple optical circuits—the number limited only by the number of wavelengths available (Figure 8.14 shows WDM using four distinct wavelengths). In addition, because WDM operates at the photonic (optical) level, different framing and transmission technologies (for example, PPP over SONET/SDH, ATM over SONET/SDH, or some as-yet-unknown techniques) may be used on each wavelength.

Figure 8.14 Wavelength-division multiplexing supports multiple optical circuits on a single fiber.

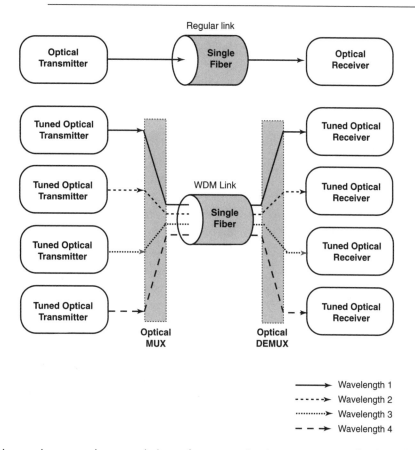

WDM is a major attraction to existing telecommunications operators who have laid various amounts of fiber around their regions in the past and would like to avoid the expense of doing so again. Additional capacity can be brought online simply by upgrading the equipment at either end of affected fiber strands—potentially a major cost saving. (The actual savings are situation dependent—not all existing fiber installations have optical properties suitable for WDM upgrades, and *some* may still require re-laying of newer fiber.) Interestingly, some newer telecommunications operators are starting out by laying their own fiber and simply installing huge numbers of strands to postpone the day when they will need WDM technology.

There has been a lot of talk about how WDM techniques will "remove the bandwidth bottleneck" and render most QoS schemes irrelevant. Although significant increases in raw capacity are available, this aggregate is made up of wavelengths each carrying *independent* circuits of finite (for example, OC-48/STM-16 or OC-192/STM-64) capacity. At the ends of these circuits sit electronic switching gear—the real bottleneck in today's backbones. If a single flow of traffic exceeds the capacity of a single circuit, dynamically distributing this load across multiple wavelengths is a nontrivial task. In reality, operators need to apply independent QoS controls to each parallel circuit, despite the fiber's aggregate capacity. (Such QoS control may be as simple as coarsely grained traffic engineering to load balance across the available wavelengths, but it is required nevertheless.)

Work is under way to develop photonic (rather than electronic) switching devices with the goal of building high-capacity networks with core-switching rates far in excess of current limits. However, it remains a fundamental truth that a heterogeneous network will always have congestion and queuing at points where bursty traffic flows converge and/or move from higher- to lower-speed links. As is observed with cars and highways, the demand usually expands to fill new capacity, and the need for congestion control techniques soon follows.

8.6 *References*

[8021D]   IEEE Std 802.1D. "IEEE Standards for Local and Metropolitan Area Networks: Common Specifications. Part 3: Media Access Control (MAC) Bridges." (1998).

[8021Q]   IEEE Std 802.1Q. "IEEE Standards for Local and Metropolitan Area Networks: Virtual Bridged Local Area Networks." (1998).

[8023]   IEEE Std 802.3. "IEEE Standards for Local and Metropolitan Area Networks: Specific Requirements. Part 3: Carrier Sense Multiple Access with Collision Detection (CSMA/CD) Access Method and Physical Layer Specifications." (1998).

[IS802]   Ghanwani, A., J. W. Pace, V. Srinivasan, A. Smith, and M. Seaman. "A Framework for Integrated Services over Shared and Switched IEEE 802 LAN Technologies." Internet Draft (work in progress) draft-ietf-issll-is802-framework-07.txt. (June 1999).

[ISSBM]   Yavatkar, R., D. Hoffman, Y. Bernet, and F. Baker. "SBM (Subnet Bandwidth Manager): Protocol for RSVP-Based Admission Control over IEEE 802-Style Networks." Internet Draft (work in progress) draft-ietf-issll-is802-sbm-08.txt. (May 1999).

[RFC1483]   Heinanen, J. "Multiprotocol Encapsulation over ATM Adaptation Layer 5." RFC 1483. (July 1993).

[RFC1577]   Laubach, M. "Classical IP and ARP over ATM." RFC 1577. (December 1993).

[RFC1619]   Simpson, W. "PPP over SONET/SDH." RFC 1619. (May 1994).

[RFC1755]   Perez, M., F. Liaw, A. Mankin, E. Hoffman, D. Grossman, and A. Malis. "ATM Signaling Support for IP over ATM." RFC 1755. (February 1995).

[RFC2022]   Armitage, G. "Support for Multicast over UNI 3.0/3.1 Based ATM Networks." RFC 2022. (November 1996).

[RFC2225]   Laubach, M., and J. Halpern. "Classical IP and ARP over ATM." RFC 2225. (April 1998).

[RFC2331]   Maher, M. "ATM Signaling Support for IP over ATM—UNI 4.0 Update." RFC 2331. (April 1998).

[RFC2379]   Berger, L. "RSVP over ATM Implementation Guidelines." BCP 24. RFC 2379. (August 1998).

[RFC2380]   Berger, L. "RSVP over ATM Implementation Requirements." RFC 2380. (August 1998).

[RFC2381]   Borden, M., and M. Garrett. "Interoperation of Controlled-Load and Guaranteed-Service with ATM." RFC 2381. (August 1998).

[RFC2382]   Crawley, E., L. Berger, S. Berson, F. Baker, M. Borden, and J. Krawczyk. "A Framework for Integrated Services and RSVP over ATM." RFC 2382. (August 1998).

[RFC2615]   Malis, A., and W. Simpson. "PPP over SONET/SDH." RFC 2615. (June 1999).

[SDL]   Doshi, B., S. Dravida, E. Hernandez-Valencia, W. Matragi, M. A. Qureshi, J. Anderson, and J. Manchester. "A Simple Data Link Protocol for High Speed Packet Networks." *Bell Labs Technical Journal* 4, no.1 (January–March 1999): 85–104.

[SDLOPT]   Carlson, J., E. Hernandez-Valencia, N. Jones, and P. Langner. "PPP over Simple Data Link (SDL) Using Raw Lightwave Channels with ATM-like Framing." Internet Draft (work in progress) draft-ietf-pppext-sdl-pol-00.txt. (June 1999).

[SDLPOS]   Carlson, J., P. Langner, E. Hernandez-Valencia, and J. Manchester. "PPP over Simple Data Link (SDL) Using SONET/SDH with ATM-like Framing." Internet Draft (work in progress) draft-ietf-pppext-sdl-03.txt. (July 1999).

CHAPTER 9

Dynamic Efficiency and Robustness

Most network customers expect that edge-to-edge QoS agreements (sometimes referred to as service level agreements, or SLAs) will be met over periods of hours, days, and months—far longer than the millisecond and microsecond intervals over which per-hop queuing and scheduling mechanisms operate. So although the focus has been on per-hop traffic differentiation mechanisms to this point in the book, there's more to deploying a robust, QoS-enabled network. In the QoS domain, robustness is a measure of how well individual edge-to-edge QoS guarantees hold up in the face of internal node and link failures (for example, whether they degrade predictably, gracefully, or suddenly). This chapter looks at how the deployment of per-hop Classify, Queue, and Schedule (CQS) capabilities in a network's routers can improve the network's robustness and allow network's to operate at higher utilization levels compared to networks using conventional Best Effort routers.

In addition, network operators still have to deal with customer-controlled end-to-end mechanisms such as Transmission Control Protocol (TCP)(flow control and reliability) operating over links with varying loss and latency characteristics. In practice, customers may not entirely understand how their own mechanisms interact with the network's edge-to-edge characteristics. This chapter reviews TCP's flow control and congestion management schemes and discusses qualitatively how TCP behaves in the face of slow, long, lossy, and asymmetric paths.

9.1   Efficient Link Utilization

Link utilization is a measure of how much of a link's available bandwidth is actually used over any given period of time—and can also be considered a measure of how efficiently a link is being used. The importance of utilizing any given link efficiently depends entirely on the link's cost and the cost of upgrading to faster (or additional) links when the existing link is overwhelmed by growing traffic levels. The goal of every network operator is to increase link utilization if doing so is cheaper than simply upgrading the existing infrastructure. Wide area backbone providers often fall into this category, especially when they must purchase link capacity in discrete bandwidth multiples from another service provider.

9.1.1   Headroom for Burstiness

A direct relationship exists between how bursty a link's traffic is, how much queuing delay is experienced at each router, and a link's average utilization. Part of this relationship is inherent—burstiness is typically a measure of the peak data rate to average data rate exhibited by a flow of traffic. Queuing delays depend on the relationship between the offered traffic's burstiness and the link's peak capacity. As noted in Chapter 2, "The Components of Network QoS," a queue forms when a transient traffic burst that exceeds the output link's capacity arrives at a Best Effort router's output port. This queue drains at the link's transmission rate, and while the queue is nonempty, the link is utilized at full capacity. However, when the burst is over and the queue is drained, the link's instantaneous utilization falls to zero. Over a number of hops, aggregation of flows with low individual burstiness can still result in high aggregate burstiness—which is significant in the core of a network.

Long-term (average) link utilization depends on the relationship between the link capacity and the traffic's average data rate. Clearly, high average link utilization can be achieved by choosing link capacity close to the traffic's expected average data rate and by using large queues to absorb bursts. However, the consequential latency and jitter are undesirable. Because queues are finite in length, this approach to increasing link utilization also tends to increase packet loss rates—an extremely undesirable trait. The desire to avoid packet loss leads most network designers to "overprovision" their links—attempting to ensure that the link has capacity *headroom* to absorb bursts, rather than using queue space in the routers. Figure 9.1 is a simplistic visualization—flows on the left are peacefully sharing the link, whereas on the right one flow is bursting and perturbs the temporal characteristics of all flows sharing the link. The additional transmission requirements of one flow's brief burst are absorbed by any unused capacity on the link.

Figure 9.1   Unused link capacity can absorb burstiness.

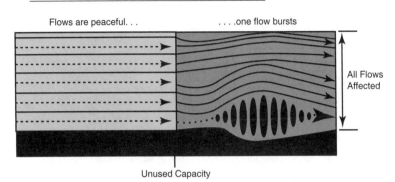

Flows are peaceful. . .   . . . .one flow bursts

All Flows
Affected

Unused Capacity

9.1.2   *Partitioning the Link*

Best Effort networks have traditionally been provisioned on the assumption that the "data" traffic is bursty. Link capacity headroom is provisioned to reduce packet loss in congested queues because end-to-end data applications have traditionally been more loss sensitive than jitter sensitive. However, the emergence of real-time streaming and interactive media poses a new issue—links can now find themselves carrying a mixture of traffic sensitive to loss, jitter, or both. Networks built around Best Effort, single-queue routers require significant link headroom on major links simply to ensure that the burstiness of the traditional data traffic does not violate jitter bounds for real-time traffic.

As discussed in Chapter 2, the key reason for introducing a CQS router architecture is to allow for controlled, independent scheduling of different traffic classes onto a link. Depending on the choice of scheduling algorithms, one or more traffic classes are isolated from the temporal characteristics of the other classes—effectively partitioning the link's capacity.

Using the router's scheduler stage to isolate bursty and jitter-intolerant traffic reduces the link headroom requirement. The scheduler ensures regular link access for jitter-sensitive traffic classes, regardless of whether the bursty traffic classes currently have a large, small, or zero backlog in their associated queue(s). Thus, compared to networks using single-queue Best Effort routers, links can be provisioned for higher average utilization. Figure 9.2 is a simplistic representation of a link fed by a multi-queue router—when one flow bursts, it doesn't end up stealing link capacity from the other flows because their link shares are guaranteed by the router's scheduler. Therefore, unused capacity on the link can be shrunk to handle only the needs of the bursty subset of the overall traffic.

Figure 9.2   Isolated traffic classes require less protective headroom than unisolated classes.

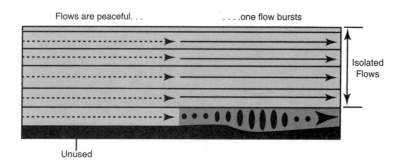

9.2   *Edge-to-Edge Path Robustness*

A major issue in network design is how the edge-to-edge service quality changes in response to internal link or router failures. Degradation of service quality may last for minutes, hours, or be barely noticeable to the customer. The degradation may be gradual or sudden, depending on which components failed and the schemes deployed to route around failures. Degradation may be limited to the traffic using the failed components or may be felt by traffic flowing through still-functioning regions of the network.

Building fault-tolerant networks is a complex endeavor. How operators choose to architect their network's fault tolerance depends on the nature of the service agreements in force with their customers. This section highlights some key issues relating to edge-to-edge QoS.

In general, restoration of edge-to-edge transport must occur quickly, usually faster than the manual intervention required to repair a failed component. This situation implies the following:

- Automated mechanisms must be deployed to rapidly *fail-over* affected traffic from the broken path to an alternative, functional path.

- Redundant capacity can be found along alternative, underutilized links until the failed component can be repaired.

IP routing protocols are the first line of defense against internal failures, ensuring that traffic is rerouted around failed components. However, QoS guarantees may apply to some of the rerouted traffic. If the alternative paths do not have spare capacity, meeting these QoS expectations is difficult. Yet redundant capacity runs counter to the goal of maximizing link utilization during regular network operation. Excess capacity requirements depend on customer expectations, how many simultaneous failures can be tolerated, and the type of traffic classification schemes being used within the network.

9.2.1 RSVP-Based Paths

Chapter 5, "Establishing Edge-to-Edge IP QoS," described how RSVP's soft state signaling can reroute a user's resource reservation when IP routing recovers from a link or router failure. Recovery depends on two factors—how quickly IP routing establishes a new shortest-path route around the failed node and how quickly RSVP can reestablish resources along the new path. From the end-user's perspective, the traffic flow first ceases completely (when the component fails) and then reappears with potentially degraded QoS (as routing reestablishes an alternative path, but without resource reservations in place). Ultimately, if adequate resources are available along the new path, the flow's requested QoS is restored after the next exchange of path establishment (PATH) and reservation (RESV) messages.

A critical assumption here is that resources are available on the alternative paths. In the absence of sufficient resources, the RESV requests are denied, and the affected sessions receive only default Best Effort service. Note that in an RSVP-IntServ environment the failed-over traffic does not disrupt the preexisting reservations along the alternative path. Because the routers perform MF classification to identify flows belonging to admitted sessions, the failed-over traffic is easily isolated into each router's Best Effort queues.

9.2.2 Differentiated Services Paths

The current Differentiated Services model does not have any dynamic signaling, per se. It relies on human configuration or out-of-band management tools for provisioning each router along a path. Provisioning requires the network operator to predict the probable paths for each traffic aggregate being mapped into the limited set of available DSCPs. Entirely independent traffic aggregates may share a common DSCP yet be provisioned separately because their probable paths across the DiffServ domain do not overlap.

Figure 9.3 shows a core of a simplified DiffServ domain. Flows 1, 2, and 3 represent flow aggregates (for example, tunnels belonging to different virtual private networks, or VPNs) being mapped to specific PHBs (and, hence, DSCPs) by upstream ingress routers (not shown in the diagram). Flows 1 and 3 traverse routers R1 and R2 before exiting the domain core, whereas flow 2 traverses router R3 to R4 and then exits the core. Based on expected shortest-path calculations, the network operator knows that flows 1 and 2 traverse entirely different sections of the network. Because they also represent traffic classes requiring similar service, flows 1 and 2 happen to share the same DSCP. Routers R1 and R2 are provisioned with resources for flow 1 and flow 3, and routers R3 and R4 are provisioned with resources for flow 2.

Figure 9.3   Unrelated flow aggregates may use the same DSCP.

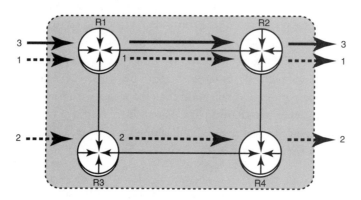

Herein lies an interesting problem. If an internal link or router fails, affected traffic is rerouted as soon as the IP routing protocols reestablish a new shortest-path forwarding tree (just as in an RSVP-IntServ network). However, some of the failed-over traffic may have the same DSCP as traffic already existing on the chosen alternative path. The failed-over and original traffic aggregates mingle in the queues of the routers along the alternative path with no way for routers to further differentiate them. If the resources assigned to the processing of each DSCP are insufficient for the total aggregate load, service degradation occurs to both the failed-over traffic and the traffic that originally used the alternative path.

Figure 9.4   Shared DSCPs may suffer fail-over degradation.

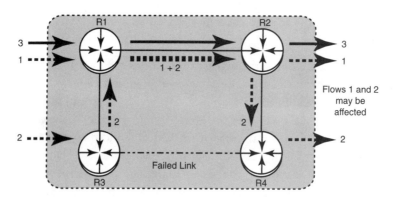

Figure 9.4 shows fail-over degradation occurring to the network of Figure 9.3. The link between R3 and R4 has failed, and the IP routing protocol has rerouted flow 2 via R1 and R2. Unfortunately, R1 cannot distinguish between flow 1 and flow 2—because they have identical DSCPs, packets from flows 1 and 2 are mingled in a single output queue toward R2. The potential exists for the network failure between R3 and R4 to degrade service for the traffic making up flow 1 as well as flow 2.

One way to prevent a fail-over from resulting in service degradation is to overprovision each alternative path, preassigning sufficient link capacity and router resources to handle flow 1 and flow 2. However, this approach requires careful network planning to predict the likely failures and the resulting alternative paths. For any realistic backbone topology, such preassignments result in a lot of unused capacity and, therefore, low average link uti-lization around the network. (For example, in Figure 9.4 the failure might have occurred in the R1-R2 link—causing flows 1 and 3 to be rerouted over the R3-R4 link. Ensuring that the R3-R4 link has capacity for all three flows means that under normal circumstances the link is potentially quite underutilized.)

A second solution exists if you want to quarantine the failure's impact and accept partial service degradation to the failed-over traffic (in this example, flow 2). Even though every PHB has an assigned DSCP, the DiffServ specifications allow multiple DSCPs to map to the same PHBs. Flows 1 and 2 could be assigned different DSCPs on ingress to the DiffServ core while still receiving the same class of PHB. Figure 9.5 shows how the failed-over scenario would appear—R1 is now able to differentiate between flow 1 and flow 2. If R1 has no specific handling rules for the DSCP used by flow 2, that flow's packets receive default Best Effort service without affecting the resources allocated to flow 1.

Figure 9.5   Different DSCPs help isolate failed-over traffic.

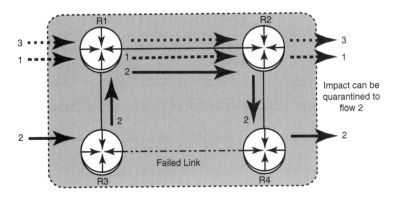

The benefit in Figure 9.5 is that R1 and the link toward R2 do not need to make any particular allowance for other traffic that might be failed-over onto the R1-R2 path—providing that the failed-over traffic and the preexisting traffic don't use the same DSCPs (in this case, flows 1 and 3). However, the DSCP space isn't particularly large. Imagine what would happen if each "flow" in Figure 9.5 represented the aggregate traffic of a distinct customer and each customer wanted to use the AF PHB group. Allowing for the class selectors, default PHB, and EF PHB, no more than four distinct customers could be supported—each consuming 12 unique DSCPs to represent its own use of AF.

In practice, DiffServ networks need to balance the use of multiple DSCPs (to isolate unrelated traffic aggregates during fail-over situations) and the overprovisioning of probable alternative paths through the network.

9.2.3 Hybrids

The level of mutual interference caused when a large block of traffic is failed-over onto an existing link clearly depends on the classification granularity of the network's QoS scheme. Part of the issue in the DiffServ example is that failed-over traffic can look the same as traffic originally expected to be on the alternative path—the use of a small DSCP space creates ambiguity. No such ambiguity exists in the RSVP-IntServ example because MF classification is used at every hop along a flow's path—failed-over traffic cannot be confused with, or steal forwarding resources from, legitimately established flows.

However, it isn't necessary to jump straight into an RSVP-IntServ network design. For example, take the scenario of Figure 9.4 but assume in addition that the following two points are true:

- Traffic belonging to each customer in Figure 9.4 comes from different source networks.

- Routers in the core can classify packets by DSCP and a prefix match on the source address field.

The network operator can configure each router so that the source address field must match an "allowed" source network before the DSCP is used to select the PHB. All other packets get Best Effort handling. In this example, flow 2 and flow 1 are assumed to be using the same DSCP. However, when flow 2 is failed-over onto the R1-R2 link, R1 fails to match the source addresses of flow 2 to anything R1 knows about; thus flow 2's packets are processed in R1's Best Effort queue. Flow 1 is unperturbed, even though the DSCPs are identical.

Obviously, you cannot take such hybrid schemes too far, or you'll have simply reinvented full MF classification. But it is not entirely unlikely for traffic aggregates to have some set of nonoverlapping source or destination network prefixes. Where IP-IP tunneling carries a customer's traffic across the backbone the source, and destination IP addresses of the tunnel endpoints are quite well known. If the flows in Figure 9.4 had been IP-IP tunnels using common DSCPs, isolation of flow 2 from flow 1 during fail-over would have simply required R1 to classify flow 1 by using its tunnel endpoint addresses in addition to the DSCP.

9.2.4 *Multiprotocol Label Switching*

Multiprotocol Label Switching (MPLS), which is discussed in Chapter 4, "Edge-to-Edge Network Models," illustrates another kind of hybrid.

A label-switching router (LSR) may use the 20-bit label, the three experimental bits, or both when classifying packets into specific output queues. If LSRs use only the experimental bits to classify MPLS frames, the outcome resembles the pure DiffServ example—a small classification key can lead to failed-over traffic being indistinguishable from original traffic in the queues of LSRs along a particular path. However, if the LSR's queue assignment takes the label into account, failed-over traffic is distinguishable because each label-switched path (LSP) has a unique label at every hop.

The main difference between MPLS and the preceding IntServ and DiffServ models is that an MPLS network must explicitly reroute and rebuild the LSPs that passed through a failed link or LSR. Basic topology-driven Label Distribution Protocol (LDP) simply rebuilds the affected LSPs to follow the new shortest paths across the network. In such an MPLS network, LSRs can use only the experimental bits for QoS (because the LDP signaling protocol assigns no particular QoS significance to any given LSP and, hence, to the per-hop label values).

Constraint-routed LSPs pose another operational challenge. They're most likely to be used for edge-to-edge traffic having specific QoS requirements. Both M-RSVP and CR-LDP install the LSPs based on constraints that include QoS requirements. Because QoS parameters may be explicitly installed along the LSPs' path, LSRs may use both the experimental and label bits to provide differentiated QoS. However, it is possible that the constraint-routed LSP's QoS requirements cannot be met along the new path. What happens next depends on the signaling protocol—the LSP might simply not be rebuilt along the fail-over path, or it might be rebuilt with Best Effort QoS explicitly installed. (Because rebuilding an LSP is expected to take many seconds, some designers are looking at preestablishing Best Effort fail-over LSPs. In theory, traffic can switch to these alternative LSPs as soon as a failure is detected. Such approaches are in the early stages of development.)

9.3 End-to-End TCP Performance

The algorithms that make up TCP are worth a closer look because most of our subjective experiences of reliability and robustness in the IP world actually reflect TCP's dynamic characteristics. From a network design perspective, you need to understand how TCP-based applications will perform in the face of your network's particular latency, jitter, and loss characteristics. Frequently a TCP connection's *goodput* (how fast the user's data is actually transferred) is less than the measured throughput (the rate at which packets can be sent) because of retransmissions and flow control.

This section provides a brief overview of TCP and then summarizes a few key interactions between TCP's flow control and common link (mis)behaviors. TCP was originally specified in RFC 793 [RFC793] but has since been augmented in a number of ways. Much of the material in this section is drawn from the work of the TCP Implementation (TCPIMPL), TCP over Satellite (TCPSAT), and Performance Implications of Link Characteristics (PILC) working groups of the Internet Engineering Task Force (IETF).

9.3.1 Reliability and Flow Control

TCP provides a reliable end-to-end connection while attempting to maximize its use of the available network capacity. User data (considered to be an unformatted stream of octets) is transmitted in segments usually sized to fit within IP packets, and each segment's reception is positively acknowledged (ACKed) by the receiver. Segments are uniquely identified by a sequence number (representing the number of bytes transmitted so far) and are retransmitted, if not positively acknowledged, within a certain time (or the receiver explicitly indicates that a segment is presumed to be lost).

TCP adapts its transmission rate to suit the available network capacity by using a congestion-sensitive, sliding-window flow control mechanism (most recently specified in RFC 2581 [RFC2581]). At any given instant, only a certain number of segments (the window) can be in transit across the network. This transmission window is the lesser of two distinct state variables—a congestion window ($cwnd$), representing the transmitter's beliefs about the network's current capacity, and a receiver window ($rwnd$), representing the receiver's current buffering and processing capacity. (The current value of rwnd is carried back to the TCP transmitter in every ACK from the receiver.) Additional segments are transmitted when ACKs come back from the receiver confirming that previous segments have successfully reached the other end. For this reason TCP is said to be *ACK clocked*.

TCP uses a cumulative ACK scheme—an ACK for segment N implicitly ACKs all previously unacknowledged segments prior to segment N (or more precisely, the segment beginning with the Nth byte transmitted). Receivers may reduce the frequency of ACK transmissions by implementing *delayed ACKs*—only ACKing every second segment (or every 500 milliseconds, whichever comes sooner) [RFC1122].

Window Control

At the beginning of a new connection, the TCP transmitter initially sets cwnd equal to 1 segment and sets the slow start threshold (*ssthresh*) equal to rwnd (because usually no other information is available about the network path at that point). To gracefully establish an optimal operating point, TCP grows cwnd as segments are successfully transferred to the receiver. There are two distinct growth modes—slow start (SS) and congestion avoidance (CA). For every ACK received by the transmitter, SS mode increments cwnd by 1 segment, whereas CA mode increments the window by (on average) 1/cwnd segment. TCP connections use SS mode to ramp up the window relatively quickly and then switch to CA mode when cwnd reaches the ssthresh. CA mode is used to carefully probe for network capacity beyond ssthresh. Note that cwnd, rwnd, and ssthresh store their values in units of bytes even though they are typically described in terms of numbers of maximally sized segments. The maximum segment size, or MSS, (in bytes) is negotiated between TCP transmitter and receiver during connection establishment.

TCP also reduces both cwnd and ssthresh if it (TCP) infers that the network path is congested between transmitter and receiver. Congestion is inferred through the existence of packet loss. (TCP's original design assumed congestive losses would vastly outweigh losses due to link errors.) The lost packet is retransmitted, and cwnd and ssthresh are modified in two different ways, depending on exactly how the loss was indicated to the transmitter.

Response to Timeouts

The default loss indication is the failure of a previously transmitted segment to be ACKed within a specific retransmission timeout (RTO) period (initially set to 3 seconds but subsequently adjusted according to the connection's estimated round trip time, or RTT [RFC1122]). In this situation, the transmitter resends the unacknowledged segment, resets ssthresh to half the current transmission window size (the lesser of cwnd or rwnd), and then resets cwnd to 1. This process forces the transmitter back into SS mode and ensures that the less aggressive CA mode is entered when the window reaches only half the window size that apparently contributed to the (presumed) congestive loss.

In addition, RTO is doubled each time a packet is retransmitted due to expiration of the timeout timer—this process is called exponential back off. This approach assumes that, if congestion caused the loss, the TCP connection should minimize the additional retransmission load it poses to the network. If RTO exceeds a certain value (for example, 100 seconds), the connection is terminated.

Duplicate Acknowledgments

A second loss indication involves the receipt of duplicate ACKs. When a receiver detects a hole in the sequence numbers of arriving segments, it ACKs the last in-sequence segment number for each new segment it receives. (These later segments are buffered at the receiver, eventually to be recombined with the missing segment.) When a transmitter sees three duplicated ACKs, it infers that a segment has been lost (specifically, the segment following the one being ACKed) and immediately retransmits the lost segment (known as *fast retransmit*). For example, if the receiver receives a sequence of segments N, {N+200}, {N+300}, {N+400}, it infers that segment {N+100} is lost. (In this example, assume the segments are 100 bytes long, segment N contained bytes N through N+99, and thus the receiver expected the next segment to contain sequence number {N+100}.) Having already ACKed segment N, the receiver sends three more ACKs for segment N—a duplicate for each out-of-sequence segment arriving after segment N.

The receipt of duplicate ACKs implies that subsequent segments are still getting through, and so the transmitter infers that congestion isn't too bad and goes into a *fast recovery* mode. Fast recovery involves setting ssthresh and cwnd to half the previous value of the current transmission window and then incrementing cwnd by one segment for each duplicate ACK that has arrived. This practice keeps TCP in CA mode (because cwnd is just above ssthresh) and ensures that traffic continues to flow at least half as fast as before the loss. (The logic behind immediately incrementing cwnd is that each duplicate ACK indicates a segment that has already exited the network, therefore, making room for more to be transmitted.)

Duplicate ACKs are not a foolproof method of detecting loss. If packets get reordered on their way to the receiver (a not-uncommon event on the Internet), the receiver will see an out-of-sequence segment arrival and issue duplicate ACKs until the reordered segment finally arrives. However, by that point the damage is done because the TCP transmitter has reduced its window and retransmitted the supposedly lost packet.

Selective Acknowledgments

Fast retransmit and fast recovery work well if no more than one segment is lost per window. However, imagine that a receiver sees segments N, {N+300}, {N+400}, and {N+500} arrive. Segment N is duplicate ACKed, causing the transmitter to fast retransmit segment {N+100}. However, the absence of segment {N+200} is not detected until the RTO timer expires at the transmitter—forcing the transmitter back into SS mode and forcing cwnd back to 1. This situation can be avoided by the use of Selective ACK (SACK) [RFC2018].

SACK allows a TCP receiver to issue an advisory in returned ACKs, indicating not only that some specific segments have been lost but also that a range of subsequent segments have been received and are being buffered at the receiver. This process allows the transmitter to optimize its retransmission strategy, focusing on missing segments. The assumption is that when the missing segments are filled in at the receiver, the receiver will resume ACKing the highest-numbered segment successfully received. This approach expedites the connection's reaction to correlated segment losses. (However, SACK doesn't mandate that a receiver continue to buffer received segments indefinitely—a receiver is allowed to "renege" on a previous SACK announcement. In this case the TCP transmitter eventually times out on the segments it may have thought were successfully transmitted, and SS mode is entered.)

9.3.2 Impact of Round Trip Time

The ideal TCP connection rapidly opens its transmission window and keeps the path between transmitter and receiver full of packets at any one time. However, long paths (such as those including geosynchronous satellite links, as documented in RFC 2488 [RFC2488]) can exhibit RTTs of hundreds, or thousands, of milliseconds—making such an ideal hard to reach. The lessons in RFC 2488 are also useful for other long-path scenarios.

Large Windows

Keeping the path full of packets requires both cwnd and rwnd to reach the effective size of the "pipe" represented by the transmission path—the so-called *bandwidth delay product* (which equals the bandwidth × RTT). Turning this relationship around, the throughput of a TCP connection is limited to window size/RTT. Traditional TCP is limited to a maximum 64KB window (cwnd and rwnd are 16-bit numbers). Taking a representative satellite path having 500-millisecond RTT, a single traditional TCP connection is unable to use more than 1.05Mbits per second (65,535 bytes/0.5 seconds) of the satellite link's capacity.

Fortunately, RFC 1323 defines a new extension for TCP (the *large windows* option) that permits significantly larger (up to 1GB) windows to be advertised and utilized [RFC1323].

Slow Window Growth

The RTT of a path also affects the growth rate of cwnd—especially important during SS mode. Because cwnd growth is clocked by the arrival of ACKs, larger RTTs cause slower cwnd growth. Many RTTs may be required before the window is large enough to fill the pipe. Depending on the amount of data to be transferred (relative to the bandwidth delay product), the transmission window might never have a chance to open fully before the transfer is complete. An experimental proposal in RFC 2414 allows the initial value of cwnd to be increased to three or four segments when a TCP connection first opens [RFC2414]. Simulation studies suggest that this change will improve the average through-put for short-lived connections [RFC2415]. (Note that this modification is not yet sup-ported as an IETF standard.)

The slow growth of cwnd is compounded when a connection is established to a receiver that implements delayed ACKs. With an initial cwnd of 1 segment, the process stalls with the transmitter sending one segment and the receiver waiting for a second segment before ACKing them both. The deadlock is broken when the receiver's delayed ACK timer expires (potentially up to 500 milliseconds later) and the connection begins regular SS behavior. The proposal in RFC 2414 (and the allowance in RFC 2581 for transmitters to now use an initial cwnd of two segments) helps to circumvent this additional startup delay.

TCP's SS mode is always a disadvantage when the amount of data to be transferred over a particular connection is of a similar size to the bandwidth delay product. Some applications have even implemented their own workarounds. (For example, early Web browsers would open multiple concurrent TCP connections to a Web site to parallel the transfer of objects on a particular Web page.) The downside to these workarounds (at least for the network) is that the source host transmits multiple streams of packets without any shared congestion-avoidance behavior.

Unfairness

RTT also affects fairness between different TCP connections. Consider two concurrent TCP connections (connA and connB) that are transmitting equivalent amounts of data. If connA has a shorter RTT, connA completes before connB because it (connA) spends less time moving through SS mode into CA mode (or reaching the maximum window size). If connA and connB share a congestion point along their paths, connA can even starve connB of capacity. Starvation occurs when connA's more aggressive evolution through SS mode congests a router shared by connA and connB. If both connections lose packets, they'll both be forced to shrink their transmission windows. However, this condition is cyclic because connA always reopens its window faster than connB does after each congestion event—ensuring that connB never reaches its potential until connA ceases transmission. (This sort of unfairness is one of the motivating factors behind the active queue management schemes described in Chapter 3, "Per-hop Packet Processing." One goal is to minimize the packet losses on connB due to the congestion caused by connA.)

Round Trip Time Estimation

Key to retransmission timeouts is the value of RTO, which must exceed each connection's RTT (otherwise pointless retransmissions are guaranteed to occur). Because the RTT can vary over time, TCP initially included relatively crude estimating machinery to create an approximate value for RTT—recalculated once every round trip. However, RFC 1323 notes that RTT estimation accuracy deteriorates markedly as the actual RTT goes up— because the number of sampled packets drops as a function of the number of packets in transit at any one time. In addition, sampling requires regular segment/ACK exchanges— which disappear after a loss event causes reversion to SS mode.

To cope with large RTT environments, RFC 1323 recommends the use of an additional time stamp carried in every transmitted segment and returned in each segment's associated ACK. Time stamps are generated from an approximately real-time time-stamp clock at the transmitter. When a nonduplicate ACK returns from the receiver, the ACK's time-stamp value is subtracted from the transmitter's current time-stamp clock value, giving a reasonable approximation of the RTT. This scheme is referred to as the round trip time measurement (RTTM) mechanism.

The RTTM mechanism does have its downsides. Time-stamping makes it difficult to efficiently compress TCP/IP headers (vital over low-speed links) because each packet's header (covering the time-stamp option) differs significantly from the previous header [PILCSLOW].

9.3.3 *Asymmetric Paths*

In a growing number of applications for TCP, the path between transmitter and receiver is asymmetric—with respect to both throughput and topology. Extreme scenarios involve satellite and public switched telephone network (PSTN) combinations—where the satellite's wide reception area is used for high-capacity downlinks to receivers that use a dial-up modem connection for the reverse path. Less-extreme scenarios include the asymmetry in home Internet connectivity using ADSL or cable modem technology. In each case the bandwidth toward the customer exceeds the bandwidth back toward the network. When the customer is a consumer of content, the TCP transmitters (at interesting Web sites and so on) send down the high-bandwidth side and the receiver's ACKs return on the low-bandwidth side.

RTT is affected when serialization delays become a significant component on the low-bandwidth path and when variable path dynamics (for example, link-level retransmissions) perturb RTT estimation. For example, a single, conventional ACK (40 bytes of TCP/IP headers) would take a little more than 5 milliseconds to transmit at 64Kbit/sec (ignoring link-framing overhead). TCP segment transmission is both window limited and ACK clocked, and so a small bandwidth on the ACK path can limit the downstream transmission rate. Consider the following scenario:

- One ACK is returned for every two segments.

- Transmit segments are 1,000 bytes long.

- ACKs are 40 bytes long.

- The ACK path is rate limited to 64Kbits per second.

Assuming a perfect return path, the transmitter never receives more than 200 ACKs per second. This rate corresponds to 400 segments being acknowledged per second, or a peak downstream rate of approximately 3.2Mbits per second even if more bandwidth is available on the downstream path. One solution is to utilize TCP/IP header compression on the slow return path (for example, RFC 1144 [RFC1144] or RFC 2507 [RFC2507]). Shrinking the ACKs to only a few bytes substantially increases the achievable ACK rate.

The return path may have two additional problems that affect the goodput achieved in the downstream direction. First, the customer (or home) site may be originating traffic of its own—outbound TCP segments, or other UDP packets, are competing with the ACKs for scarce return-path bandwidth (increasing the apparent RTT because the returning ACKs are delayed while longer segments are serialized onto the return path). Second, the return path may have its own congestion problems elsewhere within the network, causing loss of returned ACKs. Losing ACKs is never a good thing because it almost guarantees that the TCP transmitter will revert to SS mode.

9.3.4 Burstiness

On a macro level, the traditional burstiness of data networks can be partially blamed on the applications themselves—data transfers occur as a result of stop-and-start human actions (for example, typing over a remote terminal connection), completion of computational activities, and so on. On a more detailed level, TCP itself causes burstiness even while transferring large, continuous quantities of data.

Consider a TCP connection just opening up and having an unlimited supply of data to send. In the first RTT, a single segment is transmitted and then ACKed. This process causes two segments to be transmitted back to back onto the host's local network. Within the next RTT, two ACKs are likely to return back to back, causing almost immediate growth of the window to four segments. These four segments are then transmitted, again back to back. And so it goes until either rwnd is reached or a packet loss causes the TCP transmitter to revert into SS or CA mode. The net result is a sequence of longer and longer packet bursts, cycling through SS and CA modes if the connection ever suffers packet loss or reordering. (Only a loss-free path whose bandwidth delay product matches rwnd can ever reach a stable, nonbursty state. In practice, such paths do not often occur.)

The degree of burstiness during SS depends on the spacing of ACK arrivals at the transmitter. If the receiver is heavily loaded, it may space the returning ACKs far enough apart so that the transmitter's next few segments do not go out exactly back to back. Increasing TCP's initial cwnd adds to burstiness, as do "hacks" like opening multiple concurrent TCP connections to the same destination to parallel short data transfers.

Whenever the transmission window is smaller than the bandwidth delay product of the pipe, gaps occur in the transmission of segments—revealed as a bursty traffic flow from the perspective of an observer sitting in the middle of the network. Indeed, the generally uncorrelated nature of every TCP's burstiness allows statistical multiplexing to work on the Internet. When these bursts do happen to correlate, routers suffer transient congestion and require many of the mechanisms described in this book.

9.3.5 Impacts of Link Characteristics

The IETF's PILC working group is documenting the impact of different link layer characteristics on IP networks with some specific focus on TCP's behavior [PILCSLOW][PILCLTN][PILCERR][PILCLNK].

Slow Links

As noted in Chapter 6, "Link Layers Beneath IP," latency over slow links (tens to a few hundred kilobits per second) can be dominated by serialization delays rather than by propagation delays. Unlike propagation delays, serialization delays add to the RTT (inflating the RTO) but do not represent virtual buffering of packets in a pipe between transmitter and receiver.

If segments require more than 200 milliseconds to actually transmit, the receiver's delayed ACK timer often expires before the second segment arrives. Thus, the reverse path carries ACKs for every segment. In addition, if the connection's window stays less than four segments long, fast retransmit and fast recovery may never be triggered. This factor suggests that link Maximum Transmission Unit (MTU), which imposes an upper bound on the segment size, is a balancing act between implementing efficient link utilization (suggesting larger MTU) and allowing quick transmission of more than four segments in a window (suggesting smaller MTU). (Note that with the use of link-level segmentation methods discussed in Chapter 3, larger MTUs need not be an issue for mixing interactive and noninteractive traffic.)

Lossy Links

Unlike relatively low-loss wired and optical LAN/WAN technologies, many emerging wireless link technologies suffer regular and bursty packet loss unrelated to network congestion. Getting TCP to run efficiently across such links is an interesting challenge [PILCERR]. Not only does the packet loss require retransmission, but TCP insists on shrinking its windows as well—dramatically slowing the transfer (and ultimately reducing the achievable goodput). It would be nice if TCP could be changed so that packet loss simply triggered retransmissions without affecting cwnd and ssthresh. However, this modification would require all existing routers to implement an additional, explicit signal for the onset of congestion, rather than drop packets (for example, using the explicit congestion notification (ECN) proposal in RFC 2481 discussed in Chapter 3 [RFC2481]). The current installed basc of routers, and existing TCP implementations, makes such a change unlikely in the near future.

Lossy low-speed links pose a challenge to TCP header compression. With RFC 1144 packet loss disrupts the compression/decompression engine (typically forcing the receiver to discard the rest of the window's segments because they arrive with incorrectly decompressed header fields). An RTO-triggered retransmission of the lost packet is required to resynchronize the compression engine, which also forces TCP back into SS mode.

(RFC 2507 proposes an extension whereby the decompressor proactively requests a local retransmit of an uncompressed copy of the lost packet from the compressor when corruption is detected. The advantages include avoiding the RTO delay and associated window closure.)

Link-Level Loss Recovery

Hiding link-level losses so that TCP doesn't perceive any lost packets clearly has some benefits. The most general technique involves explicit, reliable transfer on every link. Where losses are due to random bit errors, the addition of forward error correction coding in every link-level frame can also reduce the average packet loss rates. However, both cases involve a trade-off between robustness and timeliness. In addition, link-level loss recovery can interact poorly with TCP's end-to-end mechanisms. The critical factors are how quickly loss is detected, how quickly loss can be rectified, and whether other link-level frames continue flowing while recovering the lost frame.

Two key considerations exist when using explicit, local frame retransmission. First, compared to a frame that is sent only once, a frame that is lost and then recovered within the link appears to take longer to traverse the link. Assuming that frame loss/recovery events are not too frequent, the delay shows up as random jitter on the interarrival times of frames flowing across the link. Second, a link might either stall all frames in flight while recovering the lost frame or continue to carry subsequent frames while recovering the lost frame.

The delay introduced by local frame recovery should not be long enough to trigger an RTO timeout at the TCP receiver. If the frame cannot be recovered within some fraction of a connection's current RTT, the link should simply declare the frame lost, and it should rely on TCP's retransmission to recover. (This practice is even more important if the link stalls the transmission of subsequent frames.)

If later frames are transmitted while recovering a lost frame, the TCP receiver may see out-of-sequence segment arrivals and generate duplicate ACKs. This situation triggers fast retransmit and fast recovery at the TCP transmitter and, thus, has a detrimental affect on overall throughput (and the link's recovery of the lost frame becomes irrelevant because TCP retransmits it anyway). Links shouldn't allow frame reordering while recovering from frame loss.

Forward error correction schemes add information redundancy within the transmitted frame to increase the likelihood of reconstructing a partially corrupted frame at the receiving end of the link. In doing so, these schemes increase the size of the transmitted frame (to accommodate the forward error correction bits), which decreases the available bandwidth and increases the transmission latency. (The latency doesn't show up as jitter, per se, because all frames generally undergo expansion by a constant factor.)

Forward error correction is a good solution over long links, where the intrinsic link latency is high. Such links make it much more attractive to simply reconstruct corrupted frames at the receiver, rather than explicitly request and wait for the frame's retransmission.

9.4 References

[PILCERR]   Dawkins, S., G. Montenegro, M. Kojo, V. Magret, and N. Vaidya. "End-to-End Performance Implications of Links with Errors." Internet Draft (work in progress) draft-ietf-pilc-error-02.txt. (October 1999).

[PILCLNK]   Karn, P., A. Falk, J. Touch, M. Montpetit, J. Mahdavi, and G. Montenegro. "Advice for Internet Subnetwork Designers." Internet Draft (work in progress) draft-ietf-pilc-link-design-01.txt. (October 1999).

[PILCLTN]   Dawkins, S., G. Montenegro, M. Kojo, V. Magret, and N. Vaidya. "Long Thin Networks." Internet Draft (work in progress) draft-montenegro-pilc-ltn-03.txt. (October 1999).

[PILCSLOW]   Dawkins, S., G. Montenegro, M. Kojo, and V. Magret. "End-to-End Performance Implications of Slow Links." Internet Draft (work in progress) draft-ietf-pilc-slow-02.txt. (21 October 1999).

[RFC793]   Postel, J. "Transmission Control Protocol—DARPA Internet Program Protocol Specification." RFC 793. (September 1981).

[RFC1122]   Braden, R. "Requirements for Internet Hosts—Communication Layers." STD 3, RFC 1122. (October 1989).

[RFC1144]   Jacobson, V. "Compressing TCP/IP Headers for Low-Speed Serial Links." RFC 1144. (February 1990).

[RFC1323]   Jacobson, V., R. Braden, and D. Borman. "TCP Extensions for High Performance." RFC 1323. (May 1992).

[RFC2018]   Mathis, M., J. Mahdavi, S. Floyd, and A. Romanow. "TCP Selective Acknowledgment Options." RFC 2018. (October 1996).

[RFC2414]   Allman, M., S. Floyd, and C. Partridge. "Increasing TCP's Initial Window." RFC 2414. (September 1998).

[RFC2415]   Poduri, K., and K. Nichols. "Simulation Studies of Increased Initial TCP Window Size." RFC 2415. (September 1998).

[RFC2481]   Ramakrishnan, K., and S. Floyd. "A Proposal to Add Explicit Congestion Notification (ECN) to IP." RFC 2481. (January 1999).

[RFC2488]   Allman, M., D. Glover, and L. Sanchez. "Enhancing TCP over Satellite Channels Using Standard Mechanisms." RFC 2488 (also BCP 28). (January 1999).

[RFC2507]   Degermark, M., B. Nordgren, and S. Pink. "Header Compression for IP." RFC 2507. (February 1999).

[RFC2581]   Allman, M., V. Paxson, and W. Stevens. "TCP Congestion Control." RFC 2581. (April 1999).

CHAPTER 10

Reflections on the Future

The hardest thing about ending a book is knowing that you could have written so much more. This situation is especially true in the area of IP QoS considering the challenges it entails for network designers and the opportunities it offers to application developers. All that is left now is to review what has been covered, contemplate on what it means to the future, and leave you with some pointers to printed and online sources of additional information.

10.1   All the Network Elements

Internet service has traditionally been Best Effort—your packets will make it to their destinations (perhaps) and will do so in some short period of time (mostly). Internet *quality* of service is about tightening those predictions—making it highly likely that certain classes of traffic will make it to their destinations and reducing the uncertainties in packet delivery times. Controlling (and rendering predictable) how the network will treat specific packet flows is critical to the deployment of time-sensitive end-user applications. Whether you're talking about latency, jitter, or loss probabilities—edge-to-edge predictability is the key to IP QoS.

In the Best Effort world, transient congestion within routers leads to latency, jitter, and loss. Latency is increased for traffic passing through congested routers (where queues are used to temporarily buffer packets). The uncorrelated nature of most transient congestion leads to random fluctuations in latency—known as jitter. When congestion is sufficiently severe, queues may overflow—causing packet loss.

To bring QoS into a Best Effort world requires new technology within existing routers. New classification mechanisms are necessary to differentiate distinct classes of traffic. Distinct queuing capabilities are also required to isolate the packets after they are classified. Also necessary is a multiple-queue scheduling feature to provide predictable link access across the queues feeding a particular link. In this book, such routers have been referred to as having a Classify, Queue, and Schedule (CQS) architecture.

You've looked at how different groups of engineers have developed the Integrated Services (IntServ) and Differentiated Services (DiffServ) architectures within the IETF. IntServ embodies the belief that routers can (and should) provide differentiated queuing and scheduling for IP traffic at the flow level—classifying packets on IP addresses, protocol type, and TCP/UDP ports. DiffServ embodies a far simpler classification scheme—presuming that sufficient differentiation can be achieved with only a 6-bit DSCP field in every packet header. The number of bits used to classify packets directly affects the granularity with which traffic can be isolated and differentiated. While IntServ provides highly granular capabilities, the number of flows and associated queues have scared many network and router designers. Conversely, DiffServ is enticing with its limited numbers of queues—but requires careful network provisioning and balancing acts to allow hundreds or thousands of demanding flows to share the limited number of queues.

Of course, a router can do only so much to affect QoS. Links between routers can have a negative impact on the traffic's temporal characteristics if not chosen and configured carefully. You have noted how ATM provides a flexible wide area service; how PPP is used over a diverse range of link technologies; and how different modulation schemes allow modems, ISDN, and ADSL to deliver data over POTS wiring. Where capacity is an issue, you've noted the emergence of 100Mbit per second Ethernet, optical SONET/SDH, and WDM techniques that can be combined to extend the capacity (and, hence, life span) of individual optical fiber strands.

Traffic engineering is also a critical part of any network design—balancing the traffic loads on routers and links within the network by using parallel, alternative paths. You've noted how MPLS provides backbone providers with a powerful tool to traffic engineer their networks—not restricted to the shortest-path forwarding of conventional, connectionless IP routers. You have also noted that CQS architectures allow higher average utilization on some paths and can help to isolate preexisting traffic from fail-over traffic on particular paths through a network—improving the network's service quality degradation characteristics during internal failures.

Finally, all these components of per-hop QoS control and traffic-engineered path control mean nothing without provisioning and signaling. Although the IETF developed RSVP a number of years ago, it is only just beginning to come into its own—shedding the legacy of being coupled tightly to IntServ and now being appreciated in other circles such as MPLS. Efforts continue in the IETF to use RSVP in hybrid IntServ-DiffServ environments, allowing for fine-grained traffic differentiation toward the edges of a network (closer to the hosts) and coarse-grained differentiation toward the core (where hundreds and thousands of flows aggregate).

10.2   A Look Ahead

We're at an interesting point in the evolution of the Internet. It has achieved explosive growth by using Best Effort IP technologies. It is encouraging us all to imagine what could be done if true QoS were available—feats like adding real-time and responsive interactive services to the existing point-and-click Web experience. But there's a Catch-22: The deployment of QoS-dependent applications has been slow because most people's IP networks don't support traffic differentiation, yet QoS capabilities won't be added until a market demand exists. To date, most IP QoS deployments have been in research test beds, and the fledgling voice and video applications space still rely on overprovisioned paths and "taking their chances." So, we're left with contemplating what will probably happen—and in few more years we can reflect on how it actually turned out.

IP QoS will become important in the service provider space during the year 2000. DiffServ techniques will be used to isolate VPN customers from each other and to allow service providers to provide service guarantees without being completely reliant on inefficient overprovisioning. A number of core providers will have their own fiber (either owned or leased) and will leverage WDM techniques to create huge capacity surpluses. However, even these providers will need basic QoS technologies in the electronic routers and switches—the congestion points at the intersections of WDM-enhanced links. For other service providers, CQS architectures within routers and switches will provide vital tools for partitioning link capacity in controllable ways.

At the other end of the spectrum is the chicken-and-egg of end-user applications and IP QoS. Without appropriate support within the end-user's operating systems, applications have limited ability to leverage network-level QoS capabilities. However, 2000 and 2001 should see emerging support for RSVP, IntServ, and DiffServ in the next generations of popular operating systems such as Microsoft Windows and Linux. With QoS-aware Ethernet switches installed throughout an enterprise network, administrators will be able to provide intra-enterprise service differentiation on a per-application basis. With the addition of bulk QoS guarantees from their service providers, enterprise sites will be able to extend these guarantees over wide area connections to far-flung sites. High-quality streaming and real-time video and audio (for example, services based on MP3 and RealAudio/RealVideo technologies) will be routinely possible across the enterprise without interference from (or to) traditional data traffic. Web-based applications and distributed gaming (for example, network-enhanced Sega, Nintendo, and Sony game appliances) will also leverage IP QoS to improve interactivity.

However, a significant amount of work remains. Understanding how to control the temporal characteristics of network traffic is only part of the problem. Admission control, resource allocation, billing for service, and generalized policy-based management of QoS remain major open issues in the IP world. The first generations of DiffServ-based WANs and 802.1Q-based LANs will whet the world's appetite for service differentiation. The challenge is to build user signaling and network management tools that can scale to hundreds, thousands, and tens of thousands of consumers across hundreds and thousands of IP networks. The challenge for us, as network designers and engineers, is to create a total business solution around the tools described in this book.

10.3   Further Reading

This book covers many topics that are explored further in existing printed works (journals and books) or are still under development (where the latest information is typically found in online sources). Here is some information that I hope readers will find useful in expanding their knowledge of subjects mentioned in this book.

10.3.1   TCP/IP Fundamentals

I've assumed some basic general knowledge of TCP, UDP, and IP networking throughout this book without providing much detail about packet formats and the history of various IP tools. The following books delve into the topics summarized in Chapter 1, "The Internet Today":

- Comer, Douglas E. *Internetworking with TCP/IP, Vol. I: Principles, Protocols, and Architecture*. 3rd ed. Upper Saddle River, NJ: Prentice Hall, 1995.

- Stallings, William. *High-Speed Networks: TCP/IP and ATM Design Principles*. Upper Saddle River, NJ: Prentice Hall, 1997.

- Stevens, Richard W. *TCP/IP Illustrated, Vol. I: The Protocols*. Reading, MA: Addison Wesley, 1994.

- Tanenbaum, Andrew S. *Computer Networks*. 3rd ed. Upper Saddle River, NJ: Prentice Hall, 1996.

10.3.2 Routing

IP routing itself is a complex area, even before including QoS considerations. The following books provide good coverage of this topic:

- Huitema, Christian. *Routing in the Internet.* 2nd ed. Upper Saddle River, NJ: Prentice Hall, 1999.

- Moy, John T. *OSPF: Anatomy of an Internet Routing Protocol.* Reading, MA: Addison Wesley, 1998.

- Perlman, Radia. *Interconnections: Bridges, Routers, Switches, and Internetworking Protocols.* Reading, MA: Addison Wesley Professional Computing Series, 1999.

- Steenstrup, Martha (ed.). *Routing in Communications Networks.* Upper Saddle River, NJ: Prentice Hall, 1995.

- Stewart, John W. *BGP4: Inter-Domain Routing in the Internet.* Reading, MA: Addison Wesley, 1998.

10.3.3 Switching

The emergence of MPLS has led to a number of useful books documenting the evolution of this standard, the underlying concepts, and details of how it all works. (Because the actual MPLS specification did not begin to stabilize until the end of 1999, books published in 2000 on this topic are likely to be more precise about MPLS itself.)

- Davie, Bruce S., Paul Doolan, and Yakov Rekhter. *Switching in IP Networks: IP Switching, Tag Switching, and Related Technologies.* San Francisco: Morgan Kaufmann Publishers, 1998.

- Malis, Andrew, and Matthew Holdrege. *Multi-Protocol Label Switching.* Indianapolis, IN: MTP, 2000.

- Metz, Christopher Y. *IP Switching: Protocols and Architectures.* New York: McGraw-Hill, 1998.

10.3.4 Quality of Service

The following titles focus on various subsets of the QoS question:

- Ferguson, Paul, and Geoff Huston. *Quality of Service: Delivering QoS on the Internet and in Corporate Networks.* New York: John Wiley & Sons, 1998.

- Bernet, Yoram. *Windows Operating Systems and Quality of Service Networking.* Indianapolis, IN: MTP, 2000.

10.3.5 Using Online Sources

A number of standards bodies and industry forums make their specifications, agreements, and working drafts available in electronic form. Online sites are very useful for obtaining up to date material. Table 10.1 is a list of useful sources in the IP and QoS arena.

Table 10.1   IP and QoS Web Sites

Body/Forum	Description	Web Site
Internet Engineering Task Force (IETF)	RFCs, Internet Drafts, and Working Group charters	http://www.ietf.org
The Internet Society (ISOC)	Policy, education, and standards issues affecting the Internet	http://www.isoc.org
Institute of Electrical and Electronic Engineers (IEEE)	For-fee access to current IEEE standards	http://www.ieee.org
IEEE Communications Society (IEEE Comsoc)	Key networking publications and conferences	http://www.comsoc.org
ATM Forum	Industry agreements (for example, LANE, MPOA)	http://www.atmforum.com
ADSL Forum	Tutorials and recommendations on the use of ADSL for data	http://www.adsl.com
CableLabs	Tutorials and recommendations on the usc of cable TV for data	http://www.cablelabs.com
International Telecommunication Union (ITU)	For-fee access to current ITU-T standards	http://www.itu.int

Many Web sites represent groups that are experimenting with new IP QoS technologies or are tracking existing IP traffic characteristics. Table 10.2 contains a few well-known North American examples.

Table 10.2   Groups Experimenting with New IP QoS Technologies

Body/Forum	Description	Web Site
Internet 2 (I2)	Next-generation IP backbone for North American R&D.	`http://www.internet2.edu`
QBone (I2 QoS backbone)	Internet 2 QoS backbone	`http://www.internet2.edu/qos`
Very High Speed Backbone (vBNS)	High-speed R&D backbone; lots of traffic and routing statistics	`http://www.vbns.net`
Abilene	High-speed R&D backbone	`http://www.ucaid.edu/abilene`
North American Network Operators Group (NANOG)	Issues, insights, and conferences regarding operating a service provider	`http://www.nanog.org`
National Laboratory for Applied Network Research (NLANR)	NSF-funded technical, engineering, and traffic analysis efforts	`http://www.nlanr.net`
QoS Forum (Stardust)	Conferences, tutorials, and marketing of IP QoS	`http://www.stardust.com/qos`

The preceding listings are by no means exhaustive. Many IP QoS–related organizations exist, are born, and disappear over time—and we can expect many more to emerge. Online search engines can help you locate regional equivalents of the organizations mentioned in the tables.

10.3.6 Special Note on Internet Drafts

References to Internet drafts crop up frequently in this book because they pertain to the latest developments in the IETF. These documents are temporary working documents—typically associated with the efforts of individual working groups but sometimes reflecting individual submissions to working groups or the IETF as a whole. Unfortunately, they may disappear, merge with other work, or morph into RFCs as they make their way through the IETF process.

Online search engines are an invaluable tool in tracking down current and old versions of Internet drafts. The IETF has a search engine interface to the current Internet draft archives (http://search.ietf.org/search/brokers/internet-drafts/query.html). Many people (often the authors) keep copies of older Internet draft versions on personal Web sites, which can sometimes be located through larger Web search engines (for example, Yahoo at http://www.yahoo.com or AltaVista at http://www.altavista.com). These search engines can sometimes also locate copies of Internet drafts stored within mailing-list archives.

Many draft names follow a simple naming convention:

```
draft-<source>-<wg>-<name>-<version>.txt
```

The <source> is a short string identifying either the author(s) (for individual submissions) or "ietf" if the document purports to represent a current working group effort. The <wg> string typically identifies the working group to which the document is directed or belongs. The <name> field is one or more hyphen-separated strings identifying the draft's contents. Finally, the <version> is a two-digit number that increments by one for each revision of the draft. Drafts always have a plain ASCII version (indicated by the trailing .txt) but may also have companion PostScript or Adobe Acrobat versions (indicated by a trailing .ps or .pdf replacing the .txt). For example, draft-ietf-mpls-vcid-atm-04.txt is revision 4 of an MPLS working group effort with -vcid-atm identifying the draft's contents.

Drop the <version>.txt when using a draft's name while searching for the latest version—this search will find all versions, which at least allows you to see whether the reference you're searching for has been superseded. If that approach doesn't work, try searching on the draft's title and its authors. Finally, if you suspect that the work became a RFC, use a RFC search engine (through www.ietf.org) and search on the words in the draft's title.

Index

M T P

New Riders *Books for Technology Professionals*

Windows NT

Windows NT Automated Deployment and Customization
by Richard Puckett
1st Edition
$32.00
ISBN: 1-57870-045-0

Learn time-saving advice that helps you install, update, and configure software on each of your clients without having to visit each client. This book includes reference material on native NT tools, registry edits, and third-party tools.

Windows NT Shell Scripting
by Tim Hill
1st Edition
$32.00
ISBN: 1-57870-047-7

A complete reference for Windows NT scripting, this book guides you through a high-level introduction to the shell language itself and the shell commands that are useful for controlling or managing different components of a network.

Windows NT and UNIX Integration
by Gene Henriksen
1st Edition
$32.00
ISBN: 1-57870-048-5

This book provides you with an all-in-one guide to integrating NT and UNIX in the same network. It begins with the fundamentals of both NT and UNIX and then proceeds with discussions of file sharing, proven solutions to the problems related to printing in an integrated environment, and more.

Windows NT Device Driver Development
by Peter Viscarola and W. Anthony Mason
1st Edition
$50.00
ISBN: 1-57870-058-2

This title begins with an introduction to the general Windows NT operating system concepts relevant to drivers. Then, it progresses to more detailed information about the operating system, such as interrupt management, synchronization issues, the I/O Subsystem, standard kernel mode drivers, and more.

Windows NT Heterogeneous Networking
by Steven B. Thomas
1st Edition
$40.00
ISBN: 1-57870-064-7

A complete reference for internetworking all major systems with Windows NT, both at the OS and protocol levels, this book tells you how to successfully develop an enterprise model as well as how to optimize hardware, domain controllers, and enterprise service traffic.

Windows NT Thin Client Solutions
by Todd W. Mathers and Shawn P. Genoway
1st Edition
$35.00
ISBN: 1-57870-065-5

Explore the cost-saving features of Windows NT Terminal Server, which allows applications to be run on a server as well as the software based on Citrix's core Independent Computing Architecture (ICA) protocol.

Win32 Perl Programming: The Standard Extensions
by Dave Roth
1st Edition
$40.00
ISBN: 1-57870-067-1

See numerous proven examples and practical uses of Perl in solving everyday Win32 problems. This is the only book available with comprehensive coverage of Win32 extensions where most of the Perl functionality resides in Windows settings.

Windows NT Domain Architecture
by Gregg Branham
1st Edition
$39.95
ISBN: 1-57870-112-0

This book contains the in-depth expertise that is necessary to both truly plan a complex enterprise domain and reconfigure current domains. It includes discussion of important domain design considerations in preparation for Windows 2000.

Windows 2000 Server: Planning and Migration
by Sean Deuby
1st Edition
$40.00
ISBN: 1-57870-023-X

Windows 2000 Server: Planning and Migration can quickly save the NT professional thousands of dollars and hundreds of hours. This title includes authoritative information on key features of Windows 2000 and offers recommendations on how to best position your NT network for Windows 2000.

Windows 2000 Quality of Service
by David Iseminger
1st Edition
$45.00
ISBN: 1-57870-115-5

Windows 2000 Quality of Service teaches network engineers and administrators how to define traffic control patterns and utilize bandwidth in their Windows-based networks.

Windows NT Applications: Measuring and Optimizing Performance
by Paul Hinsberg
1st Edition
$40.00
ISBN: 1-57870-176-7

This book offers developers crucial insight into the underlying structure of Windows NT as well as the methodology and tools for measuring, and ultimately optimizing, code performance.

Windows 2000 and Mainframe Integration
by William Zack
1st Edition
$40.00
ISBN: 1-57870-200-3

Windows 2000 and Mainframe Integration provides both mainframe and Windows computing professionals with the practical know-how to build and integrate Windows 2000 technologies into their current environment.

Windows Script Host
by Tim Hill
1st Edition
$35.00
ISBN: 1-57870-139-2

Windows Script Host is one of the first books published about this powerful tool. The text focuses on system scripting and the VBScript language using objects and server scriptlets, and includes numerous ready-to-use script solutions.

KDE Application Development
by Uwe Thiem
1st Edition
$39.99
ISBN: 1-57870-201-1

This book takes a no-nonsense approach to writing applications using the KDE and Qt KDE. Focusing on such essentials as KTsp configuration and maturation, localization and internationalization, application documentation, the automated make process, and development tools, *KDE Application Development* is for the Linux developer inexperienced with GUI or desktop programming and for the GUI developer learning to create Linux applications.

Windows NT/2000 Native API Reference
by Gary Nebbett
1st Edition, Winter 2000
$50.00
ISBN: 1-57870-199-6

Windows NT/2000 Native API Reference offers the first comprehensive look at the undocumented APIs. This essential reference enables you to develop debuggers, analysis tools, and run-time libraries; determine whether expected but seemingly missing functionality is absent or just not officially documented; and discover the API changes that accompanied the release of Windows 2000.

Windows NT/2000 ADSI Scripting for System Administration
by Thomas Eck
1st Edition, Spring 2000
$45.00
ISBN: 1-57870-219-4

Simplify redundant and solve challenging administrative tasks with *Windows NT/2000 ADSI Scripting for System Administration*. A supply of Visual Basic code segments to streamline the majority of tasks performed on Windows NT/2000, IIS, and Exchange Server is just the beginning of what this book has to offer. Its COM-based approach enables you to implement solutions in VB, ASP, and WSH. The techniques and code provided have been proven in one of the world's largest financial institutions.

Programming

Handbook of Programming Languages, Volume I
Edited by Peter Salus
1st Edition
$49.99
ISBN: 1-57870-008-6

This is the most comprehensive source on the principal object-oriented languages. It covers languages from Smalltalk to Java with explanations of the languages' histories, descriptions of their syntax and semantics, how-to information and tips, and pointers to potential traps.

Handbook of Programming Languages, Volume II

Edited by Peter Salus

1st Edition

$49.99

ISBN: 1-57870-009-4

The four most important imperative languages are covered in this title: Fortran, C, Turbo Pascal, and Icon. Evaluate them to find the best imperative language for your purpose at hand, and learn how these languages are related to each other historically and syntactically.

Handbook of Programming Languages, Volume III

Edited by Peter Salus

1st Edition

$49.99

ISBN: 1-57870-010-8

Beginning with Jon Bentley's discussion of little languages, this book continues to discuss languages "specialized to a particular problem domain"—such as Perl, sed, awk, SQL, Tcl/Tk, and Python.

Handbook of Programming Languages, Volume IV

Edited by Peter Salus

1st Edition

$49.99

ISBN: 1-57870-011-6

This book begins with the functional programming group, descended from John McCarthy's LISP of the late 1960s, and moves on to discuss its offspring: Emacs Lisp, Scheme, Guile, and CLOS.

Smart Card Developer's Kit

by Scott B. Guthery and Timothy M. Jurgensen

1st Edition

$79.99

ISBN: 1-57870-027-2

This is all the practical information a computing professional needs to write programs that use and run on smart cards. Smart card communications and commands, SDKs, terminal-side and card-side APIs, security, financial applications, and e-commerce are all covered in this title.

DCE/RPC over SMB

by Luke Kenneth Casson Leighton

1st Edition

$45.00

ISBN: 1-57870-150-3

Security people, system and network administrators, and the folks writing tools for them all need to be familiar with the packets flowing across their networks. Authored by a key member of the SAMBA team, this book describes how Microsoft has taken DCE/RPC and implemented it over SMB and TCP/IP.

Autoconf, Automake, and Libtool

by Ben Elliston, et al.

1st Edition, Summer 2000

$34.99

ISBN: 1-57870-190-2

This book is the first of its kind, authored by Open Source community luminaries and current maintainers of the tools, it teaches developers how to boost their productivity and the portability of their applications using GNU autoconf, GNU automake, and GNU libtool.

Delphi COM Programming

by Eric Harmon

1st Edition

$45.00

ISBN: 1-57870-221-6

Delphi COM Programming offers a practical exploration of COM to enable Delphi 4 and 5 developers to program component-based applications. Typical real-world scenarios, such as Windows shell programming, automating Microsoft Agent, and creating and using ActiveX controls, are explored. Discussions of each topic are illustrated with detailed example applications.

Networking

LDAP: Programming Directory-Enabled Applications

by Timothy A. Howes, Ph.D. and Mark C. Smith

$44.99

ISBN: 1-57870-000-0

This overview of the LDAP standard discusses its creation and history with the Internet Engineering Task Force as well as the original RFC standard. LDAP also covers compliance trends, implementation, data packet handling in C++, client/server responsibilities, and more.

ASDL/VSDL Principles

by Dr. Dennis J. Rushmayer

1st Edition

$44.99

ISBN: 1-57870-015-9

ASDL/VSDL Principles provides the communications and networking engineer with the practical explanations, technical detail, and in-depth insight needed to fully implement ASDL and VSDL. Coverage includes the fundamentals of the transmission theory and crosstalk in the outside plant, including the details of modeling and simulating the expected performance of ADSL and VDSL under different operating conditions.

DSL

by Dr. Walter Y. Chen

1st Edition

$54.99

ISBN: 1-57870-017-5

DSL is ideal for computing professionals who are looking for information on new high-speed communications technologies and information on the dynamics of ADSL communications in order to create compliant applications. Get calculation examples for all signal environments, coverage of ADSL, and a multitude of other xDSL technologies.

Gigabit Ethernet Networking

by David G. Cunningham, Ph.D. and William G. Lane, Ph.D.

1st Edition

$50.00

ISBN: 1-57870-062-0

Gigabit Ethernet is the next step for speed on the majority of installed networks. Explore how this technology will allow high-bandwidth applications such as the integration of telephone and data services, real-time applications, thin-client apps such as Windows NT Terminal Server, and corporate teleconferencing.

Supporting Service Level Agreements on IP Networks

by Dinesh Verma

1st Edition

$50.00

ISBN: 1-57870-146-5

An essential resource for network engineers and architects, *Supporting Service Level Agreements on IP Networks* will help you build a core network capable of supporting a range of service levels. You'll also learn how to create SLA solutions using off-the-shelf components in both best-effort and DiffServ/IntServ networks. See how to verify the performance of your SLA—as either a customer or a network service provider.

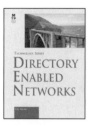

Directory Enabled Networks

by John Strassner

1st Edition

$50.00

ISBN: 1-57870-140-6

Directory Enabled Networks (DEN) is a specification for managing networks through centralized control. Written by the creator of the technology, *Directory Enabled Networks* is a comprehensive resource on the design and use of DEN. The book provides practical examples, along with a detailed introduction to the theory of building a new clan of directory enabled applications that will solve networking problems.

Understanding Public-Key Infrastructure

by Carlisle Adams and Steve Lloyd

1st Edition

$50.00

ISBN: 1-57870-166-X

This book is a tutorial on, and a guide to the deployment of, public-key infrastructures (PKIs). It covers a broad range of material related to PKIs, including certification, operational considerations, and standardization efforts as well as deployment considerations. Emphasis is placed on explaining the interrelated fields within the topic area to assist those who will be responsible for making deployment decisions and architecting a PKI within an organization.

Intrusion Detection

by Rebecca Gurley Bace

1st Edition

$50.00

ISBN: 1-57870-185-6

Written by a former key figure in the National Security Agency, this guide to the field of intrusion detection covers the foundations of intrusion detection and system audit. *Intrusion Detection* provides a wealth of information, ranging from design considerations to how to evaluate and choose the optimal commercial intrusion detection products for a particular networking environment.

Designing Addressing Architectures for Routing and Switching

by Howard C. Berkowitz

1st Edition

$45.00

ISBN: 1-57870-059-0

One of the greatest challenges for network design professionals is making the users, servers, files, printers, and other resources visible on their network. This title equips the network engineer or architect with a systematic methodology for planning the wide area and local area network "streets" on which users and servers live.

Understanding and Deploying LDAP Directory Services

by Timothy A. Howes, Ph.D., Mark C. Smith, Ph.D., and Gordon S. Good

1st Edition

$50.00

ISBN: 1-57870-070-1

This comprehensive tutorial provides the reader with a thorough treatment of LDAP directory services. Minimal knowledge of general networking and administration is assumed, making the material accessible to intermediate and advanced readers. The text is full of practical implementation advice and real-world deployment examples to help the reader choose the path that makes sense for the specific organization.

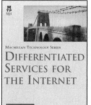

Differentiated Services for the Internet

by Kalevi Kilkki

1st Edition

$50.00

ISBN: 1-57870-132-5

Differentiated Services, an IETF standards effort, is one of the few technologies enabling networks to alter traffic patterns to suit the needs of a particular application. With the help of *Differentiated Services for the Internet*, you will understand the potential of DiffServ traffic-handling mechanisms to create a more robust, versatile, and efficient Internet infrastructure.

Switched, Fast, and Gigabit Ethernet, Third Edition

by Robert Breyer and
Sean Riley
3rd Edition
$50.00
ISBN: 1-57870-073-6

Switched, Fast, and Gigabit Ethernet,
Third Edition is the one and only solution needed to
understand and fully implement this entire range of
Ethernet innovations. Acting as both an overview of
current technologies and hardware requirement and a
hands-on, comprehensive tutorial for deploying and
managing Switched, Fast, and Gigabit Ethernet networks, this guide covers the most prominent present
and future challenges network administrators face.

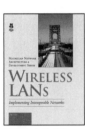

Wireless LANs: Implementing Interoperable Networks

by Jim Geier
1st Edition
$40.00
ISBN: 1-57870-081-7

Wireless LANs covers how and why to migrate from
proprietary solutions to the 802.11 standard, and it
explains how to realize significant cost savings
through wireless LAN implementation for data collection systems.

Wide Area High Speed Networks

by Dr. Sidnie Feit
1st Edition
$50.00
ISBN: 1-57870-114-7

Networking is in a transitional
phase between long-standing,
conventional wide area services and new technologies
and services. This book presents current and emerging
wide area technologies and services, makes them
understandable, and puts them into perspective so
that their merits and disadvantages are clear.

The DHCP Handbook

by Ralph Droms, Ph.D.
and Ted Lemon
1st Edition
$55.00
ISBN: 1-57870-137-6

The DHCP Handbook is an
authoritative overview and expert
guide to the setup and management of a DHCP
server. This title discusses how DHCP was developed
and its interaction with other protocols, explaining
how DHCP operates, its use in different environments,
and the interaction between DHCP servers and clients.
Network hardware, inter-server communication, security, SNMP, and IP mobility are also discussed.
Included in the book are several appendices that provide a rich resource for networking professionals
working with DHCP.

Designing Routing and Switching Architectures for Enterprise Networks

by Howard C. Berkowitz
1st Edition
$55.00
ISBN: 1-57870-060-4

This title provides a fundamental understanding of
how switches and routers operate, enabling readers to
effectively use them to build networks. The book
walks network designers through all aspects of
requirements, analysis, and deployment strategies;
strengthens readers' professional abilities; and helps
them develop skills necessary to advance in their
profession.

Software Architecture and Engineering

Designing Flexible Object-Oriented Systems with UML
by Charles Richter
1st Edition
$40.00
ISBN: 1-57870-098-1

Designing Flexible Object-Oriented Systems with UML details the UML, which is a notation system for designing object-oriented programs. The book follows the same sequence that a development project might employ, starting with requirements of the problem using UML use case diagrams and activity diagrams. The reader is shown ways to improve the design as the author moves through the transformation of the initial diagrams into class diagrams and interaction diagrams. The author continues offering tips and strategies for improving the design and ultimately incorporating concurrency, distribution, and persistence into the design example.

Constructing Superior Software
Paul C. Clements, et al.
1st Edition
$40.00
ISBN: 1-57870-147-3

This title presents a set of fundamental engineering strategies for achieving a successful software solution with practical advice to ensure that the development project is moving in the right direction. Software designers and development managers can improve the development speed and quality of their software by using this book, and they can improve the processes used in development.

A UML Pattern Language
Paul Evitts
1st Edition
$45.00
ISBN: 1-57870-118-X

While other books focus only on the UML notation system, this concepts and illustrates their use through patterns. It provides an integrated, practical, step-by-step discussion of UML patterns with real-world examples to illustrate proven software modeling tehniques.

How to Contact Us

Visit Our Web Site

www.newriders.com

On our Web site, you'll find information about our other books, authors, tables of contents, indexes, and book errata. You can also place orders for books through our Web site.

Email Us

Contact us at this address:

nrfeedback@newriders.com

- If you have comments or questions about this book
- To report errors that you have found in this book
- If you have a book proposal to submit or are interested in writing for New Riders/MTP
- If you would like to have an author kit sent to you
- If you are an expert in a computer topic or technology and are interested in being a technical editor who reviews manuscripts for technical accuracy

nrmedia@newriders.com

- For instructors from educational institutions who want to preview New Riders/MTP books for classroom use. Email should include your name, title, school, department, address, phone number, office days/hours, text in use, and enrollment in the body of your text along with your request for desk/examination copies and/or additional information.
- For members of the press who want to review copies of New Riders/MTP books. Email should include your name and the publication or Web site you work for.

Write to Us

New Riders/MTP
201 W. 103rd St.
Indianapolis, IN 46290-1097 USA

Call Us

Toll-free (800) 571-5840 + 9 + 4511
If outside U.S. (317) 581-3500. Ask for New Riders/MTP.

Fax Us

(317) 581-4663

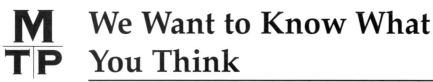

We Want to Know What You Think

To better serve you, we would like your opinion on the content and quality of this book. Please complete this card, and mail it to us or fax it to 317-581-4663.

Name _____

Address _____

City _____ State _____ Zip _____

Phone _____

Email Address _____

Occupation _____

Operating system(s) that you use _____

What influenced your purchase of this book?

- ❏ Recommendation
- ❏ Table of Contents
- ❏ Magazine Review
- ❏ MTP's Reputation
- ❏ Cover Design
- ❏ Index
- ❏ Advertisement
- ❏ Author Name

How would you rate the content of this book?

- ❏ Excellent
- ❏ Good
- ❏ Below Average
- ❏ Very Good
- ❏ Fair
- ❏ Poor

How do you plan to use this book?

- ❏ Quick reference
- ❏ Classroom
- ❏ Self-training
- ❏ Other

What do you like most about this book? Check all that apply.

- ❏ Content
- ❏ Accuracy
- ❏ Listings
- ❏ Index
- ❏ Price
- ❏ Writing Style
- ❏ Examples
- ❏ Design
- ❏ Page Count
- ❏ Illustrations

What do you like least about this book? Check all that apply.

- ❏ Content
- ❏ Accuracy
- ❏ Listings
- ❏ Index
- ❏ Price
- ❏ Writing Style
- ❏ Examples
- ❏ Design
- ❏ Page Count
- ❏ Illustrations

What would be a useful follow-up book for you? _____

Where did you purchase this book? _____

Can you name a similar book that you like better than this one, or one that is as good? Why?

_____

_____

How many MTP books do you own? _____

What are your favorite computer books? _____

_____

What other titles would you like to see us develop? _____

_____

Any comments for us? _____

_____

Fold here and tape to mail

New Riders Publishing/MTP
201 W. 103rd St.
Indianapolis, IN 46290